722-0958

Daniel

REFORMED EXPOSITORY COMMENTARY

A Series

Series Editors

Richard D. Phillips
Philip Graham Ryken

Testament Editors

Iain M. Duguid, Old Testament
Daniel M. Doriani, New Testament

Daniel

IAIN M. DUGUID

P&R
PUBLISHING
P.O. BOX 817 • PHILLIPSBURG • NEW JERSEY 08865-0817

Page design by Lakeside Design Plus

Printed in the United States of America

Library of Congress Cataloging-in-Publication Data

Duguid, Iain M.
Daniel / Iain M. Duguid.
    p. cm. — (Reformed expository commentary)
Includes bibliographical references and indexes.
ISBN-13: 978-1-59638-068-4 (cloth)
1. Bible. O.T. Daniel—Commentaries. I. Title.
BS1555.53.D84 2008
224'.5077—dc22

                    2007028713

To Ken & Yoori Han,
Faithful fellow-laborers in the service of the gospel

CONTENTS

Series Introduction

In every generation there is a fresh need for the faithful exposition of God's Word in the church. At the same time, the church must constantly do the work of theology: reflecting on the teaching of Scripture, confessing its doctrines of the Christian faith, and applying them to contemporary culture. We believe that these two tasks—the expositional and the theological—are interdependent. Our doctrine must derive from the biblical text, and our understanding of any particular passage of Scripture must arise from the doctrine taught in Scripture as a whole.

We further believe that these interdependent tasks of biblical exposition and theological reflection are best undertaken in the church, and most specifically in the pulpits of the church. This is all the more true since the study of Scripture properly results in doxology and praxis—that is, in praise to God and practical application in the lives of believers. In pursuit of these ends, we are pleased to present the Reformed Expository Commentary as a fresh exposition of Scripture for our generation in the church. We hope and pray that pastors, teachers, Bible study leaders, and many others will find this series to be a faithful, inspiring, and useful resource for the study of God's infallible, inerrant Word.

The Reformed Expository Commentary has four fundamental commitments. First, these commentaries aim to be *biblical*, presenting a comprehensive exposition characterized by careful attention to the details of the text. They are not exegetical commentaries—commenting word by word or even verse by verse—but integrated expositions of whole passages of Scripture. Each commentary will thus present a sequential, systematic treatment of an entire book of the Bible, passage by passage. Second, these commentaries are unashamedly *doctrinal*. We are committed to the Westminster Confession of Faith and Catechisms as containing the system of doctrine taught in the Scriptures of the Old and New Testaments. Each volume will teach, promote, and defend the doctrines of the Reformed faith as they are found in the Bible. Third, these commentaries are *redemptive-historical* in their orientation. We believe in the unity of the Bible and its central message of salvation in Christ. We are thus committed to a Christ-centered view of the Old Testament, in which its characters, events, regulations, and institutions are properly understood as pointing us to Christ and his gospel, as well as giving us examples to follow in living by faith. Fourth, these commentaries are *practical*, applying the text of Scripture to contemporary challenges of life—both public and private—with appropriate illustrations.

The contributors to the Reformed Expository Commentary are all pastor-scholars. As pastor, each author will first present his expositions in the pulpit ministry of his church. This means that these commentaries are rooted in the teaching of Scripture to real people in the church. While aiming to be scholarly, these expositions are not academic. Our intent is to be faithful, clear, and helpful to Christians who possess various levels of biblical and theological training—as should be true in any effective pulpit ministry. Inevitably this means that some issues of academic interest will not be covered. Nevertheless, we aim to achieve a responsible level of scholarship, seeking to promote and model this for pastors and other teachers in the church. Significant exegetical and theological difficulties, along with such historical and cultural background as is relevant to the text, will be treated with care.

We strive for a high standard of enduring excellence. This begins with the selection of the authors, all of whom have proven to be outstanding communicators of God's Word. But this pursuit of excellence is also reflected in a disciplined editorial process. Each volume is edited by both a series editor and a testament editor. The testament editors, Iain Duguid for the Old Testament and Daniel Doriani for the New Testament, are accomplished pastors and respected scholars who have taught at the seminary level. Their job is to ensure that each volume is sufficiently conversant with up-to-date scholarship and is faithful and accurate in its exposition of the text. As series editors, we oversee each volume to ensure its overall quality—including excellence of writing, soundness of teaching, and usefulness in application. Working together as an editorial team, along with the publisher, we are devoted to ensuring that these are the best commentaries our gifted authors can provide, so that the church will be served with trustworthy and exemplary expositions of God's Word.

It is our goal and prayer that the Reformed Expository Commentary will serve the church by renewing confidence in the clarity and power of Scripture and by upholding the great doctrinal heritage of the Reformed faith. We hope that pastors who read these commentaries will be encouraged in their own expository preaching ministry, which we believe to be the best and most biblical pattern for teaching God's Word in the church. We hope that lay teachers will find these commentaries among the most useful resources they rely upon for understanding and presenting the text of the Bible. And we hope that the devotional quality of these studies of Scripture will instruct and inspire each Christian who reads them in joyful, obedient discipleship to Jesus Christ.

May the Lord bless all who read the Reformed Expository Commentary. We commit these volumes to the Lord Jesus Christ, praying that the Holy Spirit will use them for the instruction and edification of the church, with thanksgiving to God the Father for his unceasing faithfulness in building his church through the ministry of his Word.

Richard D. Phillips
Philip Graham Ryken
Series Editors

3yrs old

pg 4

my mom — the "exiled" life — taken fr. her
parents, separated fr. her
family, stripped of her Jewish
identity + all relationships to
grandparents — aunts/ uncles, etc
→ given a new name — made a
   Gentile
   - frightened -
   - insecure -
   far away fr home
   Alone

No wonder she would hide behind the trees!

PREFACE

The Book of Daniel is both familiar and unfamiliar to most Christians, and consequently poses its own unique challenges to preachers. The stories of Shadrach, Meshach, and Abednego in the fiery furnace and Daniel in the lion's den are the staples of children's Bible story books and Sunday school classes, and so are well-known even in an age of increasing biblical illiteracy. Most have been taught to read them as tales intended to encourage believers to "Dare to be a Daniel," to live for Christ in a hostile world. That is indeed part of their purpose: they provide models for believers living in an alien world as to how they can both serve the culture in which they find themselves and at the same time live lives that are distinctive from that culture. They encourage believers to remain faithful, no matter what the cost. Yet the reality is that few of us can really claim to come close to the standard set for us by Daniel and his friends: we are all compromised in many ways by the pressures of our environment. It is important therefore to be reminded at the same time of the one greater than Daniel who has perfectly lived the exilic life of service and separation for us, Jesus Christ.

The latter chapters of Daniel's vision are more unfamiliar and daunting to most believers. They may have been exposed to a variety of end-times speculations constructed from an amalgam of these texts and others drawn from elsewhere in the Bible, but few have been encouraged to consider how these apocalyptic passages encourage all believers, whether or not they find themselves living during the final pages of world history. Here too, seeing the centerpiece of these visions as the exalted heavenly Son of Man who took flesh amongst us in the person of Jesus Christ can bring these often puzzling visions to bear on our everyday lives in a whole new way. It is my prayer that this commentary will help Christians to see how the gospel of Jesus Christ is at the heart of the Book of Daniel.

These sermons were originally preached at Grace Presbyterian Church in Fallbrook, California, shortly before I moved to Pennsylvania. I would like to thank the elders and the congregation of that church for their constant love and encouragement. We all miss you greatly but are encouraged to see God's grace continuing to be poured out upon you through the ministry of my former co-pastor, Rev. Ken Han. This book is dedicated to Ken and his wife, Yoori, with gratitude to God for sending you to our church and equipping you with the gifts and character necessary for the work of gospel ministry.

I would also like to thank my wife, Barb, for her part in my own ongoing spiritual growth and development. Her ability to be open and unstintingly honest about her own sinful heart and her consequent passionate love for the grace of God in the gospel is a constant inspiration to me: I pray that as I grow in the Lord I may learn increasingly to share her humility, love, and compassion. My children have patiently endured the trials and joys of being part of a pastor's family. Thank you Jamie, Sam, Hannah, Rob, and Rosie for regularly making us look much better parents than we are. We thank the Lord for his continued work in each of your hearts and pray that you may daily grow in your knowledge of the depth of your own sin and the magnificence of your Savior, Jesus Christ.

Daniel

FAITH ENDURING THROUGH ADVERSITY

genre)

1

WHEN THE WORLD
DOES ITS WORST

Daniel 1:1—21

But Daniel resolved not to defile himself with the royal food and wine, and he asked the chief official for permission not to defile himself this way. (Dan. 1:8)

→ novels

*T*here is a fascinating genre of literature that goes by the name "Alternative Histories." These novels imagine what life would be like if history had turned out differently from the way that it did. In the alternative history novel *SS-GB*,[1] Len Deighton imagines, "What if Adolf Hitler had focused all of his attention on invading Britain in 1940 and had not started a second front against Russia?" Very possibly, he would have made a successful assault, and the result would be a very different face for Britain and Europe today. In all likelihood, people in those countries would have grown up in a repressive police state, living in constant fear of the authorities.

For some Europeans, of course, that is not such an alternative history. I regularly teach in a small seminary in Latvia, and the young men in this

---

1. Len Deighton, *SS-GB: Nazi Occupied Britain, 1941* (New York: Knopf, 1979).

country know precisely what it is like to grow up under a repressive regime. After having a brief spell of independence between the two world wars, their small country was annexed by the Russians in 1940 and spent most of the next fifty years under alien rule until they were finally able to regain their freedom in 1991. It was a time of terror and intense suffering for all Latvians, and especially for the church, as their world was overrun by enemies who were determined to stamp out their culture, their language, their identity, and their religion. Anyone who was a potential leader was either executed or exiled to some distant part of the Soviet empire.

Latvia

when mother was taken @ 3 yr of age

Can you imagine what it must have been like to be exiled from home to a foreign city, to be alone and scared, a long way from familiar surroundings? How would you cope in such a hostile setting? What truths could you cling to? Would you remain faithful to your former identity or simply be assimilated into your new surroundings?

THE EXPERIENCE OF EXILE

This is not entirely an imaginative exercise for us either, however. Even though our Western experience of the hostility of this world is certainly not normally as extreme as that of postwar Latvia, it nonetheless remains true for all of us that we are exiles here on earth. As citizens of heaven, Christians live as aliens and strangers in a land that is not their own, and there are times when the world's enmity to the people of God becomes evident. The hostility of the world is often shown in the efforts it makes to squeeze us into its mold. It wants to make us conform to its values and standards and not to stick out from the crowd. The pressure is on us, in school and at work, to be like everyone else in the way that we dress and the language that we use. We are expected to laugh at certain kinds of jokes and gossip about certain kinds of people. If we want to get on and be promoted in the world of business, we are pressured to leave our values and religious beliefs at the front entrance and to live a lifestyle entirely assimilated to the business community. We are expected to value the things the surrounding culture values, to pursue passionately its glittering prizes, and generally to live in obedience to its idols. We have to choose daily whether to be part of this world in which we live, or to take the difficult path of standing against it.

Why I was fired out of a job I had @ 1 @ 26 yrs.

4

How do you cope in the midst of the brokenness and alienation that is life here on earth? What truths can you cling to when the jagged edges of existence are twisting against you and cutting into your flesh? What do you need to know to live a life of faith in an alien world, a world that is frequently a place of sickness and pain, of broken relationships and bitter tears, of sorrow and death? These are the questions to which the Book of Daniel will give us the answers. It is a book written to God's Old Testament people, Israel, when they were experiencing the brokenness and pain of life in exile, far away from home. It was designed to encourage them in their walk with God, who was with them in the midst of their pain.

GOD'S FAITHFULNESS IN JUDGMENT

Daniel's own story of exile began like this:

> In the third year of the reign of Jehoiakim king of Judah, Nebuchadnezzar king of Babylon came to Jerusalem and besieged it. And the Lord delivered Jehoiakim king of Judah into his hand, along with some of the articles from the temple of God. These he carried off to the temple of his god in Babylonia and put in the treasure house of his god.
> Then the king ordered Ashpenaz, chief of his court officials, to bring in some of the Israelites from the royal family and the nobility—young men without any physical defect, handsome, showing aptitude for every kind of learning, well informed, quick to understand, and qualified to serve in the king's palace. He was to teach them the language and literature of the Babylonians. The king assigned them a daily amount of food and wine from the king's table. They were to be trained for three years, and after that they were to enter the king's service. (Dan. 1:1–5)

To live faithfully in exile, we first need to know God's faithfulness. This is not altogether as comforting a truth as you might imagine, since the first aspect of God's faithfulness that we see in this chapter is God's faithfulness in judgment. Judah's exile from the land in Daniel's time was not merely an accident of fate or the tragic result of the expansionist policies of imperial Babylon in the late seventh century B.C. As Daniel 1:2 makes clear, the exile came upon Judah because the Lord handed King Jehoiakim over to the power of Nebuchadnezzar. God gave his people into the hand of their enemies.

5

The Lord had warned Israel of the sure consequences of their sins in the Book of Leviticus. At the beginning of Israel's history as a nation with God, he made a covenant with them, a covenant that included blessings for obedience and curses if they disobeyed (Lev. 26). If they served the Lord faithfully and kept the terms of the covenant, then they would experience his favor and blessing (26:3–13). However, if they abandoned him and violated his covenant, they would experience his wrath and disfavor (26:14–39). Their crops would be ruined and they would become prey for wild animals and for their enemies (26:19–25). If they persisted in their disobedience, the Lord would scatter them among the nations and they would waste away in exile (26:33, 39). This was exactly Israel's fate as it unfolded. Because of their persistent disobedience and rebellion against God over many generations, the Lord finally handed them over into the power of their enemies, and so they went into exile.

Yet the fate of Daniel and his friends in being dragged off into exile was not merely a fulfillment of the general covenantal curse of Leviticus 26. It was also the specific fulfillment of the prophecy of Isaiah in 2 Kings 20:18. Judah's King Hezekiah had received envoys and a gift from Merodach-Baladan, king of Babylon. In response, Hezekiah showed them everything that was of value in his storehouses and all of his treasures (20:13). For this action, he was roundly condemned by the prophet Isaiah.

Why was the Lord so upset with Hezekiah? What was the problem with giving the envoys from Babylon a royal tour of the palace? The answer is that in the world of ancient diplomacy, nothing came free. When Merodach-Baladan sent envoys and a gift to Hezekiah, it wasn't merely a friendly gesture of goodwill on his recovery from sickness. Rather, he was soliciting Hezekiah's help and support in his ongoing struggle against Assyria.[2] So when Hezekiah showed his envoys around his treasure houses, he was responding positively to Merodach-Baladan's overtures of alliance and seeking to show him that he had the resources to be a useful ally against Assyria. In spite of the Lord's miraculous deliverance of Jerusalem from the surrounding armies of Sennacherib and the Assyrians in the previous chapter of the Book of Kings, Hezekiah was now looking to political means for solving the Assyrian problem, through alliances with Babylon. Politics had replaced trust in the Lord.

---

2. T. R. Hobbs, *2 Kings*, Word Biblical Commentary (Waco, TX: Word, 1985), 294.

This is not merely an ancient temptation. Modern people too may be tempted to place their hopes in political alliances rather than wholeheartedly trusting in the Lord. The cost may be the loss of our distinctive spiritual voice as the church becomes just one more political action committee. Alternatively, we may invest our career hopes in adopting the world's methods of getting ahead, only to discover much later the cost of these methods to our homes and families.

Isaiah's word of judgment on Hezekiah's strategy was specific and severe. Because Hezekiah sought to preserve his treasures by trusting in Babylon, the Babylonians would come and carry off everything in his palace (2 Kings 20:17). Far from assuring the security of his line, his foolish spiritual alliance would result in some of his own offspring being taken off to become eunuchs in the palace of the Babylonian king (20:18). It is this specific word of judgment that is fulfilled in the opening verses of the Book of Daniel. Nebuchadnezzar, king of Babylon, came to Jerusalem and carried off treasures from the temple of God to put in the house of his own god (Dan. 1:2), and he took some of the royal family and nobility—the descendants of Hezekiah—and put them under the charge of Ashpenaz, the chief of his court officials, or eunuchs (1:4).[3] God's judgment upon the line of Hezekiah had been faithfully carried through, just as Isaiah had said.

JUDGMENT AND HOPE

Yet the recognition that their fate came from the hand of God as a faithful act of judgment was itself an encouragement to the exiles. Their future was not controlled by Babylon or its gods, but by the Lord, the God of heaven (Dan. 2:19). The one who had sent them into exile had also promised to be with them there, and ultimately to restore them from exile after a time of judgment. An implicit parallel is drawn between the sacred articles stolen from the temple and the people who were taken by Nebuchadnezzar: the young men are described as "free from defect" (*me'um*), a word more

3. The Hebrew word for "official" and "eunuch" is the same. It is not clear whether Daniel and his friends were literally made genderless in preparation for their new assignments. Some but not all of the Babylonian officials would have been literal eunuchs. The essential point of the text, however, is that what Isaiah prophesied had now come true.

commonly used of sacrifices (1:4).[4] Just as the Lord allowed Nebuchadnez-zar to carry away the temple vessels, he also allowed him to carry off some of the best of his people. That parallel further implies that just as the temple vessels would inevitably eventually make their way home (see Ezra 1:7), so too would his exiled people.[5] God will not abandon what is his own.

This is an important point. During its hardest moments, life often seems out of control. Our fate may sometimes seem to lie in the hands of hostile people, or in the outworking of impersonal forces of one kind or another. Yet the reality is that our every experience in this world, from the apparently coincidental at one end of the spectrum, to the determined acts of wicked men and women on the other, lies under the control of our sovereign God. The sparrow does not fall to the ground without his permission (Matt. 10:29), which demonstrates that even the most trivial of events are within his view. At the other extreme, though, even the most wicked act of all time, the crucifixion of Jesus, was also the outworking of God's predetermined purpose (Acts 4:28). No sinful act ever catches God by surprise or thwarts his sovereign will. Everything that we experience in life, no matter how difficult or apparently meaningless it may seem, is God's purpose for us. For believers in Christ, each circumstance is the Lord's means of furthering his sanctifying goals. He has not abandoned or forgotten us. On the contrary, he will walk through these trials and preserve us through them by his grace.

RESISTING REPROGRAMING

So it was that in the will of God, Daniel and his three friends found themselves exiled in Babylon: "Among these were some from Judah: Daniel, Hananiah, Mishael and Azariah. The chief official gave them new names: to Daniel, the name Belteshazzar; to Hananiah, Shadrach; to Mishael, Meshach; and to Azariah, Abednego" (Dan. 1:6–7).

The four were probably still only young teenagers at the time, and in Babylon they were to be exposed to an intense program of reeducation.

4. Tremper Longman III, *Daniel*, New International Version Application Commentary (Grand Rapids: Zondervan, 1999), 49.

5. On the importance of the theme of the temple vessels, see P. R. Ackroyd, "The Temple Vessels—A Continuity Theme," in *Studies in the Religion of Ancient Israel* (Leiden: E. J. Brill, 1972), 166–79.

First, their very names were changed. In place of their good Hebrew and Yahwistic names, Daniel ("God is my judge"), Hananiah ("the Lord is gracious"), Mishael ("Who is what God is?"), and Azariah ("The Lord is a helper"), they were assigned pagan, Babylonian names: Belteshazzar, Shadrach, Meshach, and Abednego (1:7). These Babylonian names invoked the help of the Babylonian gods, Marduk, Bel, and Nebo, rather than Israel's Lord.[6] The four young men were also instructed in the language and literature of the Babylonians, so that its myths and legends would take the place of the Scriptures as the source of their wisdom and worldview (1:4). Third, they were to be royally supplied from the king's table, with a daily allowance of food and wine, so that they would become accustomed to a life of dependence on their new master (1:5). At the end of this three-year initiation process, with their previous identity fully obliterated, they would enter the service of Nebuchadnezzar (1:5).

This provides us with a picture of the world's strategy of spiritual reprograming. At its most effective, it consists of a subtle combination of threat and promise, of enforcement and encouragement. Those who are totally recalcitrant may be sent to prison camps or gulags if necessary, but the majority of the population are far more easily assimilated if they are well fed and provided for. After all, more flies are caught with honey than with vinegar. The fundamental goal of the whole procedure, though, was in one way or another to obliterate all memory of Israel and Israel's God from the lips and the minds of these young men, and to instill into them a sense of total dependence on Nebuchadnezzar for all of the good things in life.

Isn't this how Satan still operates today? He may violently persecute believers in some parts of the world, yet often he works more effectively by seducing and deceiving us into forgetting God and thinking that our blessings come from somewhere else. He wants us to forget the truths expressed in those Hebrew names, that God is our judge, as well as the one who shows us his grace. He wants us to forget the uniqueness of our God and the help that only he can provide. He wants to control the educational process, so

---

6. On the origin of the names, see John Goldingay, *Daniel*, Word Biblical Commentary (Dallas: Word, 1989), 5; on the literary significance of the renaming, see B. T. Arnold, "Word Play and Characterization in the Hebrew Bible," in S. B. Noegel, ed., *Puns and Pundits: Word Play in the Hebrew Bible and the Ancient Near East* (Bethesda, MD: CDL Press, 2000), 243–47.

A b o r t i o n
↓ L G B T A g e n d a

that our children grow up immersed in his worldview and his philosophy of life. If he can further instill in us a sense of dependence upon the material comforts that make up our way of life, or certain pleasures of this world that we have grown to love, then he can far more effectively draw us away from the Lord. His fundamental goal is always to obliterate our memory of the Lord, to reeducate our minds to his way of thinking, and to instill in us a sense that all of the good things in life come from the world around us and from the satisfaction of the desires of our own flesh.

Recognizing the Babylonian strategy helps us to see and evaluate the strategy of resistance formulated by the four young men. To be sure, they did not outwardly resist the Babylonian system. They did not refuse to work for the Babylonians, perhaps because they recognized the hand of God in their situation. They understood the word that the Lord gave through Jeremiah, that those whom he had sent to Babylon should labor there for the blessing of the place in which they found themselves (Jer. 29:4–7). As far as possible these young men sought to work within the system in which they had been placed, being good citizens of Babylon as well as of heaven. They didn't kick against the challenging providence of God, but rather accepted it as their present calling, with all of its trials, pains, and limitations. This reminds us that our calling is not to form Christian ghettoes that are isolated from the world around us. On the contrary, we should be active in pursuing the common good of the community in which God has placed us, whatever challenges may face us.

Maintaining Dual Identities

Yet at the same time the four friends accepted the will of God for their lives and served the Babylonian community, they also inwardly resisted the assimilation process of the Babylonian empire in a number of specific ways. In the first place, they resisted the total renaming program of the Babylonians. They didn't refuse to answer to their Babylonian names, to be sure, but they did maintain their Jewish names (and identities) as well. Daniel did not *become* Belteshazzar, even though he answered to that name, nor did Hananiah, Mishael, and Azariah *become* Shadrach, Meshach, and Abednego. They preserved their Hebrew names amongst themselves as a marker of who they really were (see 1:11, 19; 2:17); they lived with dual names as a

*Just like Jews of today—
a secular + a ? name within
the family*

DANIEL 1:1–21

reminder of their dual identities, and more fundamentally as a reminder of the true nature of their God.

How can we learn from them and maintain our dual identity as citizens of two kingdoms? Surely one way is by taking every opportunity that we can to celebrate our heavenly citizenship with other believers. It is a well-observed phenomenon that exiles are often more profoundly patriotic than those who have never left the mother country. St. Patrick's Day is certainly celebrated with more enthusiasm in Boston than it ever is in Dublin, and the Fourth of July means more to Americans abroad than it does at home. Exiles desire and need opportunities to celebrate and preserve their true identity. So, as citizens of heaven, we need to take every opportunity to gather with our fellow exiles, so that we can remind one another of "home." We cannot preserve our heavenly identity on our own: left to ourselves, the pressure of the world will inevitably crush us into its mold. But together we can help one another to keep the memory of heaven strong.

We remind one another of our true citizenship when we gather week by week in our homes and in our churches. There, we talk of our true home-land and remind one another of heaven. In our church services, our goal is not simply to be equipped for more effective lives here on earth, but also, or even more, to be reminded of the heavenly realities that truly define who we are. We do not simply come together to be taught in practical steps how to be more effective husbands and wives, fathers and children, employers and employees, but also to be pointed towards our true home. To be sure, if our heavenly identity is strong, it will transform our marriages, our parenting, and our work relationships (see Eph. 5:22–6:9), for in the kingdom to which we belong, these things are done differently than they are in this world. However, the primary focus of our coming together as the church is to fix our eyes together on the kingdom of heaven, our true home.

This is done as the signs of the kingdom are displayed in our worship services, through the preaching of the Word and the celebration of the sacraments. As the Word is preached, a heavenly wisdom is proclaimed that runs counter to the wisdom of the world around us. In baptism, the sign of heavenly citizenship is placed upon us and upon our children, reminding us where our true citizenship lies. In the Lord's Supper, we eat our native food, reminding one another of the cost at which our citizenship was bought and

11

of the ultimate feast that awaits us at home. All of these things help us to preserve and to remember our true identity.

The four young men also preserved biblical knowledge and perspectives in the midst of a thoroughly pagan educational system. This is a challenge that increasingly faces families in our community as well. Different families will resolve to meet that challenge in different ways. Some will homeschool their children, or send them to a school with a godly, Christian ethos. Others will walk with their children through a public school setting, helping them to stand firm as believers in the midst of the world. Each of those choices may be the right one for a particular child from a particular family in a particular setting, yet each family needs to recognize the need to train their children not simply in an outward conformity to Christian morality but in a true countercultural Christian identity as citizens of heaven, living on earth. Wherever they are educated, our children need to know and understand the contemporary "language and literature of the Babylonians" and to be armed with biblical discernment into its follies and flaws.

STAYING DEPENDENT UPON GOD

The second way in which the four young men resisted assimilation into the Babylonian system, though, was that they resolved not to eat the food from the king's table nor to drink his wine:

> But Daniel resolved not to defile himself with the royal food and wine, and he asked the chief official for permission not to defile himself this way. Now God had caused the official to show favor and sympathy to Daniel, but the official told Daniel, "I am afraid of my lord the king, who has assigned your food and drink. Why should he see you looking worse than the other young men your age? The king would then have my head because of you."
>
> Daniel then said to the guard whom the chief official had appointed over Daniel, Hananiah, Mishael and Azariah, "Please test your servants for ten days: Give us nothing but vegetables to eat and water to drink. Then compare our appearance with that of the young men who eat the royal food, and treat your servants in accordance with what you see." So he agreed to this and tested them for ten days.
>
> At the end of the ten days they looked healthier and better nourished than any of the young men who ate the royal food. So the guard took

away their choice food and the wine they were to drink and gave them vegetables instead. (Dan. 1:8–16)

The issue here was not simply that the Babylonian food was not kosher—that is, prepared according to the Jewish dietary laws. Nor was the issue that the meat and wine had first been offered to Babylonian idols, for that would have been the case with the vegetables as well.[7] If there had been something intrinsically evil about the Babylonian food, then Daniel would have had to abstain permanently from royal meat and wine, which does not seem to have been the case (see Dan. 10:3). The key to understanding why the four young men abstained from the royal food and wine is noticing that instead they chose to eat only those things that grow naturally—grains and vegetables—and to drink only naturally occurring water (1:12). This suggests that the goal of this simple lifestyle was to be constantly reminded of their dependence upon their creator God for their food, not King Nebuchadnezzar.[8] Dependence on Nebuchadnezzar's rich food would have been defiling because it would have repeated in their own lives the sin of King Hezekiah that brought this judgment upon God's people in the first place (see 2 Kings 20:17).

So also we need to build into our daily routines constant reminders of our dependence upon God for all of the good things in our lives. Even such a simple act as giving thanks for our food may be a profound reminder of who has provided it for us. Keeping a daily record of the Lord's gifts to us, from the trivial to the profound, can be another way of keeping our eyes fixed on our Creator. The practice of fasting—deliberately choosing to abstain from some of the legitimate pleasures and satisfactions in this world—can also be a powerful means in which we too can remind ourselves that this world is not our home and that its gifts are not our real treasure. Omitting a meal and instead devoting the time to prayer is a potent way of keeping our eyes fixed on our true inheritance and our hearts longing for the true feast.

Once again, though, Daniel and his friends sought to maintain their faithfulness to God by working *within* the Babylonian system, not against it. They sought permission from the chief official for their personalized diet

7. Goldingay, *Daniel*, 18.
8. Jacques Doukhan, *Daniel: The Vision of the End* (Berrien Springs, MI: Andrews University Press, 1989), 74.

plan (Dan. 1:8). The official was sympathetic to their request, but, like many government bureaucrats, he was also afraid of the potential consequences of bucking the system (1:10). Yet at the same time his response was not an outright refusal of their request, so Daniel went further down the chain of command to the guard who looked after them and proposed a ten-day test. At the end of that trial period, he could evaluate their progress. Surprisingly, at the end of this time, Daniel and his friends looked fitter (which in that context meant fatter; see 1:15) than those who had been indulging in a high-calorie lifestyle. So the guard agreed to continue to provide the four young men with the means for their alternative way of life, by which they could maintain their constant awareness of the one true God.

God's Faithfulness in Mercy

The focus throughout this chapter is not simply the faithfulness of these four young men to their God, however. It is on God's faithfulness to them. It was God who caused them to find mercy (*rahamim*) in the eyes of their captors (Dan. 1:9). This was an explicit answer to King Solomon's prayer at the dedication of the temple. On that occasion, Solomon prayed that when the people ended up in exile, as they surely would because of their sinfulness, then the Lord would cause their captors to show them mercy (*rahamim*; 1 Kings 8:50). This mercy is exactly what the chief official showed Daniel and his friends. What is more, the outcome of their dietary test was clearly not what ordinarily would have been expected: normally people don't get fat on a simple diet of fruit and vegetables. This outcome too was a mark of God's faithfulness to these young men, honoring their commitment to him.

In addition, it was God who gave all four of them exceptional knowledge and understanding of Babylonian literature and learning and gave Daniel the unique ability to discern visions and dreams of all kinds:

> To these four young men God gave knowledge and understanding of all kinds of literature and learning. And Daniel could understand visions and dreams of all kinds.
>
> At the end of the time set by the king to bring them in, the chief official presented them to Nebuchadnezzar. The king talked with them, and he found none equal to Daniel, Hananiah, Mishael and Azariah; so they entered the king's service. In every matter of wisdom and understanding about which the

king questioned them, he found them ten times better than all the magicians and enchanters in his whole kingdom.

And Daniel remained there until the first year of King Cyrus. (Dan. 1:17–21)

God's favor upon them enabled them to answer all of Nebuchadnezzar's questions, so that he found them ten times better than all of his other advisors (1:20). God thus placed them in a unique position where they could be a blessing to their captors and build up the society in which they found themselves, while at the same time enabling them to remain true to him in the midst of extraordinary pressures.

We are perhaps so familiar with the stories of Daniel and his three friends that we may fail to realize what a remarkable work of the Lord's faithfulness their testimony was. As a result, we miss the comfort and encouragement that we can gain from their lives. If the Lord could keep these young men faithful to him in their situation, then he is surely able to keep us faithful to him in our much lesser trials and difficulties. No matter how overwhelming our situation may seem, God is able to keep us through it. It is his work from beginning to end, and he will do it.

This theme of the faithfulness of God emerges again in the brief note with which the chapter closes, which literally says: "Daniel lived until the first year of Cyrus" (Dan. 1:21). The first year of Cyrus was the year in which the decree was issued that enabled the Jews to return home (see 2 Chron. 36:22–23), some seventy years after the time when Daniel and his friends were taken into exile. We are thus reminded that God's faithfulness proved sufficient for Daniel throughout the entire time of the exile. Babylonian kings came and went. Indeed, the Babylonians themselves were replaced as the ruling world power by the Medo-Persians in the person of Cyrus, yet God sustained his faithful servant throughout the whole time. In the same way, he is able to preserve us throughout the trials and tribulations that we face, no matter how intense they may be or how long they may last. When the world does its worst, God's faithfulness is enough.

God's Faithfulness in Our Salvation

There is one final note that we must not miss in all of this. The reality for most of us is that when we look at our lives, we find we are *not* like

Daniel and his three friends. We are far more like the nameless multitude who were deported along with Daniel, who adopted foreign names, ate the king's food, and altogether became like the Babylonians. In many respects, we are assimilated to the world system in which we live, and our futures are mortgaged to it. So if the message of this book is simply "Be like Daniel and all will be well," then we might as well stop reading now. The more we get to know Daniel, the more we come to realize that we are not Daniels.

The good news of the gospel, however, is not simply that God is faithful to those who are faithful to him. It is that a Savior has come to deliver faithless and compromised saints like us. Our salvation rests not on our ability to remain undefiled by the world, but rather on the pure and undefiled offering that Jesus has provided in our place. Jesus Christ came voluntarily into this world, with all of its pains and trials. He endured far greater temptations and sufferings than Daniel did, or than we ever will (Heb. 4:15). Yet he remained entirely faithful and pure until the very end, without spot or blemish, and grants the perfection of his obedience to all those who trust in him by faith (1 Peter 1:19). What is more, Jesus has already returned from his time of exile and now sits at the Father's right hand in heaven. He has prepared our places there, and his presence there already is the guarantee that one day we will be with him there as his people. The cross is the means by which God's faithfulness redeems the unfaithful; the resurrection and ascension are the surety of our inheritance in heaven.

Remind yourself often of this gospel. Fix your eyes on Jesus Christ crucified, raised, and exalted. He has not only pioneered the route home; he *is* the route home. Trust in him and ask him to work in you a true faithfulness. Ask him to put you in places where you can be a blessing to your community. Be a breath of heavenly wisdom in your home, your school, your workplace. Be constantly dependent upon his sanctifying work, looking to him to keep you faithful, not to your best efforts to "Be a Daniel." Finally, long for the day when his heavenly kingdom will invade this earth and bring the fullness of your inheritance.

2

INTERESTING TIMES

Daniel 2:1–23

*Then Daniel returned to his house and explained the matter to
his friends Hananiah, Mishael, and Azariah. He urged them to
plead for mercy from the God of heaven concerning this mystery,
so that he and his friends might not be executed with the rest of
the wise men of Babylon. (Dan. 2:17–18)*

n old Chinese saying goes like this: "May you live in interesting times." Is the saying a blessing or a curse? I'm not sure.
On the one hand, young people tend to dream of living in
"interesting times." We hope to find a place in history where we are able to
make a difference in the flow of world events. But as we grow older, sometimes we wish that the times in which we live were a little less "interesting."
Living in "interesting times" is often challenging and sometimes painful.

It was Daniel's calling, for better or for worse, to live in interesting times.
At least, that is the impression we get from the biblical book that bears his
name and recounts some of the challenging situations he faced. Of course,
we shouldn't overstate the case. After all, Daniel lived a long life, spanning
from the days of Nebuchadnezzar when he was carried off into exile from
Judah to the time of Cyrus when the exile came to an end. His adult life

thus covered some seventy years. Much of that time was probably not very interesting at all. During many of those years, as far as we know, nothing special happened. There was just the difficult regular routine of Daniel's faithfulness in a faraway land, trying to balance the demands of his two masters, the Babylonians and the Lord.

THE BLESSING OF INTERESTING TIMES

We don't have any record of these ordinary times, however. The times in Daniel's life that Scripture records for us are the "interesting times"— the moments when Daniel's two loyalties clashed sharply with each other, or when his life was threatened in some way or another. It was not as if God was not also with Daniel in exile during the other times. However, at these special times of stress and trial, it was made evident to all those around Daniel that the Lord was working in and through his life in a special way.

The same may be true in our own lives as well. Do you want friends and neighbors to be able to see the difference that being a Christian makes? That is really a prayer to live in "interesting times," for it is most often in our trials and difficulties that the difference that our faith in God makes to us becomes evident. For example, it has been said that the reason God sends cancer to Christians as well as to non-Christians is so that the world may see the difference in how they deal with it. Certainly, such times of trial do provide the opportunity for our faith to make a visible difference in our lives. As long as the world can find a perfectly good explanation for our peace in the circumstances of our lives, it will not be puzzled by us. The world will be forced to sit up and take notice only when we have a peace that is clearly *not* the result of our comfortable circumstances, a peace that evidently transcends the peace that the world gives.

As the apostle Peter put it, "These [trials] have come so that your faith— of greater worth than gold, which perishes even though refined by fire— may be proved genuine and may result in praise, glory and honor when Jesus Christ is revealed" (1 Peter 1:7). It is in the "interesting times" of life that the world sees the genuineness of our faith in God put on open display. It is then that our faith and our peace may shine out clearly as a beacon of hope to those around us.

Daniel 2 was certainly one of those "interesting times" through which God put on display the difference between Daniel and those around him. In fact, the triumph of Daniel's wisdom over the wisdom of the Babylonians is the primary point of this chapter: the content of the dream itself, to which we will come in our next exposition, is secondary to the conflict between Daniel and the Babylonian wise men. This is evident from the fact that the story conforms closely to the genre of a "court tale of contest," much like that of Joseph's interpretation of Pharaoh's dream in Genesis 41 and similar stories from the ancient Near East.[1]

The conflict was initiated when King Nebuchadnezzar dreamed a dream (Dan. 2:1). In the ancient world, such dreams were thought to be shadows that the future cast in front of itself, tipping its hand to show what lay ahead. The interpretation of the dream was therefore important, in order that the king might take whatever steps could be taken to counteract the events the dream anticipated, or at least to be ready for them. In preparation for such eventualities, many of the kings of the ancient Near East had specialist dream interpreters on their payroll, and Nebuchadnezzar was no exception. He employed a staff of diviners, whose job it was to interpret the significance of such dreams, and whatever other omens might occur.

NEBUCHADNEZZAR AND THE DIVINERS

The opening of the story proceeds predictably enough, with the king's dreams:

> In the second year of his reign, Nebuchadnezzar had dreams; his mind was troubled and he could not sleep. So the king summoned the magicians, enchanters, sorcerers and astrologers to tell him what he had dreamed. When they came in and stood before the king, he said to them, "I have had a dream that troubles me and I want to know what it means."

1. Tremper Longman III, *Daniel*, New International Version Application Commentary (Grand Rapids: Zondervan, 1999), 73–74. Of course, the fact that events are reported according to a more or less standard fashion has no bearing on the historicity or otherwise of the events themselves. In our own time, newspaper obituaries have a fairly standard form, yet the lives they recount are nonetheless historical. So too, ancient story genres can be utilized by biblical authors to describe real, historical events.

Then the astrologers answered the king in Aramaic, "O king, live forever! Tell your servants the dream, and we will interpret it."

The king replied to the astrologers, "This is what I have firmly decided: If you do not tell me what my dream was and interpret it, I will have you cut into pieces and your houses turned into piles of rubble. But if you tell me the dream and explain it, you will receive from me gifts and rewards and great honor. So tell me the dream and interpret it for me." (Dan. 2:1–6)

After Nebuchadnezzar awoke from his dream, he summoned his professional interpreters—the "magicians, enchanters, sorcerers and astrologers" (Dan. 2:2)—and told them that he needed their services. They responded, as they doubtless had many times before, "O king, live forever! Tell your servants the dream and we will interpret it" (2:4).[2] At this point, however, Nebuchadnezzar introduced an extraordinary complication. Instead of telling the diviners the dream, which they could then seek to interpret by reference to their books of dream interpretation and other such resources, he declared that they would have to find out the dream itself as well as its interpretation.[3] If the diviners succeeded, then they would be given great rewards. However, if they failed to tell the king the dream and its interpretation, then they would be horribly executed and their houses would be destroyed (2:5–6). The word translated "turned into piles of rubble" here is uncertain: other alternatives are that it means that their houses would be "turned into a dunghill" or "confiscated and turned into a royal grant," to be given by the king to someone else. Either way, though, the prospects for the diviners were bleak. It is as if Nebuchadnezzar suspected all along the emptiness of

2. From this point through the end of chapter 7, the text switches from Hebrew into Aramaic, for reasons that are not entirely clear. Certainly, this underlines the foreignness of Daniel's setting; yet if that is the purpose, why not switch earlier (in 1:10 for example) or write the whole account in Aramaic? Perhaps the change indicates that these chapters address matters of universal significance, rather than those of more specifically Israelite concern (Jacques Doukhan, *Daniel: The Vision of the End* [Berrien Springs, MI: Andrews University Press, 1989], 33 n.66). Alternatively, the switch has been explained by Bill Arnold in terms of a shift in the literary point of view, with the narrator using Aramaic to provide distance between himself and the events of chapter 2–7 (B. T. Arnold, "The Use of Aramaic in the Hebrew Bible: Another Look at Bilingualism in Ezra and Daniel," *Journal of Northwest Semitic Languages* 22 (1996:1–16).

3. Some commentators have argued that Nebuchadnezzar had actually forgotten the dream, at least in its details, but the Aramaic in v.5 is more plausibly rendered "the matter is firm" rather than "the matter has gone from me" (see Stephen R. Miller, *Daniel*, New American Commentary [Nashville: Broadman, 1994], 81).

the diviners' alleged ability to foretell the future and was determined to put them to the test.

The Babylonian wise men were horrified at this unreasonable demand. They could not meet it, for they were diviners and not prophets.[4] That is, they sought to discern patterns in events and dreams that foreshadowed the future, but they claimed no direct access to the mind of the gods. Such a demand was too difficult, according to their theology, and they told the king so: "There is not a man on earth who can do what the king asks! No king, however great and mighty, has ever asked such a thing of any magician or enchanter or astrologer. What the king asks is too difficult. No one can reveal it to the king except the gods, and they do not live among men" (Dan. 2:10–11). Unlike the God of Israel, the gods of the Babylonians were not so accommodating as to reveal their plans ahead of time through their representatives on earth (see Amos 3:7). Thus in their view what the king asked of them was something impossible for human wisdom to accomplish. Here we see the uniqueness of the God of the Bible, who is both able and willing to reveal his plans and purposes to mankind.

Nebuchadnezzar was so infuriated by this response that he "ordered the execution of all the wise men of Babylon" (Dan. 2:12). As was already evident in the scale of the rewards that he promised and the punishments he threatened, Nebuchadnezzar did nothing by halves. In line with the king's normal pattern of overreaction—it is tempting to say "overkill"—the decree of death involved far more people than those who had faced the original demand to interpret the dream. Perhaps he concluded that if the wisdom of his counselors was insufficient for this crisis, what good was it in any situation? The failure of his diviners to reveal his dream and its meaning thus resulted in a decree of death for all of his wise men, including Daniel and his three friends (2:13).

DANIEL'S FAITH, GOD'S FAITHFULNESS

When the bad news came to Daniel, he responded with a wisdom and faith in God far beyond his years:

4. Longman, *Daniel*, 74.

21

When Arioch, the commander of the king's guard, had gone out to put to death the wise men of Babylon, Daniel spoke to him with wisdom and tact. He asked the king's officer, "Why did the king issue such a harsh decree?" Arioch then explained the matter to Daniel. At this, Daniel went in to the king and asked for time, so that he might interpret the dream for him.

Then Daniel returned to his house and explained the matter to his friends Hananiah, Mishael and Azariah. He urged them to plead for mercy from the God of heaven concerning this mystery, so that he and his friends might not be executed with the rest of the wise men of Babylon. During the night the mystery was revealed to Daniel in a vision. Then Daniel praised the God of heaven. (Dan. 2:14–19)

Put yourself in Daniel's shoes for a moment. At first sight, this decree must have seemed proof of the monumental meaninglessness of life. Daniel and his three friends had been preserved out of the holocaust of the destruction of Judah and then miraculously protected in the king's court despite their commitment to eat only vegetables, but now they were condemned to death along with all the other wise men of the court. Simply because the king had a sleepless night and a fit of unreasonableness, their lives were now at risk—a "decree was issued to put the wise men to death, and men were sent to look for Daniel and his friends to put them to death" (Dan. 2:13).

Yet in the face of these adverse circumstances, Daniel didn't panic. He understood that in spite of all appearances to the contrary, this bizarre event too was under the sovereign control of God, who had a purpose in all of it. This purpose turned out to be not simply to show Nebuchadnezzar the future through this dream, but to demonstrate clearly the difference between Daniel and the rest of the wise men of Babylon, and between his God and theirs. Nebuchadnezzar's dream and his decree of death for the wise men was not a meaningless tragedy; rather, it would provide the context for God to display publicly his power.

In the first place, God showed his power by granting Daniel initial favor before King Nebuchadnezzar. When the king's wise men told him, "Let the king tell his servants the dream, and we will interpret it," Nebuchadnezzar accused the diviners of "trying to gain time, because you realize that this is what I have firmly decided: If you do not tell me the dream, there is just one penalty for you. You have conspired to tell me misleading and wicked things, hoping the situation will change. So then, tell me the dream, and I will know that you can interpret it for me" (Dan. 2:7–9). Yet when Daniel asked for time to interpret the dream, he received what he asked from the king. By itself, however, this merely provided a stay of execution for Daniel and his three friends, Hananiah, Mishael, and Azariah (Dan. 2:17). Here they are given their Hebrew names, rather than the more familiar Babylonian names: Shadrach, Meshach, and Abednego. Perhaps this is because they will need to remember the Lord's grace, uniqueness, and willingness to help his people in distress—attributes to which these names allude.[5]

In search of a more permanent answer to their situation, they therefore pleaded for mercy (*rahamin*; 2:18) from the God of heaven that they might not be executed with the rest of the Babylonian wise men. In making this request, they were echoing Solomon's prayer at the dedication of the temple in 1 Kings 8:50, that in the times to come God would cause their captors to show his exiled people mercy (*rahamim*; the Hebrew equivalent of the Aramaic word used here). In other words, in their prayer they pleaded with God to be faithful to his Word and to deliver them in their hour of need. With the stark clarity that such "interesting times" bring, they knew that their hope rested in God alone: if he did not reveal the dream to them, then there was nowhere else for them to turn. No mere human wisdom could deliver them from their predicament.

It is particularly amazing that they echoed Solomon's prayer at this point, for the temple for which Solomon prayed was then in ruins, abandoned by the Lord and destroyed by the Babylonians. Yet even in the complete absence of earthly signs of God's favor, they nonetheless trusted in his bare word of promise to be their God in the midst of their distress, no matter where they might find themselves.

Trusting in God alone like this is never a comfortable situation to be in, for by definition it means that all human means of support have been knocked away. It means that we have no one else to whom we can turn. Yet who could be better to turn to in a time of trial? Who is like the Lord as a helper and deliverer? God is both faithful and able to support us in our hour of need and to deliver us from our great distress. As we will see as we go further in the Book of Daniel, he doesn't always deliver us from our trials in the way that he delivers Daniel and his friends here. Sometimes he

---

5. On these names, see the exposition of Daniel 1.

delivers us by walking through the fiery trial with us, rather than saving us out of it (see Heb. 11). Yet the Lord is always faithful to his Word, and whenever we find ourselves at our wit's end, it is always a good strategy to gather our friends and flee to God, pleading the promises of his Word and trusting in his sure faithfulness.

In this case, the Lord answered Daniel's prayer by revealing the mystery to him (Dan. 2:19). Yet Daniel did not immediately rush off to Nebuchadnezzar with the answer. Even with his life in the balance, Daniel took the time to give thanks to God for the answer he had received. This is where we so often fall short, isn't it? We may pray passionately for a deliverance from our trials, but when that deliverance comes, we fail to return our thanks to God. Like nine out of ten of the lepers healed by Jesus (Luke 17:12–19), we go on our way rejoicing that our problems are solved. Eager to get on with life, we forget the one from whom our healing comes. Not so Daniel. He takes the time to praise God for the awesome deliverance he has received before he brings the answer to the king.

THE POWER AND WISDOM OF GOD

Specifically, Daniel praises God for his power and his wisdom:

Praise be to the name of God for ever and ever; wisdom and power are his. He changes times and seasons; he sets up kings and deposes them. He gives wisdom to the wise and knowledge to the discerning. He reveals deep and hidden things; he knows what lies in darkness, and light dwells with him. I thank and praise you, O God of my fathers: you have given me wisdom and power, you have made known to me what we asked of you, you have made known to us the dream of the king. (Dan. 2:20–23)

The Lord alone possesses the power to control world events. The future does not rest in the hands of the Babylonian gods, to whom the diviners looked. Their gods are empty idols, with no power either to bless or to curse their followers (see Isa. 46:5–10). They cannot affect the future, for they themselves are blind, dumb, and impotent (Isa. 44:18). For all the pomp and show of the Babylonian diviners, their claims to anticipate the future are empty and void. The Lord is the one who raises up kings and deposes them. He sets the times and seasons for everything under the sun (Dan. 2:21; compare Eccl. 3).

Yet Israel's God does not merely control the future; he also *reveals* the future to his servants. He gives wisdom to the wise and reveals the mysteries of the future, as he has done in this case for Daniel (2:21–22). This was precisely what the Babylonian diviners wrote off as impossible, because the gods do not dwell with men (2:11). Yet Israel's God, even though he is transcendent and exalted high above the heavens, *does* dwell with the humble and contrite of spirit (Isa. 57:15). The one who governs the future has made it known to Daniel by revealing both the dream and its interpretation.

This assertion that Israel's God is the one who possesses all power and wisdom was an important reminder for Daniel's hearers. As exiles in Babylon, they were surrounded by alternative religions that claimed to offer access to the hidden mysteries of the universe. The events of this chapter exposed the emptiness of these claims: there is only one God who reveals the future, because there is only one God who controls the future. However outwardly impressive the "wisdom" and "power" of the world may seem, they have no ultimate substance. Babylon's gods were a sham and a lie.

The same message is important in our own day and time. We too are surrounded by the power and wisdom of the world. Sometimes it takes explicitly religious shape and promises us enlightenment and deeper experience of life through New Age meditation or practices borrowed from Eastern religions. Sometimes it takes the form of an explicit denial that God can really know and control the future, preferring to imagine an "open" God who is struggling his way through the historical process alongside us. At other times, it comes to us in secular forms, promising power and success through applying its strategies in business and in personal relationships. It often presents impressive credentials and, like the Babylonian diviners, comes to us strongly endorsed by the society in which we live. The wisdom of the world looks outwardly very impressive, with its qualifications and influence in high places in our society. Yet at root the wisdom of the world is always an empty sham. It neither understands the true nature of humanity, nor the true nature of the world in which we live. How can it, when it denies the existence or ignores the relevance of the one true God who created and controls all things? His power works all things according to his will (Rom. 8:28). His wisdom is the true source of insight for skillful living (Prov. 1:7).

Pursuing Wisdom

Where are we to find that wisdom for our own lives? The Lord has revealed that wisdom to us in his Word, the Bible. We don't need to flounder around seeking to piece together our own wisdom when we have this book. Nor do we need to be able to interpret strange dreams. Instead, we need to dive into its depths and ponder its profundity. We need to store it in our hearts and treasure its riches. This is not exactly a new observation, yet it is one that we need constantly to recall. For in practice, even as Christians, we often live our lives according to the wisdom of the world. If we pursued God's wisdom with half of the enthusiasm with which we seek to progress in the world, we would be much wiser than we are. If we spent even half the passion on seeking God that we spend on seeking amusement, our lives would be far different from those of the people around us. Think back over this past week and see what pursuits have filled your hours and minutes. Have you sought the Lord's wisdom and power, or poured yourself into the pursuit of the world's emptiness?

If we pursue God's wisdom with a passion, then we too, like Daniel, will be distinct from the culture around us, and we will be better able to give those around us the answer to questions that are beyond them. People around us may not be having the same dreams as Nebuchadnezzar, but they are nonetheless regularly faced with questions they cannot answer. They wonder, "Why am I here? What happens to me when I die? How should I live in this world?" These are profound questions that keep intruding themselves into our lives, especially in times of trial, and they are questions for which the wisdom of the world is always insufficient. Only the wisdom of the world's Creator, the one for whom and by whom all things exist, will suffice. He reveals this wisdom to all in his Word and gives it to us to read. Should we not, like Daniel, thank and praise God for the richness of his gift to us, treasure this source of heavenly wisdom, and share it with our puzzled neighbors?

God's wisdom has a subjective as well as objective aspect to it. Objectively, his revealed Word tells me who God is and who I am, what I should believe about him, and how I should please him. This is a wonderful gift. Yet in order to live wisely in this world, I also need to be able to apply the principles of the Word subjectively in the various situations of life. Given the mandate to share the gospel with my neighbors, how should I best approach them with the good news of Jesus Christ? Given the commandment to love my wife and sacrifice myself for her, what does that mean for the way in which I order my time and my priorities today? Out of the various choices of employment or career in front of me, what does God want me to do with my life?

Christians often tend to gravitate towards one aspect of wisdom to the neglect of the other. Some Christians place a great deal of stress on the objective aspect of wisdom: they rightly revere the Bible as God's Word, the normative source of true wisdom. Yet these Christians may at the same time neglect to depend on God for the subjective aspect of it, how to apply it in particular circumstances. In practice, they may be functionally dependent on their own wisdom for these "circumstantial" issues, rather than leaning on God's Spirit for guidance, moment by moment. Other believers place a great deal of stress on the subjective aspect of God's wisdom: they affirm that God guides them moment by moment, perhaps through intuitions, or by other means through which they sense that the Spirit is directing them. Yet these believers may sometimes place so much stress on these subjective sources of guidance that the normative character of the objective Word of God is in practice placed in a secondary, and even subordinate, position.[6]

Daniel had a grasp of both objective and subjective wisdom: objectively, he knew the Word of God, a knowledge that must surely have been implanted within him in his childhood, before he was carried into exile. He was thoroughly grounded in the Scriptures and ordered his behavior on the basis of them. Subjectively, though, he also recognized that God is able to guide indirectly through circumstances and, in this unique case, by dreams and visions as well as directly through the Word. Such a balance of objective and subjective wisdom does not come to us through education or qualifications (though Daniel had both and we should not despise them). It comes in response to prayer. It is by humble petition that we come to

6. For a helpful discussion, see Vern S. Poythress, "Modern Spiritual Gifts as Analagous to Apostolic Gifts: Affirming Extraordinary Works of the Spirit within Cessationist Theology," *JETS* 39 (1996): 71–102.

understand the more challenging and difficult aspects of God's revealed Word, as Daniel 9 will make clear. Yet it is also by humble petition that we seek to understand how God would have us apply that Word in the complex and challenging world in which we live. We need to learn to grow in our constant dependence upon God to live wisely, both as we read his Word and as we live our lives.

Jesus Christ: The Wisdom of God

Simply living his life wisely would not have saved Daniel by itself. After the decree for his death went forth from the king, nothing but the direct intervention of God could save him. If God had remained at a distance and had not revealed to him the king's dream, Daniel would have faced the same fate as the Babylonian diviners. But God did not remain at a distance: he came to Daniel and revealed the dream, delivering him from death.

This part of the Book of Daniel points us forward to Christ. In Christ, God definitively came to live among men, thereby disproving once and for all the theology of the Babylonian diviners that the gods do not dwell among men (see Dan. 2:11). In Christ, God became flesh and made his dwelling among us. In him, we saw revealed the glory of the one and only true God (John 1:14). He came and lived the perfect life of wisdom, the perfect combination of obedience to God's Word and constant dependence upon the Spirit's guidance. Just as Daniel gave thanks to God for his deliverance, Jesus modeled for us an entire life of thanksgiving to God, even giving thanks for a trial from which there would be no deliverance for him. At the Last Supper, Jesus gave thanks for the bread when he was about to break it—an action that symbolized the breaking of his body for our sin (Matt. 26:26). When he took the cup, the cup that would mean life for us but suffering and woe for him, Jesus gave thanks for it (Matt. 26:27). Jesus thus gave thanks ahead of time for the cross, the most unjust and agonizing trial that has ever faced a person!

When Jesus gave thanks for the cross, it was not because he minimized its awful cost. Later that same evening, in the Garden of Gethsemane, its horror caused him to sweat as if he were shedding drops of blood (Luke 22:44). Nothing we will ever face could match up to that event. Yet Jesus nonetheless gave thanks for the cross because he recognized that it was not a meaningless trial; he saw ahead of time its reward. He gave thanks for the cross because he knew that by it God would redeem for himself a holy people that would be his for all eternity. By the cross, God would deliver us from death and fit us for eternal life in heaven.

When Jesus prayed that God might show him mercy and allow the cup to pass from him, he had no friend to share his burden, as Daniel did. He had to pray his prayer alone, for the disciples were all too tired to stay awake with him and pray. What is more, Jesus' prayer for deliverance was not answered in the way that Daniel's prayer was. He was not delivered from the undeserved sentence of death in his hour of need. Yet the reason his prayer was not answered was simple: it was so that we might be delivered in our hour of need and might receive undeserved mercy from the divine king. Through his death, we received our lives.

Daniel and his friends weren't the only ones whose lives were spared by God's intervention, though. The Babylonian diviners were delivered as well. What did the Babylonian diviners do with their stay of execution? Did they give worship and praise to Daniel's God, as Nebuchadnezzar did (Dan. 2:46–47)? Or did they ascribe Daniel's success in discovering the dream to a lucky guess or insider information? We don't know, because it is not important for us to know their story. The more important point is what we will do with our stay of execution. What will we do with the good news of the gospel? We need to respond to the news that someone has come to bear our sins and to give us the righteousness we need to stand before a holy God as a free gift. We must repent and abandon our love affair with the gods of this world and the wisdom and power they offer and bow down to Jesus. We must throw ourselves on God's mercy and ask for the death of Jesus to cover our sins. It is the only way to receive the life that he offers.

Yet there is also a challenge in this passage to those of us who are believers, particularly as we face the trials and challenges of life—the "interesting times." We need to recognize, as Jesus did, that these times are never meaningless but come to us from our Father's hand. We must receive these trials not merely with submission, but also with thanksgiving. We too can give thanks for the cup that our Father has set before us.

The only way to suffer with thankfulness is to remember the cup that Jesus has drained in our place, the cup of God's wrath toward our sins. As a result of that sacrifice, we know that whatever suffering we now encounter

29

is an outworking of God's grace towards us. The sovereign God has brought us into this trial, and he will either deliver us out of it or sustain us by his grace through the midst of it. He is not distant and uncaring, nor is he powerless to deliver us. On the contrary, in Christ God has come to dwell among us and with us, precisely in order to deliver us from our deepest trial: our alienation from him. Even now, he indwells us by his Holy Spirit. So we must depend on his Spirit to give us the heavenly wisdom that we need to face each day. We need to look to him for objective wisdom from his Word and subjective direction in every moment of our lives. We should praise him daily for his guidance and his help, his protection and his power. If we remember these things, then we will have peace for the present, and a sure inheritance stored up for us in heaven, when our "interesting times" will finally be done.

3

GONE WITH THE WIND

Daniel 2:24–49

In the time of those kings, the God of heaven will set up a king-
dom that will never be destroyed, nor will it be left to another
people. It will crush all those kingdoms and bring them to an end,
but it will itself endure forever. This is the meaning of the vision
of the rock cut out of a mountain, but not by human hands—
a rock that broke the iron, the bronze, the clay, the silver and
the gold to pieces. (Dan. 2:44–45)

Margaret Mitchell's epic novel *Gone with the Wind* is a lament for a lost culture. It is a eulogy for the beautiful but doomed society of the antebellum South, swept away by the devastation of the American Civil War. Yet in the midst of the carnage and devastation on all sides, the memorable characters of the book are the inveterate survivors, Rhett Butler and Scarlett O'Hara, who are able to swim with and against the currents around them, surviving one disaster after another with indomitable spirit. In the midst of tragedy, they defiantly declare, "Tomorrow is another day."

Had it been written at the time, the exiles of Judah might well have found *Gone with the Wind* compelling reading. The images of Atlanta in flames would certainly have been painfully familiar to those who saw Nebuchadnezzar destroy Jerusalem, and they might well have been able to identify with Scarlett and Rhett's struggles in a postwar world filled with carpetbaggers and compromisers. They too needed encouragement to believe, with Scarlett, that "Tomorrow is another day." In essence, that encouragement of a new future is what Nebuchadnezzar's dream gave to them, and through them to us also.

DANIEL AND ARIOCH

To recap the events of Daniel 2, Nebuchadnezzar king of Babylon had a dream (Dan. 2:1). He summoned his wise men to interpret the dream for him but refused to tell them its contents (2:5–6). This task they declared impossible, because the gods who give such dreams do not live among men to reveal such information (2:11). In his rage at their refusal, Nebuchadnezzar sentenced all of his wise men to death, a fate which included Daniel and his three friends, Hananiah, Mishael, and Azariah (2:12–13). But when Daniel learned of this decree, he asked the king for more time and went to the Lord in prayer, seeking the dream and its interpretation (2:16–18). The Lord answered his prayer and gave him both the dream and its meaning, and Daniel responded with praise and thanksgiving (2:19–23).

This brings us to the point in the chapter where Daniel went in to the king to interpret the dream for him:

> Then Daniel went to Arioch, whom the king had appointed to execute the wise men of Babylon, and said to him, "Do not execute the wise men of Babylon. Take me to the king, and I will interpret his dream for him."
>
> Arioch took Daniel to the king at once and said, "I have found a man among the exiles from Judah who can tell the king what his dream means."
>
> The king asked Daniel (also called Belteshazzar), "Are you able to tell me what I saw in my dream and interpret it?"
>
> Daniel replied, "No wise man, enchanter, magician or diviner can explain to the king the mystery he has asked about, but there is a God in heaven who reveals mysteries. He has shown King Nebuchadnezzar what will happen in days to come." (Dan. 2:24–28)

At this juncture, we should note Daniel's demeanor in approaching the king, which is to deflect all credit from himself to the Lord. The narrator has highlighted this for us by contrasting Daniel's humility with the words of Arioch, the commander of the king's guard. Arioch approached the king and declared, "I have found a man among the exiles from Judah who can tell the king what his dream means" (Dan. 2:25). Actually, Arioch did nothing of the sort. He was ready to execute Daniel, along with the rest of the wise men. It was Daniel who went and found Arioch, not vice versa (2:24). Yet Arioch was eager to claim at least some of the credit for this stunning turn of events for himself. This is the way the world works, isn't it? Pass as much of the blame for your failures on to other people, and claim as much credit as you can for other people's success!

Arioch's self-promoting attitude provides a vivid foil for Daniel, however. For when Nebuchadnezzar asked Daniel, "Are you able to tell me what I saw in my dream and interpret it?" (Dan. 2:26), Daniel could easily have answered "Yes" to that question and claimed the credit for himself. Yet instead he responded to the king: "No wise man, enchanter, magician or diviner can explain to the king the mystery he has asked about, but there is a God in heaven who reveals mysteries. He has shown King Nebuchadnezzar what will happen in days to come" (2:27–28). Instead of promoting himself, Daniel took the opportunity publicly to exalt his God: "As you were lying there, O king, your mind turned to things to come, and the revealer of mysteries showed you what is going to happen. As for me, this mystery has been revealed to me, not because I have greater wisdom than other living men, but so that you, O king, may know the interpretation and that you may understand what went through your mind" (Dan. 2:29–30).

TRUE HUMILITY

There is a model here for all of us in our relationships with those who do not know our God. In contrast to the self-promoting way of the world, we should constantly seek occasions to exalt and declare publicly the praises of our God. Whatever gifts and abilities we have, whatever successes we may meet with in life, all of them are ultimately the work of the one who gave us those gifts and opportunities, along with the diligence and perseverance to pursue them. We are simply God's servants, doing the work he has assigned to us; he deserves all of the praise and adoration. The biblical word for this attitude is *humility*: the perspective that sees our own size rightly in comparison to the surpassing greatness of our God.

One caveat is important at this point, which is that our humility must be sincere. Ben Franklin once said of humility, "I cannot boast of much success in acquiring the reality of this virtue, but I had a good deal with regard to the appearance of it." Sadly, the same is true of many of us as well. We are not truly humble, but we certainly know how to fake it. I know this temptation exists in my own heart. I see it when I serve in some way in the church and then find myself looking to see if anyone is noticing my service. I see it when I publicly tell people that anything good in my sermons is a gift of God's grace—and then prepare the next one as if it were all up to me. I see it when I am even tempted to become proud of my own humility! Truly my heart is a cauldron of all kinds of self-promotion.

True humility comes, however, when we look away from ourselves towards God and towards the one who is God revealed in human flesh, Jesus Christ. He shows us genuine humility at work in his constant attitude of dependence upon his heavenly Father. He shows us authentic lowliness of heart that turns away from the spotlight and the position of glory to serve the outcasts and the unacceptable, the lepers and the notorious sinners. The Lord of all eternity demonstrated that servant's heart all the way to an inglorious death on the cross, reviled and spat upon, abandoned and alone. When I ponder his humility, my own attempts at humility are revealed as a mere baby step downwards, and I marvel afresh at the glory of God's plan of salvation, which has absolutely nothing to do with my merit and everything to do with Christ's work in my place. How can I exalt myself when I stand beside the cross?

Paradoxically, as I look at the humility of Christ, which is a quantum order of magnitude greater than anything I have attained, a true perspective on my own place in God's work becomes possible. When I see the richness of God's grace shown to me, a sinner, then real humility can start to grow. As the hymn writer Isaac Watts understood, it is precisely "when I survey the wondrous cross" that I begin to be able to "pour contempt on all my pride." This is the same genuine humility that shone out from Daniel's life, a humility that enabled him to give all of the glory to God for revealing the dream and its interpretation to him, and not to take any of the credit for himself.

NEBUCHADNEZZAR'S DREAM AND ITS INTERPRETATION

Daniel then recounted to Nebuchadnezzar his dream, which was precisely what Nebuchadnezzar's wise men had claimed was impossible:

> You looked, O king, and there before you stood a large statue—an enormous, dazzling statue, awesome in appearance. The head of the statue was made of pure gold, its chest and arms of silver, its belly and thighs of bronze, its legs of iron, its feet partly of iron and partly of baked clay. While you were watching, a rock was cut out, but not by human hands. It struck the statue on its feet of iron and clay and smashed them. Then the iron, the clay, the bronze, the silver and the gold were broken to pieces at the same time and became like chaff on a threshing floor in the summer. The wind swept them away without leaving a trace. But the rock that struck the statue became a huge mountain and filled the whole earth. (Dan. 2:31–35)

Having described the content of the dream, Daniel went on and told the king its interpretation:

> This was the dream, and now we will interpret it to the king. You, O king, are the king of kings. The God of heaven has given you dominion and power and might and glory; in your hands he has placed mankind and the beasts of the field and the birds of the air. Wherever they live, he has made you ruler over them all. You are that head of gold.
>
> After you, another kingdom will rise, inferior to yours. Next, a third kingdom, one of bronze, will rule over the whole earth. Finally, there will be a fourth kingdom, strong as iron—for iron breaks and smashes everything—and as iron breaks things to pieces, so it will crush and break all the others. Just as you saw that the feet and toes were partly of baked clay and partly of iron, so this will be a divided kingdom; yet it will have some of the strength of iron in it, even as you saw iron mixed with clay. As the toes were partly iron and partly clay, so this kingdom will be partly strong and partly brittle. And just as you saw the iron mixed with baked clay, so the people will be a mixture and will not remain united, any more than iron mixes with clay.
>
> In the time of those kings, the God of heaven will set up a kingdom that will never be destroyed, nor will it be left to another people. It will crush all those kingdoms and bring them to an end, but it will itself endure forever. This is the meaning of the vision of the rock cut out of a mountain, but not

by human hands—a rock that broke the iron, the bronze, the clay, the silver and the gold to pieces. (Dan. 2:36–45)

The dream and the interpretation given to Daniel were actually quite simple, at least if we focus our attention on its central message, and yet at the same time incredibly profound. What Nebuchadnezzar saw in his dream was an enormous statue of a man made up of four parts (Dan. 2:31). It had a head of gold, chest and arms of silver, belly and thighs of bronze, and legs of iron with feet of iron mixed with baked clay (2:32–33). While Nebuchadnezzar was watching, a rock was cut out but not by any human agency (2:34). It struck the statue on its feet, and the whole statue disintegrated into pieces, which the wind blew away like chaff. Meanwhile, the rock grew into a huge mountain and filled the earth (2:35).

Daniel interpreted this picture as follows: the head of gold is Nebuchadnezzar (Dan. 2:37). God is the one who gave him great dominion and power and glory. In fact, his power and glory are described in terms reminiscent of what was granted to Adam at the beginning of the world, with dominion not only over human beings but the birds of the air and the beasts of the field (2:38). After Nebuchadnezzar's time there would be more kingdoms, each of which would be inferior to the one that went before it in glory, though still strong and of wide-ranging power. The last of these kingdoms will be strong as iron, yet in the end it will prove to be an unstable composite of different peoples who cannot hold together. At that time, God will establish his final kingdom, which will ultimately destroy all other kingdoms. Though it starts small, it will grow to fill the earth and, unlike the earthly kingdoms, it will endure forever.

At this point, the temptation is to start inquiring about the identity of the four kingdoms in the vision. If the first kingdom is Babylon, can we also identify the other three? Some people argue that the four kingdoms are Babylon, Media, Persia, and Greece, while others say that they are Babylon, Medo-Persia, Greece, and Rome.[1] If the last kingdom is Rome, then who

---

1. The former scheme is widely accepted by critical scholars, who date the book as a whole during the Maccabean crisis in the middle of the second century B.C. (e.g., André Lacocque, *The Book of Daniel*, trans. D. Pellauer [Atlanta: John Knox, 1979], 51), while the latter more traditional view is generally argued by conservative scholars (e.g., Stephen R. Miller, *Daniel*, New American Commentary [Nashville: Broadman, 1994], 55–56). Nevertheless, some conservative scholars have argued in favor of the former view (see R. J. M. Gurney, "The Four Kingdoms of Daniel 2 and 7," *Themelios* 2 [1977]: 39–45; John Walton, "The

are the ten toes? It doesn't take long before we find our heads spinning with the variety of interpretations offered, all of which go far beyond the interpretation and application that Daniel himself gave here. It is important to notice, however, that the passage itself gives us virtually no data about the specifics of any of these kingdoms, because it intends to give a philosophy of history rather than a precise analysis of history ahead of time. As John Goldingay puts it, "In the drama of the story the description has to be allowed to remain allusive. People miss the point when they spend time arguing who the empires were."[2] The focus of the dream itself and its interpretation are more concerned with *what* the future holds than *when* it will come to pass. In our analysis, we shall focus our attention on the interpretation of the vision that the passage itself gives to us rather than pursuing broader and more speculative connections.

THE RISE AND FALL OF EARTHLY EMPIRES

So what, according to Daniel 2, does this dream seek to teach us? First, it shows us that God gives every earthly kingdom its glory and power: they do not come from their own strength. God gave Nebuchadnezzar his unparalleled sovereignty, power, strength, and glory (Dan. 2:37). In fact, the height of Nebuchadnezzar's authority is underlined by the creation language used to describe it: like Adam, he has been given authority not only over people, but over nature itself, so that the beasts of the field and the birds of the air are placed in his hands (2:38).[3] Yet that same creation imagery also underlines the dependent and transient nature of his position: like Adam, if he sins, he too can be cast down from his exalted position.[4] Even if he is

---

Four Kingdoms of Daniel," *JETS* 29 [1986]: 25–36). As Walton correctly notes, the identification of the kingdoms in Daniel 2 does not flow out of information contained within the passage itself but depends on attempts to correlate subsequent events with this passage and other complex prophetic texts.

2. John Goldingay, *Daniel*, Word Biblical Commentary (Dallas: Word, 1989), 58. See also Tremper Longman III, *Daniel*, New International Version Application Commentary (Grand Rapids: Zondervan, 1999), 82, and E. C. Lucas, *Daniel*, Apollos Old Testament Commentary (Downers Grove, IL: InterVarsity, 2002), 79. A similar scheme, with four successive ages of gold, silver, bronze, and iron, where the key point is their character rather than their identity, is also found in Hesiod, a Greek poet of the eighth century B.C.

3. The claim to this authority over nature was perhaps the rationale behind the royal game parks that Assyrian and Babylonian monarchs established (see A. L. Oppenheim, *Ancient Mesopotamia* [Chicago: University of Chicago, 1964], 46).

4. This is comparable to the exalted Adamic language used to describe the King of Tyre in Ezekiel 28, which likewise precedes anticipation of his fall.

history's head of gold, he can still be brought down to the dust. To use the language of Daniel's prayer, the same God who set him up as king can also depose him (2:21).

In fact, the transient nature of all worldly authority is one of the central features of the dream: it reminds us that every earthly kingdom has an "after this."[5] No earthly kingdom is forever: the gold gives way to the silver, which in turn gives way to the bronze and the iron. What is more, the progress of the history of man in rebellion from God is not simply a pattern of change but of regress. It is not simply that you can never step in the same river twice, as the Greek philosopher Heraclitus famously pointed out; it is that the river keeps getting more and more polluted as it travels from its source. Far from journeying onward and upward until we finally reach the great city of man, we go from one transient kingdom to another, proceeding downward from gold to silver to bronze to iron, rather than in a positive direction. The final kingdom in the sequence is not only inferior in glory to the first—iron compared to gold—but inferior in unity as well: it is made of iron mixed with baked clay, an uneven mixture that cannot hold together (Dan. 2:42–43).

The one thing that remains constant about these various kingdoms is their lust for power and their desire to dominate the world (Dan. 2:39–40). The desire to rule and crush remains undiminished throughout the sequence, but ultimately that ambition will go frustrated. In the final analysis, the kingdoms of this world, however glorious or powerful they may seem, have "feet of clay," as we say, and will not stand.

In fact, by linking these different kingdoms together as parts of a single statue in the form of a man, the dream says something profound about the whole human enterprise viewed as a unity, from beginning to end. In a real sense, this is not simply a vision of the decline and fall of the Babylonian empire and its immediate successors, but an epitaph for human history. The entire human endeavor, though gifted and blessed by God in the beginning with unparalleled glory and dominion, ends up in nothing but division and dissolution. This pattern is evident already in the early chapters of Genesis. The glory of Adam in Genesis 1–2 gives way to the judgment of the flood in Genesis 6–9 and the chaos of life after Babel in Genesis 11. According to this

---

5. Jacques Doukhan, *Daniel: The Vision of the End* (Berrien Springs, MI: Andrews Universitiy Press, 1989), 47.

pattern, our world is not destined to end with a glorious bang but rather with a pitiful whimper.

The depiction of these changing and ultimately failing earthly kingdoms stands in stark contrast to what replaces them, however. The kingdom of God enters the chaos and hopelessness of human history and brings fresh and lasting hope to humanity. After the despair of Genesis 11 comes the new hope of God's call to Abram in Genesis 12. Nebuchadnezzar's dream comes to a similar conclusion. The final word of history does not lie with a new and improved version of the statue of man. Rather, it lies with something radical that God will do: a rock that is not hewn by human hands will strike and demolish the statue and then grow to fill the earth (Dan. 2:34–35). This rock clearly points to the kingdom that God will establish in the last days, a kingdom that starts small and lacking in glory but grows through the power of God until it ultimately dominates the entire globe and becomes the ultimate fact of history. Only that divine kingdom is eternal.

SIC TRANSIT GLORIA MUNDI

How should we respond to this dream? In the first place, Nebuchadnezzar's dream encourages us to see reality around us more clearly. The transient nature of all earthly glory and power is an important reminder to modern readers, as well as ancient. *Sic transit gloria mundi* ("So passes the glory of the world") applies to modern America and Europe as well as to ancient Babylon. Whether our present earthly context is an actively hostile dictatorship or a relatively benevolent democracy, one day the glory and power of this kingdom too will come to an end, and there may be others after it. This world and its constantly changing kingdoms are not what life is all about.

This reality challenges the focus of our priorities and values. Which kingdom are we building? Are we pouring ourselves into the pursuit of the power and the glory of this world's kingdoms, a power and glory that must inevitably decay and topple into obscurity? Or are we instead pouring ourselves into the pursuit of God's kingdom, the only kingdom that will truly last? What is more, are we measuring our success by the fickle standards of present appearances, or do we have our eyes fixed on ultimate things? It is easy to become discouraged in our pursuit of God's kingdom if we measure things by the present. The church here on earth often seems powerless and weak, beset by problems. Our own lives too may evidence little progress in holiness. Yet the answer to that temptation to despair is to fix your eyes on the glorious promises of God and trust that in his own time he will build his kingdom, both in our own lives and in this world. No one and nothing can prevent him from accomplishing his purposes, for the final chapter of history has already been written.

There are two particular circumstances where we most need to hear and heed that truth. One is when things are going badly for us in this life. When our earthly hopes and dreams are in tatters, and our lives are being crushed painfully under the jackboot of the kingdoms of this world, we need to remember that this world is not ultimate. When we face sickness, isolation, and disability, even death itself, we need to remember that there is a kingdom that lasts beyond the grave. There is a time coming when the kingdom of this world will become the kingdom of our God and of his Christ (see Rev. 11:15).

Yet paradoxically we also need to be reminded of this truth when life is going well for us. This dream had a message not just for the Israelites who were squirming under the foot of the statue, but also for Nebuchadnezzar himself, who was the head of gold. In times when we may feel like the head of gold, when this world showers its honors and favors upon us, we need to remember that there will be an "after this." There will come a day when all of our little triumphs and glories will lie in the dust and we will stand before the great Creator to give an account. When that day comes, what will count will not be our standing in the statue but our standing on the rock.

GOD'S ROCK

The rock in this picture is none other than Jesus Christ. As Paul reminds us, the mystery of the ages that has now been revealed to those of us who live in the fullness of times is God's plan to bring all things in heaven and earth together under one head, even Jesus Christ (Eph. 1:9). Jesus came proclaiming that, with his arrival, the kingdom of God was at hand (Mark 1:15). In Luke 20 Jesus told the parable of the son of the vineyard owner whom the tenants rejected and killed. He then quoted Psalm 118, "The stone the builders rejected has become the capstone," and added, "Everyone who falls on that stone will be broken to pieces, but he on whom it falls will be crushed" (Luke 20:17–18). The last words in that prophecy come straight from Daniel 2:44–45, and by quoting them Jesus was identifying himself as Israel's Messiah, the stone which crushes the kingdoms of this world.

Paradoxically, as Luke 20 also makes clear, Jesus brings about the establishment of his kingdom through his rejection by the Jews and his sacrificial death. The son of the vineyard owner accomplishes his mission by dying (Luke 20:15). His kingdom is thus not like the kingdoms of this world. The kingdoms of this world advance by power and conquest, and glory in their strength. The kingdom of God advances through suffering and death, a pattern in which Jesus' own death led the way. By that death, he brings life to all who will come and bow down before him, receiving his kingdom as a free gift that comes by faith. To be sure, his kingdom starts out small, as Jesus pointed out in the parable of the mustard seed. The mustard seed begins as the tiniest of seeds, yet it grows into the mightiest of trees (Matt. 13:31–32). So it is with the kingdom that Jesus came to establish: it may start small but it grows into an unstoppable force. The passing glory of this world may seem outwardly impressive in the present, but the future belongs to God's kingdom.

Luke 20 also reminds us that those who stubbornly refuse to submit to Jesus and who place their trust in any other source of salvation will ultimately be rejected by him. Those who refuse to recognize the capstone will be crushed by it. Or, to use the imagery of Daniel 2, the kingdoms of this world and all those who have placed their trust in them will be shattered by the stone that God has appointed and will be blown away like chaff (Dan. 2:35). Like the straw that is separated from the grain by the winnowing process, the wicked—all those whose sins have not been washed away and replaced by Christ's righteousness imputed to them—will not stand in the day of judgment (Ps. 1:4). On the last day, they will be blown away, literally "gone with the wind."

If that is true, then we should be straining our eyes in anticipation of the return of the one who has come and is to come. For Daniel, the coming of the Rock was a future event, something to which he could look forward in the midst of the messiness of life. For us, however, the coming of the Rock is both past and future. Jesus Christ has come into the world and established his kingdom. God calls us even now to submit to the Rock and seek first his kingdom. If you have never bowed your heart to Jesus Christ and asked for his pardon and forgiveness, then now is the time to take that step. Yet we also look forward to the return of the Rock. We must recognize that even though the kingdom of God is growing throughout the world, the present will continue to be a time of trials and difficulties until Christ's return. We are therefore to long for the return of the Rock, the coming in fullness of Christ's kingdom, and to pray passionately for that day.

WAITING FOR THE ROCK

In the meantime, however, we should be careful not to let this eschatological focus on the coming of God's kingdom take us away from seeking to serve our present community. It is not coincidental that the chapter ends with Daniel and his friends promoted to responsible positions within the Babylonian system: "Then the king placed Daniel in a high position and lavished many gifts on him. He made him ruler over the entire province of Babylon and placed him in charge of all its wise men. Moreover, at Daniel's request the king appointed Shadrach, Meshach and Abednego administrators over the province of Babylon, while Daniel himself remained at the royal court" (Dan. 2:48–49). These men didn't isolate themselves from the kingdom of this world as they waited for God to establish his kingdom; rather, they poured themselves into seeking the welfare of their temporary home in Babylon.

This attitude of seeking the peace of their present city, even though it was not their home, and certainly not yet the city of God, is exactly the attitude that the prophet Jeremiah urged the exiles in Babylon to adopt when he wrote to them:

> Build houses and settle down; plant gardens and eat what they produce. Marry and have sons and daughters; find wives for your sons and give your daughters in marriage, so that they too may have sons and daughters. Increase in number there; do not decrease. Also, seek the peace and prosperity of the city to which I have carried you into exile. Pray to the LORD for it, because if it prospers, you too will prosper. (Jer. 29:5–7)

One of the major challenges in the Christian life is keeping these two emphases in balance. Some Christians have their eyes fixed on the return of Christ so intently that they are literally of no earthly use. These believers need to be reminded that if God intended our attention to be exclusively focused on him right now, he would take us to be with him immediately, where we could fulfill that purpose far more adequately. The fact that he has not chosen to do so suggests that he has earthly work for us to complete in the meantime. We therefore need to take seriously our duty to pursue the blessing of the earthly communities in which we find ourselves. We need to ask ourselves, "If I were gone, would anybody outside my immediate family be affected?" If our church were to be removed from our community, would anybody around us notice and lament the loss? What earthly use are we?

On the other hand, some Christians are so busy pursuing programs of earthly transformation for Christ that they have lost sight of the heavenly goal. They are busy polishing the statue instead of looking for the Rock. These believers need to be encouraged to remember that whatever improvements we may legitimately make in our society, we are still looking for the establishment of a kingdom which is heavenly and will not be here in fullness until Christ returns. This world is not our home, merely a lodging point along the way. Seeking to transform our culture can sometimes become an idolatrous pursuit that takes our eyes off God.

In the meantime, while we await the coming of the kingdom, our primary calling is to bow down and worship God. This was Nebuchadnezzar's response to the dream and its interpretation: he "fell prostrate before Daniel and paid him honor and ordered that an offering and incense be presented to him." He acknowledged, "Surely your God is the God of gods and the Lord of kings and a revealer of mysteries, for you were able to reveal this mystery" (Dan. 2:46–47). This same response should be ours as well. As Handel's *Messiah* so gloriously reminds us, there is only one appropriate response to the declaration "For the Lord God omnipotent reigneth." It is "Hallelujah! Hallelujah! Hallelujah! Hallelujah!"

How do we respond to the news of a great sporting triumph or an earthly political victory? We naturally celebrate, and we find it hard to keep the wonderful news to ourselves. How much more, then, should we respond with an overflowing joy to the reminder that God's kingdom is ultimate and that in Jesus Christ his sovereignty is established forever! God is bringing all things together under the feet of Christ, and our eyes too shall see him reign! The Rock reigns! Our hearts should be ready to burst with gladness at the news, our feet ready to run to share it, our voices ready to shout the good news. Our God reigns! Those who oppose him he shatters in pieces, but those who trust in him will reign with him forever and ever! How astounding and wonderful is that vision! To that joyous declaration, what is there to add except our own personal "Hallelujah! Amen! Come soon, Lord Jesus, to take your throne!"

4

THROUGH THE FIRE

Daniel 3:1—30

Shadrach, Meshach and Abednego replied to the king, "O Nebu-chadnezzar, we do not need to defend ourselves before you in this matter. If we are thrown into the blazing furnace, the God we serve is able to save us from it, and he will rescue us from your hand, O king. But even if he does not, we want you to know, O king, that we will not serve your gods or worship the image of gold you have set up." (Dan. 3:16–18)

Some movie quotes are universally recognized, even if we can't remember the movie from which it came or the actor who delivered the line. Phrases like "Toto, we're not in Kansas anymore" or "Here's looking at you, kid," or "Do you feel lucky, punk?" are known and recognized even by people who have never seen the movies from which they were drawn. Another great movie quote is: "A man's gotta do what a man's gotta do." Even if we can't quite remember who said it (Alan Ladd) or which movie it was from (*Shane*), the quote conjures up an indelible image of someone standing up for what is right, no matter what the consequences may be. Such bold action immediately inspires our respect.

In the same way, many people know the basic story of Shadrach, Meshach, and Abednego in the fiery furnace, even if their general knowledge of the Old Testament is a bit sketchy. It is a familiar story of three young men who were willing to stand up for their faith, even if it might cost them their lives. Yet, as we shall see, there is much more to this story than three men simply "doing what a man's gotta do."

NEBUCHADNEZZAR'S STATUE

The story starts with King Nebuchadnezzar making an enormous golden image on a Babylonian plain:

> King Nebuchadnezzar made an image of gold, ninety feet high and nine feet wide, and set it up on the plain of Dura in the province of Babylon. He then summoned the satraps, prefects, governors, advisers, treasurers, judges, magistrates and all the other provincial officials to come to the dedication of the image he had set up. So the satraps, prefects, governors, advisers, treasurers, judges, magistrates and all the other provincial officials assembled for the dedication of the image that King Nebuchadnezzar had set up, and they stood before it.
>
> Then the herald loudly proclaimed, "This is what you are commanded to do, O peoples, nations and men of every language: As soon as you hear the sound of the horn, flute, zither, lyre, harp, pipes and all kinds of music, you must fall down and worship the image of gold that King Nebuchadnezzar has set up. Whoever does not fall down and worship will immediately be thrown into a blazing furnace." (Dan. 3:1–6)

The idea of an enormous golden statue reminds us immediately of Nebuchadnezzar's dream in the previous chapter. In that dream, the statue had a head of gold, which represented Nebuchadnezzar, while the rest of the body was made of other materials, which depicted the lesser kingdoms that would come after him and end up in fragmentation, destroyed by the coming of God's kingdom (Dan. 2:31–35). Nebuchadnezzar's statue, however, was made entirely of gold in an apparent attempt to counteract the dream. It was a defiant statement asserting that there would be no end or "after this" with respect to his kingdom, but rather that his glory would continue forever.[1]

---

1. E. C. Lucas, *Daniel*, Apollos Old Testament Commentary (Downers Grove, IL: InverVarsity, 2002), 93.

The identity of the statue was not made clear: presumably it represented Nebuchadnezzar or his god (or both). Perhaps that vagueness was deliberate to allow people to interpret the significance of the statue however they wished, and thereby accommodate it more easily into their own diverse religious beliefs. Most pagan religions were pluralistic, allowing for the easy incorporation of additional gods into their pantheon. One thing was repeatedly stressed, however: this was "the image that King Nebuchadnezzar set up" (Dan. 3:1–3, 5, 7, 12, 15, 18).[2] In other words, even if the statue represented a god, no one was left in any doubt as to whose power lay behind its existence. In contrast to Daniel's confession that it was the God of heaven who set up kings and deposed them (2:21), the statue was Nebuchadnezzar's defiant declaration that as king he could set up gods for his people to worship.

What is more, the location of the statue was significant, for the Babylonian plain was the location for the building of the Tower of Babel in Genesis 11:2. The Tower of Babel had a twofold function in the mind of its builders: it was a defiant attempt to make a name for the people who built it as a lasting legacy to their glory, and also to prevent the people from being scattered throughout the earth, as God had decreed (Gen. 11:4). Nebuchadnezzar's statue had the same two goals in mind: it was designed to establish a lasting testimony to his glory and to provide a unifying focus for the kingdom.[3] This is why he summoned not merely local dignitaries but all of the leading officials from throughout his empire—the satraps, the prefects, the governors, the advisors, the treasurers, the judges, the magistrates, and all the other provincial officials—to gather before the statue for its dedication (Dan. 3:2). This occasion was a public statement that the unity of Nebuchadnezzar's empire was rooted in the common worship of his image, a religious unity which he was willing to enforce with the threat of death if necessary (3:6).

Symbols of Unity

Totalitarian states have continued to operate on the same basis throughout history. There are visual symbols of unity—often statues of the dictator

---

2. Dana Nolan Fewell, *Circle of Sovereignty: Plotting Politics in the Book of Daniel* (Nashville: Abingdon, 1991) 41.

3. Joyce G. Baldwin, *Daniel*, Tyndale Old Testament Commentaries (Downers Grove, IL: InterVarsity, 1978), 99.

or national symbols—to which homage must be paid if you want to progress in society, or even to stay alive. Before his death, Mao's statue dominated China, just as the image of Lenin was (and in some places still is) pervasive throughout the former Soviet Union. This homage to the national government can often be combined with religious affiliations, so long as it is clear which loyalty has priority. Thus, the ancient Romans would force people to choose between *kyrios Caesar* ("Caesar is Lord") and *kyrios Christos* ("Christ is Lord"). In a similar way, the Japanese invaders in Korea and Manchuria between the two world wars imposed the requirement of emperor worship on conquered Christians, Confucians, and Buddhists. Contemporary China permits Christians to worship freely—but only in state-sponsored and state-regulated "official" churches; the underground "house churches" remain heavily persecuted. Like Nebuchadnezzar, these empires don't require people necessarily to change their religion or their beliefs: they just have to subordinate them to their allegiance to the empire. People can serve whatever god they choose, so long as it is clear that he takes second place to the state.

When put in these terms, it becomes evident that our culture places the same pressure on each one of us to put our God in second place, albeit in more subtle ways. We too find ourselves constantly pressed to keep our beliefs private, and therefore secondary. We are told that the public sphere must be kept untainted by any religion, for any other opinion threatens the unifying dogma of the separation of church and state. We can believe whatever we want, by all means. However, we are strongly discouraged from talking about it or trying to influence the beliefs of others. In our public schools, any hypothesis may be taught in a science class, except the idea that the universe shows the hallmarks of intelligent design. Similarly, my son was once told that he could read any book he liked in study hall of his public school, so long as it was not the Bible. Thankfully, in our society, we are not likely to get shot or thrown into a fiery furnace for being the odd one out, and we still have a remarkable amount of freedom, but we still feel other kinds of pressure to conform and put the demands of our God in second place.

At first, Nebuchadnezzar's golden image seemed to be accomplishing its purpose successfully. We are told that the diverse group of officials he summoned came in response to his decree, a point underlined by the repetition of the lengthy list of titles.[4] They were there not merely as political officials, but as representatives of "peoples, nations and men of every language" (Dan. 3:4). This language emphasizes the theme that this act of worship was designed to reverse the consequences of the original Tower of Babel by unifying the whole world in an act of submission to this statue. When the music of a cacophony of different instruments sounded,[5] everyone was to bow down to the statue. Sure enough, when the music rang out, "all the peoples, nations and men of every language fell down and worshiped the image of gold that King Nebuchadnezzar had set up" (3:7). For a moment, the whole world was united in bowing to Nebuchadnezzar's statue. The curse of Babel had, it seemed, successfully been reversed.

HERE THEY STAND

Yet at this point some of the Babylonian officials came forward and revealed a small detail that the narrator had previously passed over as he surveyed the vast crowd:

> At this time some astrologers came forward and denounced the Jews. They said to King Nebuchadnezzar, "O king, live forever! You have issued a decree, O king, that everyone who hears the sound of the horn, flute, zither, lyre, harp, pipes and all kinds of music must fall down and worship the image of gold, and that whoever does not fall down and worship will be thrown into a blazing furnace. But there are some Jews whom you have set over the affairs of the province of Babylon—Shadrach, Meshach and Abednego—who pay no attention to you, O king. They neither serve your gods nor worship the image of gold you have set up." (Dan. 3:8–12)

Even while the whole world was busily bowing before Nebuchadnezzar's image of gold, one small group of three individuals had resisted the decree, standing with unbowed heads at the crucial moment. Shadrach, Meshach, and Abednego—or Hananiah, Azariah, and Mishael, to give them

---

4. Fewell, *Circle of Sovereignty*, 39.

5. In this lengthy list of exotic musical instruments, there is more than a little fun being poked at the strange forms of pagan worship. None of these instruments were used individually in Israel's worship (John Goldingay, *Daniel*, Word Biblical Commentary [Dallas: Word, 1989], 70), let alone together in such a bizarre orchestra.

their proper, Hebrew names—had failed to prostrate themselves in accordance with the king's decree, thereby disrespecting Nebuchadnezzar's gods and Nebuchadnezzar's statue (Dan. 3:12). The three Jews were accused of ingratitude ("some Jews whom you have set over the affairs of the province of Babylon") and impiety ("they neither serve your gods nor worship the image of gold you have set up"), but the fundamental element of both charges was their offense against Nebuchadnezzar. How would the empire respond to this act of disobedience?

It is worth noticing that there were only three men in the whole vast crowd who refused to bow down to Nebuchadnezzar's statue.[6] This highlights the fact that standing up for God will often be a lonely activity. There are times in every life when to do what is right we cannot simply hide in the crowd; we have to stand more or less alone. Sometimes it will seem that the whole world is watching, as when Martin Luther stood before the church authorities at the Diet of Worms. Called upon to abandon his commitment to justification by faith alone before a gathering of the Catholic authorities, Luther boldly declared, "Unless I am convicted by Scripture and plain reason . . . my conscience is captive to the Word of God, I cannot and will not recant anything, for to go against conscience is neither right nor safe. God help me. Amen."[7] Luther's example shows us that at times we may even have to stand alone for what is right within the church itself.

At other times, however, no one outside our immediate circle of acquaintances will ever be aware of whether we stand up for our faith or crumple under pressure. Our testimony for the faith may seem completely unobserved. Yet in either case—whether the human crowd of watchers is large or small—we should not forget that the most important audience, God himself, will always be watching us. He always observes our faithful testimony or our craven submission.

THE CONSEQUENCES OF NONCONFORMITY

In the case of Shadrach, Meshach, and Abednego, their trial of faith was very public:

6. It is not clear where Daniel was when this event took place. Perhaps he had been sent (or had arranged to be) on business elsewhere in the Babylonian empire.

7. See Roland H. Bainton, *The Reformation of the Sixteenth Century* (Boston: Beacon, 1952), 61.

50

Furious with rage, Nebuchadnezzar summoned Shadrach, Meshach and Abednego. So these men were brought before the king, and Nebuchadnezzar said to them, "Is it true, Shadrach, Meshach and Abednego, that you do not serve my gods or worship the image of gold I have set up? Now when you hear the sound of the horn, flute, zither, lyre, harp, pipes and all kinds of music, if you are ready to fall down and worship the image I made, very good. But if you do not worship it, you will be thrown immediately into a blazing furnace. Then what god will be able to rescue you from my hand?"

Shadrach, Meshach and Abednego replied to the king, "O Nebuchadnezzar, we do not need to defend ourselves before you in this matter. If we are thrown into the blazing furnace, the God we serve is able to save us from it, and he will rescue us from your hand, O king. But even if he does not, we want you to know, O king, that we will not serve your gods or worship the image of gold you have set up." (Dan. 3:13–18)

When the matter was brought to the king's attention, he immediately flew into a rage at the challenge to his authority and national unity. He inquired of Shadrach, Meshach, and Abednego if it was indeed true that they refused to serve his gods or bow down to his statue (Dan. 3:14). Without giving them time to answer, Nebuchadnezzar set before them a final choice. If, when the music sounded, they were willing to fall down and worship the image he had made, their lives would be spared; if not, they would be thrown into the blazing furnace, and then what god would rescue them from his hand (3:15)?

Shadrach, Meshach, and Abednego responded to King Nebuchadnezzar's challenge with one of their own. They replied, "If the God whom we serve is willing to save us, then he will do so, but even if he does not choose to do so, we still will not serve your gods or bow down to the image of gold you have made" (Dan. 3:17–18; author's translation). The proper translation of the conditional clause of Daniel 3:17 ("If the God whom we serve is willing to save us . . . ") has been much debated. The most common alternative among conservative translations has been to render it: "If it be so [i.e., if we are indeed going to be thrown into the furnace], our God is able to save us and he will do so" (see KJV, ESV, NIV). Another alternative is to translate it, "If the God we serve exists, then he can rescue us . . . " (HCSV). However, neither of those translations renders a suitable parallel for the "But if not . . . " of the next verse, which we expect to negate the conditional element of the sentence (being thrown into the fire, or God existing), not the unconditional element (our God is able to save us).[8] They have therefore not found favor with most recent commentaries. Linguistically, a more likely translation is, "If the God whom we serve is able to save us, then he will."[9]

However, such a translation inevitably raises the question of what aspect of God's ability to save is here in doubt. No one reading the rest of the Book of Daniel can seriously suggest that God's *power* to save his people from the fire is ever in doubt in this book. This is the God who raises kings and casts them down (2:21), and who is able to rescue Daniel from the mouth of the hungry lions (6:27). Rather, as C. F. Keil pointed out more than a century ago, the reference is to "ethical ability, i.e. the ability limited by divine holiness and righteousness, not the omnipotence of God as such."[10] The Hebrew cognate verb, *yakol*, clearly has a broader sense which describes willingness rather than ability. For example, in Genesis 37:4 we are told that Joseph's brothers were not able (*yakol*) to speak a civil greeting to him. Obviously their inability to speak to Joseph lay in their will, not in a physical weakness in their vocal cords. So also here in Daniel the question in the minds of the three young men was not whether God had the physical ability to rescue them, but rather whether using that ability is part of the divine plan. It is thus similar to Jesus' prayer in the Garden of Gethsemane, "If it be possible, let this cup pass from me" (Matt. 26:39). In terms of absolute possibility, the Father was certainly able to deliver the Son from drinking that cup. Yet given the Father's will to save sinners, the cross became a consequent absolute necessity, for that goal could not be accomplished in any other manner.

There was thus no doubt in the young men's minds as to God's power to save them: they had confessed it with Daniel in the previous chapter (see Dan. 2:20–23). Yet the actual way in which God's plans for them would work themselves out in this situation was far less clear. God's power is sometimes extended in dramatic ways to deliver his people, as when he parted the Red

8. Though see Tremper Longman III, *Daniel*, New International Version Application Commentary (Grand Rapids: Zondervan, 1999), 101; and Stephen R. Miller, *Daniel*, New American Commentary (Nashville: Broadman, 1994), 119.

9. See P. W. Coxon, "Daniel 3:17: A Linguistic and Theological Problem," *Vetus Testamentum* 26 [1976] 400–409; this rendering is accepted even by such a conservative commentator as E. J. Young (*The Prophecy of Daniel. An Introduction and Commentary* [Grand Rapids: Eerdmans, 1949], 91).

10. *The Book of Daniel*, trans. M. G. Easton (Grand Rapids: Eerdmans, 1988 reprint), 127.

Sea for Israel on the way out of Egypt. Yet at other times that same power is withheld and his people are allowed to suffer.

Shadrach, Meshach, and Abednego did not presume to predict what the outcome would be in their case. If God were our servant, or our accomplice, he would be predictable: he would always do our bidding. Shadrach, Meshach, and Abednego understood that since God is sovereign, however, it was his choice whether he opted to be glorified in their deaths or through their dramatic deliverance. Either way, it didn't make a difference to their decision. Whether they were miraculously delivered or left to burn in the fire, Shadrach, Meshach, and Abednego would not compromise their commitment to the Lord. Live or die, they would be faithful to their God.

THE PRESSURE TO CONFORM

As a child and a young person, I sometimes used to wonder and worry about what it would be like to be in their position. What would I do, if I were faced with a similar choice between denying Christ and a painful death? I doubted whether I would be so bold in service of the Lord as these young men were; I feared rather that I would cave under the pressure. As I have grown older, however, I have come to realize two things. First, God has not promised to give us the grace to face all of the desperate situations that we might imagine finding ourselves in. He has promised to sustain us only in the ones that he actually brings us into. He therefore doesn't promise that we will be able to imagine how we could go through the fire for his sake, but he does promise that if he leads us through the fire, he will give us sufficient grace at that time. Like manna, grace is not something that can be stored up for later use: each day receives its own supply.

Second, though, I have also come to see that the same battle is actually being fought out daily in my heart over much lesser issues. Am I going to declare the Lord to be my God, my primary allegiance, come what may, or will I bow down to the multitude of glittering idols that the world presents to me? These idols are not physical statues in our setting, of course. They are the various pleasures, the desires, and the attitudes that society tells me I need to have if I am to be fulfilled and lead a worthwhile life. They promise to bless me if I will bow down to them, but to curse me and ruin my life if I fail to meet their demands.

For some, the golden image is the respect and admiration of others. As young people, we often feel the pressure to be one of the "in-crowd" at school, even though the cost of admission to this club is that we mustn't show respect for our parents, or talk about God, or keep ourselves mentally and physically pure until marriage. "Bow down to me," the image says, "or I will throw you into the fiery furnace of the mockery and ridicule of your peers." This idolatry was described by C. S. Lewis as the allure of "The Inner Ring," the desire to be on the right side of an invisible line that divides "insiders" from "outsiders."[11] Indeed, the power of this idol is such that, in the opinion of Lewis, "of all the passions, the passion for the Inner Ring is most skillful in making a man who is not yet a very bad man do very bad things."[12]

Pastors feel the demands of this idol of respect and admiration just as much as other people. We are constantly bombarded with mailings suggesting that the measure of our pastoral success is the size of our church. Sometimes they suggest that perhaps if we just toned down the Bible-centered nature of our message a little and supplemented it with something a little lighter and more palatable to "seekers," then our churches would be larger and we would therefore be more "successful." Using this approach, the world's methods of bringing people together have invaded the church repeatedly over the centuries, and we who are supposed to be the shepherds are the ones who opened the gate and invited the wolves in to dinner. The same idol also shows its ugly face when people ask me how large the church I serve is, and I find myself tempted to exaggerate the numbers a little bit to make myself sound more of a "success," as if numbers were an accurate measure of ministry. Whenever I give in to that temptation, I'm bowing down to an idol rather than wholeheartedly submitting myself to God.

Other idols play their blaring worship music through our unsanctified desires and appetites. We may become obsessed with food or with drink, with sexual satisfaction or with romantic daydreams, because these idols tell us that if we don't give in to them they will leave us burning in the fiery furnace of frustration. There is no gun pointed at our head, but in our case none is needed, for we are often easily cajoled into putting the Lord second

---

11. C. S. Lewis, "The Inner Ring," in *The Weight of Glory and Other Essays* (Grand Rapids: Eerdmans, 1949), 55–66.

12. Lewis, "Inner Ring," 63.

to our idol. In fact, our hearts are all the more condemned by the very smallness of the pressure under which we buckle and bow down. Not for us the grand declaration that, come what may, we will never bow down to the idols of our hearts. We are not like Shadrach, Meshach, and Abednego. Instead, we often slip almost unthinkingly into a daily obeisance to our idol's demands, like the rest of the crowd on the plain of Babylon.

When we do stand up to our idols, though, we had better be prepared to experience their wrath. Nebuchadnezzar was "furious with Shadrach, Meshach, and Abednego, and his attitude toward them changed. He ordered the furnace heated seven times hotter than usual and commanded some of the strongest soldiers in his army to tie up Shadrach, Meshach and Abednego and throw them into the blazing furnace. So these men, wearing their robes, trousers, turbans and other clothes, were bound and thrown into the blazing furnace" (Dan. 3:19–21).[13] In fact, Nebuchadnezer's command was "so urgent and the furnace so hot that the flames of the fire killed the soldiers who took up Shadrach, Meshach and Abednego, and these three men, firmly tied, fell into the blazing furnace" (Dan. 3:22–23). There is a great irony here, to be sure. The ones who obeyed Nebuchadnezzar's commands died, while those whom he condemned to death emerged alive! What a vivid demonstration of Jesus' dictum that "Whoever wants to save his life will lose it, but whoever loses his life for me will find it" (Matt. 16:25). The issue is not whether Israel's God can keep his servants alive, but whether Nebuchadnezzar can! In a similar way, our own idols often turn out to be liars, unable to deliver either the rewards that they promise or the judgments they threaten.

IMMANUEL: GOD WITH US

The unexpected death of the soldiers was not what was truly surprising about the fiery furnace, however. The truly amazing twist of events came when Nebuchadnezzar watched Shadrach, Meshach, and Abednego fall into the fire. Not only did he see that they were free and unharmed, but they were also joined in the fire by a fourth individual, who had the appearance of a divine being: "Then King Nebuchadnezzar leaped to his feet in

---

13. "Seven times hotter" is typical biblical hyperbole, in which seven is the number of completeness. See André Lacocque, *The Book of Daniel*, trans. D. Pellauer (Atlanta: John Knox, 1979), 66.

amazement and asked his advisers, 'Weren't there three men that we tied up and threw into the fire?' They replied, 'Certainly, O king.' He said, 'Look! I see four men walking around in the fire, unbound and unharmed, and the fourth looks like a son of the gods.' (Dan. 3:24–25)

The question of whether this fourth person is a Christophany (a physical appearance of Christ before his incarnation) or merely an angel cannot be resolved from the text, which would fit either instance equally well. In either case, however, it is a physical demonstration of God's presence with believers in their distress. God did not simply rescue his servants from the fire, he sent his personal emissary to pass through the fire with them, a presence that takes richer dimensions in the New Testament, when God comes to dwell physically with us as Immanuel.[14] As a result of his presence with them, Shadrach, Meshach, and Abednego emerged safely at the end of their time in the furnace:

> Nebuchadnezzar then approached the opening of the blazing furnace and shouted, "Shadrach, Meshach and Abednego, servants of the Most High God, come out! Come here!"
>
> So Shadrach, Meschach and Abednego came out of the fire, and the satraps, prefects, governors and royal advisers crowded around them. They saw that the fire had not harmed their bodies, nor was a hair of their heads singed; their robes were not scorched, and there was no smell of fire on them. (Dan. 3:26–27)

They were not merely physically unharmed: their clothing did not even smell of smoke, a powerful testimony to the comprehensiveness of their salvation by God.

This experience was a fulfillment of the words the Lord had spoken to his people through the prophet Isaiah two centuries earlier: "When you pass through the waters, I will be with you; and when you pass through the rivers, they will not sweep over you. When you walk through the fire, you will not be burned; the flames will not set you ablaze" (Isa. 43:2). Notice that God didn't promise to take his people around the waters or to keep the fire far from them. On the contrary, tribulation was the anticipated path for God's saints, then and now (see Acts 14:22). Trials

---

14. Longman, *Daniel*, 103.

provide the context in which the faith of believers shines with unmatched clarity before the eyes of a watching world, as 1 Peter 1:6–7 makes clear. It is precisely in the furnace that the reality of our faith is displayed most clearly. Yet, in the midst of those trials and difficulties, the Lord promised that his people could count on his presence with them, ensuring that their trials would not utterly overwhelm them. The Lord does not stand far off from his people in need: he has promised to be "God with us," Immanuel. As a result, nothing in all creation can separate us from God's love (Rom. 8:38–39).

That commitment to be with us, of course, found its richest fulfillment in the coming of Christ, the one who was himself "Immanuel." In Jesus, the promise of "God with us" took flesh and walked along the weary paths of this world. He experienced all of the pressures and temptations of this world, yet remained utterly without sin. This was not because his commitment to holiness went untested. On one occasion, Satan came to him and offered to give him all the kingdoms of this world if Jesus would just bow down and worship him (Matt. 4:9). Think of what Satan was offering: the kingdom of the world could have become the kingdom of Christ without the agony of the cross. Wasn't that the reason why he had come? Not at all. He had come so that the kingdom of this world could become the kingdom of *our Lord* and of his Christ (Rev. 11:15), a goal that could come only by way of the path that wound towards the cross of Calvary. So, unbowed, Jesus responded to Satan with words of Scripture: "It is written, 'Worship the Lord your God, and serve him only'" (Matt. 4:10).

Jesus felt the full range of the pains and sorrows of life in this fallen world, stretching out his hand to touch the leper (Luke 5:13) and weeping with Martha and Mary at the tomb of their brother Lazarus (John 11:35). He faced the difficulties and frustrations that we all feel, without once bowing his head to an idol. He never surrendered, even under the greatest temptation and pressure. However, even this humbling of himself was not sufficient identification with us in our trials. To complete the process, Jesus Christ was himself falsely accused, condemned to death by the Roman authorities, and then nailed to a cross. Like Shadrach, Meshach, and Abednego, his obedience was tested and found faithful unto death.

ABANDONED BY GOD

Yet Jesus went through his own personal furnace experience completely alone. God was with Shadrach, Meshach, and Abednego in the fire, and we have the promise of the Lord's sustaining presence with us in our trials, but on the cross Jesus felt the utter aloneness of total abandonment by God. When he passed through the waters, there was no one by his side. When the fire of God's wrath burned him to the core and blazed unchecked over him, he was entirely alone. There was no companion to share his burden, no angel sent to relieve his agony, no saving hand from God stretched down to preserve his faithful servant in his moment of greatest need. For Jesus, there was no deliverance from experiencing the power of the final enemy, death itself.

Now why would God be with Shadrach, Meshach, and Abednego, but not with his own Son? Why would he be faithful to his promise to be with Israel, sinners as they were, and then abandon Jesus, his perfect chosen one? You would expect it to be the other way around.

The answer to that question is that on the cross Jesus was taking into himself the fiery pains that we deserve for our compromise and idolatry. Unlike Daniel's three friends, I am no hero of the faith. Every time I bow down to the idols of my heart, I merit for myself God's judgment curse. I choose to escape the fiery threat of my idol, but only at the cost of earning the fiery judgment of God for my unfaithfulness. Nebuchadnezzar is not the only one who condemns to the fire those who will not bow the knee to him: our God rightfully demands the wholehearted homage of those whom he has created. Yet in the case of his people, God took all of our fiery judgment curse and laid it on his own Son. He personally paid the price of my hell during those six hours on the cross so that I might pass through the threatening fire unburned and emerge safely out on the other side. What is more, his perfect faithfulness is now credited to my account as if it were my own. A faithfulness that far exceeds that of Shadrach, Meshach, and Abednego is now mine as a free gift. I am welcomed into God's presence for Christ's sake.

THE TRUE SOURCE OF UNITY

The result of Jesus' faithful sacrifice is that in his own flesh he now provides the ultimate answer to Babel's tower and Nebuchadnezzar's idol. What they sought to achieve in vain—making a lasting name for themselves and binding together the peoples, nations, and men of every language in one united worshiping society—is now accomplished by God through Christ. In the church, God brings glory to his name by saving a hopeless and helpless band of ragtag sinners. In the church, men and women from every tribe and nation and language group come together across social, racial, and ethnic lines as the one new people of God. Together, we stand before the throne of the Lamb, a united multitude from all nations, gathered to sing praises to the God of heaven and earth. No one has to tell us to bow before Christ. It is our joy and delight to throw ourselves down at his pierced feet. The cross is the towering symbol that binds God's empire together as one.

Not all respond to God's act of redemption at the cross in the same way, though. It is certainly something we cannot simply ignore, any more than Nebuchadnezzar could ignore the remarkable miracle that had happened in front of his eyes. Nebuchadnezzar was forced to confess the greatness of the God of Shadrach, Meshach, and Abednego. He gave praise to him and threatened any who spoke against their God with death:

> Then Nebuchadnezzar said, "Praise be to the God of Shadrach, Meshach and Abednego, who has sent his angel and rescued his servants! They trusted in him and defied the king's command and were willing to give up their lives rather than serve or worship any god except their own God. Therefore I decree that the people of any nation or language who say anything against the God of Shadrach, Meshach and Abednego be cut into pieces and their houses be turned into piles of rubble, for no other god can save in this way."
>
> Then the king promoted Shadrach, Meshach and Abednego in the province of Babylon. (Dan. 3:28–29)

This is a somewhat ironic threat, since death was precisely the sanction that he had just proved unable to enforce on Shadrach, Meshach, and Abednego themselves! Yet even great miracles don't have the power in themselves to change people's hearts. People will always find a way to explain them away. So too Nebuchadnezzar's heart was not changed at a deep level by this experience. The God of whom he spoke was still "the God of Shadrach, Meshach, and Abednego," or "their God," not his own. He still would not fall down in the face of this revelation of the Lord's power and confess, "My Lord and my God."

59

Sadly, there are many who respond in exactly the same way to the message of the cross and resurrection of Christ, and other demonstrations of God's mighty power. When you tell them what the Lord has done, they say, "I'm glad you've found something that works for you. I'm happy for you. But don't ask me to submit to your God." Sooner or later, though, they will be forced to bow their knee before the Lord and confess his power and his glory. Such a confession on that day will save no one: it will be a bare recognition of the nature of reality. The confession that saves is the one that bows joyfully now before the Lord and confesses him, "My Lord and my God, my only hope in life and death."

Yet for those who believe, God's power is at work both to save us from the threat of God's judgment that we so richly deserve and also to carry out his perfecting plans in us. In bringing all nations together in his one new people, the church, the Lord will not leave us as he finds us, in bondage to our idols. He promises that progressively through the course of our lives he will purify our hearts. That work will not be completed on this side of heaven, of course. Our idols continue to have a powerful grip, and their continuing hold over us is one of the key means that the Lord uses to show us just how desperate our situation would be without him. Through bitter experiences of personal failure and compromise, we come to see the depth of our own personal depravity and the extent of the Lord's grace to save us. Yet, at the same time, in the midst of the fires of life we have the assurance of his presence with us in the present, and of a glorious future with him in heaven. How should you and I respond to that news? Surely we should delight to bow our knees to the Lord and sing his praises daily, even if everyone around us refuses to bow. We should be willing to give up our very lives rather than give in even once to the demands of our idols. And we should celebrate the one who went through the fire of God's wrath alone in our place: Jesus Christ, our Redeemer and Savior.

5

THE FALL AND RISE OF NEBUCHADNEZZAR

Daniel 4:1—37

At the end of that time, I, Nebuchadnezzar, raised my eyes toward heaven, and my sanity was restored. Then I praised the Most High; I honored and glorified him who lives forever. His dominion is an eternal dominion; his kingdom endures from generation to generation. All the peoples of the earth are regarded as nothing. He does as he pleases with the powers of heaven and the peoples of the earth. (Dan. 4:34–35)

on't you just hate some of those glowing family newsletters that you receive every year during the holiday season? You know, the ones that run like this:

It's been a great year for the Lamplighters! Greg had been hoping for a promotion, but what a surprise when the CEO came to his desk and begged him to take over the company. The whole office chipped in and gave the family a week in Paris to celebrate. Wasn't that nice? Of course Jeanne has been busy as well. You probably saw that news item about how she rescued a school bus full of children from a kidnapper, armed only with a plastic comb. Nice to think, too, that the poem she wrote for last year's holiday letter will be chiseled into the wall of the Library of Congress. The twins did so well at the state tap-dance championship that Spielberg is crafting a movie around them, while Greg Jr.'s science fair project was the topic of much excitement in the *New England Journal of Medicine.*[1]

When I get letters like that, I want to take the Lamplighters' perfect little family picture, set it on fire, and jump up and down on the ashes. Why is that? Pride. The problem is not simply the Lamplighters' pride in their achievements: the Lord will deal with them (or not) as he sees fit. No, what my response to the letter reveals is the pride within my own heart. Pride inherently compares our own achievements and rewards to those of others around us: it boasts if we have achieved greater accomplishments and recognition than our companions, and sulks enviously if we have done less or seem to have been passed over. The Lamplighters' letter makes me feel like a hopeless underachiever and so challenges my pride.

Pride is one of the few sins that is still almost universally recognized as being wrong. The remainder of the seven traditional "deadly sins"—lust, sloth, greed, and so on—have long since been recategorized as being harmless peccadilloes, or even virtues, but pride is still generally reckoned deservedly to go before a fall. In fact, even people who would not regard themselves as religious find pride offensive. Yet at the same time few people actually recognize the sin of pride within themselves; we may see it readily enough in others, but it often deceptively slides undetected into our own hearts.[2] In God's grace and mercy to us, however, he sometimes uses life's difficult experiences to remove the blinders from our eyes and show us what our hearts really contain. He exposes and confounds our pride in order to transform us from the inside out.

Beginning at the End

Daniel 4 is about one such journey from pride to humility, by way of a great fall. The narrative actually begins at the end of the story, with the letter of praise to God that Nebuchadnezzar wrote after his recovery:

1. The letter comes from Frederica Mathewes-Green, "Pride: The Anti-Self-Esteem," <http://www.beliefnet.com/story/110/story_11056_1.html>. Accessed August 18, 2005.
2. See C. S. Lewis, "The Great Sin," in *Mere Christianity* (New York: Macmillan, 1982), 108–14.

King Nebuchadnezzar,

To the peoples, nations and men of every language, who live in all the world:
May you prosper greatly! It is my pleasure to tell you about the miraculous
signs and wonders that the Most High God has performed for me. How great
are his signs, how mighty his wonders! His kingdom is an eternal kingdom;
his dominion endures from generation to generation. (Dan. 4:1–3)

Normally, a doxology like this comes at the conclusion of the events
to which it refers, a fact which led the person numbering the chapters in
the Hebrew Bible to put these verses together with the events of the previous chapter. He assumed that Nebuchadnezzar's letter must be describing
the deliverance of Shadrach, Meshach, and Abednego. The division of the
chapters in our English Bibles is probably the right one, but don't miss
the connections that are made at the outset with the events of the previous chapter. The letter is addressed to "peoples, nations and men of every
language, who live in all the world," the same group that were summoned
to bow down to King Nebuchadnezzar's image (4:1; see 3:7). In speaking
of the "miraculous signs and wonders" that the Lord has performed, the
letter immediately makes us think of the fiery furnace. The key difference,
however, is that now Nebuchadnezzar speaks of "signs and wonders that
the Most High God has performed *for me*" (4:2). From being a persecutor
of the faithful in the previous chapter, Nebuchadnezzar has now himself
become a witness to the faith.[3]

This is a striking shift in the life of the most powerful man in the
world. It is as dramatic as the transformation in the New Testament of
Saul, the persecuting Pharisee, to Paul, the apostle to the Gentiles. How
did such an incredible change take place? In both cases, the change was
not wrought merely by witnessing the power of God as an observer. King
Nebuchadnezzar watched Shadrach, Meshach, and Abednego emerge
unscathed from the fiery furnace (Dan. 3), even as Saul saw the Lord's
grace sustain Stephen through his violent death (Acts 8:1), yet neither
man was immediately converted by the experience. Miraculous demonstrations of God's power can certainly stop people in their tracks and
make them think, but true conversion can only be accomplished by a

3. Danna Nolan Fewell, *Circle of Sovereignty: Plotting Politics in the Book of Daniel* (Nashville:
Abingdon, 1991), 63–64.

personal experience of God's power and grace. That personal experience in Nebuchadnezzar's life is what we will see in Daniel 4.

In Nebuchadnezzar's case, the transformation required the stripping away of everything in which he once gloried. He began the chapter with everything he desired, contented and prosperous, at home in his palace: "I, Nebuchadnezzar, was at home in my palace, contented and prosperous. I had a dream that made me afraid. As I was lying in my bed, the images and visions that passed through my mind terrified me. So I commanded that all the wise men of Babylon be brought before me to interpret the dream for me" (Dan. 4:4–6). Nebuchadnezzar was, quite literally, the lord of all that he surveyed. Can you imagine reading Nebuchadnezzar's annual holiday letter? It would surely have made the Lamplighters slink off in shame! Yet that situation of contentedness and prosperity was an obstacle to the work of God in his life that had to be addressed if his heart was to be changed.

This is an important point for us to recognize in our own experience. Discontent and disaster, or at the least profound personal discomfort, are very often the necessary precursors of spiritual growth and change. As long as we are comfortable and at ease in this world, we are not normally ready to examine our hearts and institute deep changes. On the other hand, when God disturbs the calm waters of our lives we begin to be ready to seek different paths to pursue. It is often when our career hopes are dashed, or our marriage relationship is in shreds, or the doctor announces that we have only a few more months to live that we are finally persuaded to become serious about spiritual things. If that is true, however, it suggests that we should approach these troubled times of our lives with a far more positive outlook than we normally do. These shattering experiences should prompt within us the expectation and hope that God is going to do something important in our lives. It is precisely through the storms of life that God will show us who we really are and, even more importantly, who he really is.

Nebuchadnezzar's Second Dream

The first challenge from the Lord in Nebuchadnezzar's life was directed at his contentedness. It came in the form of another disturbing dream:

I looked, and there before me stood a tree in the middle of the land. Its height was enormous. The tree grew large and strong and its top touched the sky; it was visible to the ends of the earth. Its leaves were beautiful, its fruit abundant, and on it was food for all. Under it the beasts of the field found shelter, and the birds of the air lived in its branches; from it every creature was fed.

In the visions I saw while lying in my bed, I looked, and there before me was a messenger, a holy one, coming down from heaven. He called in a loud voice: "Cut down the tree and trim off its branches; strip off its leaves and scatter its fruit. Let the animals flee from under it and the birds from its branches. But let the stump and its roots, bound with iron and bronze, remain in the ground, in the grass of the field.

"Let him be drenched with the dew of heaven, and let him live with the animals among the plants of the earth. Let his mind be changed from that of a man and let him be given the mind of an animal, till seven times pass by for him.

"The decision is announced by messengers, the holy ones declare the verdict, so that the living may know that the Most High is sovereign over the kingdoms of men and gives them to anyone he wishes and sets over them the lowliest of men." (Dan. 4:10–17)

Like his earlier dream in Daniel 2, this vision terrified Nebuchadnezzar. The king was frustrated, he said, because "when the magicians, enchanters, astrologers and diviners came, I told them the dream, but they could not interpret it for me" (Dan. 4:7). Acknowledging that Daniel possessed an ability that the others did not, Nebuchadnezzar turned to him for help: "Finally Daniel came into my presence and I told him the dream. (He is called Belteshazzar, after the name of my god, and the spirit of the holy gods is in him.) I said, 'Belteshazzar, chief of the magicians, I know that the spirit of the holy gods is in you, and no mystery is too difficult for you. Here is my dream; interpret it for me'" (Dan. 4:8–9).[4]

4. The transformation in Nebuchadnezzar's thinking that takes place in the course of the chapter is underlined by the names that Nebuchadnezzar uses for Daniel. In the narrative frame, written after his experience of humbling, Nebuchadnezzar calls Daniel by his Judean name (meaning, "God is my judge"), whereas in the reported conversations that took place earlier, he called him "Belteshazzar (meaning "Bel, guard his life"). In the same way, prior to his humbling, Nebuchadnezzar describes Daniel in pagan terms as one "in whom is the spirit of the holy gods" (Dan. 4:8). See Tremper Longman III, *Daniel*, New International Version Application Commentary (Grand Rapids: Zondervan, 1999), 118.

After Nebuchadnezzar told Daniel of his dream, he reiterated his confidence in Daniel's ability to tell him what it meant: "This is the dream that I, King Nebuchadnezzar, had. Now, Belteshazzar, tell me what it means, for none of the wise men in my kingdom can interpret it for me. But you can, because the spirit of the holy gods is in you" (Dan. 4:18). The vision itself was fairly straightforward: in his dream, Nebuchadnezzar saw an enormous tree that stretched up until its top touched the heavens. The tree was both beautiful and useful, providing food and shelter for the beasts of the field and the birds of the air (4:10–12). While Nebuchadnezzar was looking on, however, a heavenly figure came down and ordered that the tree should be cut down: its fruit was to be scattered and its leaves stripped from it, the birds and beasts that had found shelter in it scattered in all directions. The tree was not utterly destroyed, however; its stump was to remain in the ground (4:13–15).[5]

Although Daniel was "greatly perplexed for a time, and his thoughts terrified him," Nebuchadnezzar attempted to reassure him: "Belteshazzar, do not let the dream or its meaning alarm you" (Dan. 4:19). In his interpretation Daniel provided the key to understanding the dream. The enormous tree represented Nebuchadnezzar himself. Thus far, it was good news, for Nebuchadnezzar would have been quite happy to see himself in the role of cosmic tree, the center and pivotal point of the entire universe.[6] As with the king's dream of a statue in Daniel 2, where Nebuchadnezzar was the head of gold, this dream acknowledged Nebuchadnezzar's power and might. Daniel said,

> The tree you saw, which grew large and strong, with its top touching the sky, visible to the whole earth, with beautiful leaves and abundant fruit, providing food for all, giving shelter to the beasts of the field, and having nesting places in its branches for the birds of the air—you, O king, are that tree! You have become great and strong; your greatness has grown until it reaches the sky, and your dominion extends to distant parts of the earth.

5. The "fetter of iron and bronze" that binds the stump is most likely to be understood as a figurative representation of the bondage of insanity to which Nebuchadnezzar is to be given over (C. F. Keil, *The Book of Daniel*, trans. M. G. Easton [Grand Rapids: Eerdmans, 1988 reprint], 152).

6. The image of a cosmic tree is a common one, both elsewhere in the Bible (e.g., Ezek. 31) and more broadly in the ancient Near East. See André Lacocque, *The Book of Daniel*, trans. D. Pellauer (Atlanta: John Knox, 1979), 77–78.

You, O king, saw a messenger, a holy one, coming down from heaven and saying, "Cut down the tree and destroy it, but leave the stump, bound with iron and bronze, in the grass of the field, while its roots remain in the ground. Let him be drenched with the dew of heaven; let him live like the wild animals, until seven times pass by for him." (Dan. 4:20–23)

Yet the image of the cosmic tree also has a dark side, as Daniel recognized when he said, "My lord, if only the dream applied to your enemies and its meaning to your adversaries!" (Dan. 4:19). The description of the tree reaching to the heavens (4:11) reminds us once again of the attempt of the builders of the Tower of Babel to construct an edifice whose top would enter the heavens (Gen. 11:4). Such acts of hubris inevitably end in disaster. In this case, the image itself suggests the appropriate metaphor for its downfall: the divine lumberjack will bring the mighty tree crashing to the ground, removing it from its place of influence and glory.[7]

According to the vision, Nebuchadnezzar would be brought down low indeed. He would not only lose his power and glory; his very humanity would be removed from him. Daniel said, "This is the interpretation, O king, and this is the decree the Most High has issued against my lord the king: You will be driven away from people and will live with the wild animals; you will eat grass like cattle and be drenched with the dew of heaven. Seven times will pass by for you until you acknowledge that the Most High is sovereign over the kingdoms of men and gives them to anyone he wishes" (Dan. 4:24–25). Cast down from his place as the cosmic tree, Nebuchadnezzar would then make his home with the birds and the beasts that in the metaphor once found shelter in his branches. The one who thought of himself in godlike terms as the very center of the universe will be transformed into a beast so that he can learn that he is merely human after all.[8]

However, when the tree is cut down, the stump and the roots are allowed to remain (Dan. 4:15). There was therefore the hope of new growth emerging from the stump. So too God's act of judgment on King Nebuchadnezzar would not be a final cutting off, for the "command to leave the stump of the

---

7. The same metaphor of a cosmic tree felled by God is adopted in Ezekiel 31 to describe the fate of Pharaoh and of Egypt. There is not necessarily any direct link between the two passages, since the image of a tree to represent the king is a widespread one (compare Ezek. 17), which lends itself naturally to the imagery of felling.

8. Fewell, *Circle of Sovereignty*, 72.

tree with its roots means that your kingdom will be restored to you when you acknowledge that Heaven rules" (Dan. 4:26). Nebuchadnezzar would experience a full period of judgment in this animal-like state, expressed in typical Hebrew fashion as "seven times," since seven is the Hebrew number of completeness. Yet when that time was complete, and he acknowledged that "heaven rules"—that God is in charge of the universe and he is not— his kingdom would be restored to him (4:26).

ROOM FOR REPENTANCE

The somber fate depicted for King Nebuchadnezzar in the dream was not inevitable, though. The purpose of the dream was to provide Nebuchadnezzar with a warning shot across his bow, so that he might repent of his pride. He could demonstrate that repentance by doing what was right and showing concern for the oppressed. Daniel pleaded with him, "Therefore, O king, be pleased to accept my advice: Renounce your sins by doing what is right, and your wickedness by being kind to the oppressed. It may be that then your prosperity will continue" (Dan. 4:27). If Nebuchadnezzar humbled himself, then God would not need to further humble him. If he did not repent, however, then he would find out who is really in control of the universe.

In the same way, God sometimes presses in upon our hearts the likely outcome of our present course. Perhaps he shows us someone else who is further along the same path that we are headed down and we catch a glimpse of what we too may look like ten or twenty years from now. As a pastor, there is nothing more sobering to me than to see elders and ministers who have now made shipwreck of their lives. These men were friends and colleagues who once faithfully preached the gospel and encouraged the saints, but are now disqualified from ministry because of moral failure. It brings me up short and challenges my pride, for I know that I am no better than they were, and only God's grace will keep me from a similar fate.

Alternatively, sometimes God gives you a glimpse of the depravity of your own heart, as you catch yourself thinking (or even saying) something truly vile. You haven't yet committed the act, perhaps, but in your secret thoughts, you see the seeds of that sin within yourself. It is a shot across your bow, a challenge to repent and humble yourself before the Lord while there is still time, asking for his strength to hold you up and keep you faithful to him.

PRIDE AND FALL

Sadly, the warning of the dream went unheeded by Nebuchadnezzar. A whole year went by, during which Nebuchadnezzar had plenty of opportunity to live his life differently. Instead, he mistook the merciful delay of God's judgment as a sign that the threat could safely be ignored. Yet everything that had been prophesied "happened to King Nebuchadnezzar. Twelve months later, as the king was walking on the roof of the royal palace of Babylon, he said, 'Is not this the great Babylon I have built as the royal residence, by my mighty power and for the glory of my majesty?' " (Dan. 4:28–30).

From that vantage point, there was much for him to contemplate, including one of the seven wonders of the ancient world: the famous hanging gardens he had built for his wife, whom he had brought from her mountainous home in Media to the flat plain of Babylon. Another of his building exploits was the outer wall of Babylon, which was wide enough to enable a chariot driven by four horses to turn around on the top, according to the Greek historian Herodotus.[9]

The boastful words were hardly out of Nebuchadnezzar's mouth before the sentence of judgment was announced from heaven: "This is what is decreed for you, King Nebuchadnezzar: Your royal authority has been taken from you. You will be driven away from people and will live with the wild animals; you will eat grass like cattle. Seven times will pass by for you until you acknowledge that the Most High is sovereign over the kingdoms of men and gives them to anyone he wishes" (Dan. 4:31–32). This was exactly what happened: "Immediately what had been said about Nebuchadnezzar was fulfilled. He was driven away from people and ate grass like cattle. His body was drenched with the dew of heaven until his hair grew like the feathers of an eagle and his nails like the claws of a bird" (Dan. 4:33). Nebuchadnezzar lost his power and position, being

9. Longman, *Daniel*, 121.

driven away from Babylon, and even his humanity, eating grass and living wild in the open air like the beasts of the field and growing his hair and his nails unchecked like the birds of the air. Many commentators have sought to establish parallels between Nebuchadnezzar's behavior and recognized mental illnesseses of one kind or another. The story itself, however, is much more interested in the unique inhuman bestiality of Nebuchadnezzar's condition than in providing us the means of diagnosis. His sickness is, after all, a direct judgment of God, not a naturally occurring phenomenon. Finally, at the end of God's appointed time of judgment, Nebuchadnezzar raised his eyes to heaven and his mind was restored.

It is worth noticing where Nebuchadnezzar's eyes are directed at the beginning and end of his time of judgment. At the beginning of the episode he is on a lofty perch, the rooftop of his house, from where his eyes roam sideways and downwards, comparing his glory to that of other men and glorifying himself. He thought of himself as the center of the universe, the tree from which everything else receives its sustenance. This is exactly what pride does: it locates the self at the center of the universe, glorying in its own achievements, and putting everyone else in second place. Its eyes are always directed sideways and downwards, comparing ourselves with others, and endlessly trying to outdo them.[10] In its very nature, pride has to be cleverer than someone else, or more attractive than other people, or a better cook, or a faster runner, or a more skillful gardener, or whatever. Pride is never satisfied in what has been accomplished because its essence always lies in defeating others, not in achieving the thing itself. The eyes of pride are thus always fixed on myself and my performance, in a way that leaves no room for looking upwards to God.

RESTORATION

Nebuchadnezzar's pride was stripped away along with his achievements, until he came to recognize that whatever he possessed or accomplished before was the gift of God, who can exalt the lowliest of men to kingship or bring down the mightiest of men:

10. Lewis, *Mere Christianity*, 109–10.

At the end of that time, I, Nebuchadnezzar, raised my eyes toward heaven, and my sanity was restored. Then I praised the Most High; I honored and glorified him who lives forever. His dominion is an eternal dominion; his kingdom endures from generation to generation. All the peoples of the earth are regarded as nothing. He does as he pleases with the powers of heaven and the peoples of the earth. No one can hold back his hand or say to him: "What have you done?"

At the same time that my sanity was restored, my honor and splendor were returned to me for the glory of my kingdom. My advisers and nobles sought me out, and I was restored to my throne and became even greater than before. Now I, Nebuchadnezzar, praise and exalt and glorify the King of heaven, because everything he does is right and all his ways are just. And those who walk in pride he is able to humble. (Dan. 4:34–37)

It is significant that the end of Nebuchadnezzar's humbling and the return of his reason came when he took his eyes off himself and lifted them to heaven in an act of supplication and dependence.

This looking away from oneself is the essence of true humility, and the means by which we can distinguish it from the counterfeit form. Counterfeit humility may confess cringingly, "Oh how worthless I am," yet its eyes are still fixed on itself. In counterfeit humility, I am caught up in my weakness rather than my strength, but I am still as focused on myself as I was in my pride. True humility, in contrast, looks away from myself to heaven. True humility recognizes not only that I am nothing, but also that God is everything. It acknowledges that I cannot stand by myself, but God can make even me stand firm and strong. Humility sees that apart from Christ I can do nothing, but in Christ I can accomplish whatever God designs for me.

The end result of Nebuchadnezzar's humbling was even greater exaltation. Once brought low by God, he could safely be elevated back to the heights and restored to control of his kingdom (Dan. 4:36). The Lord demonstrated in his life that he is indeed able both to humble the proud, and to exalt the humble. This became Nebuchadnezzar's own personal confession of faith in Israel's God, and it is the last word we hear from his lips in the Bible. The great and mighty persecutor of Israel, the destroyer of Jerusalem, had at last been humbled by God's grace and brought to confess God's mercy. His personal experience showcases God's power: if someone like Nebuchadnezzar can be humbled and restored, then surely no one is beyond the reach of God's mercy.

NEBUCHADNEZZAR, ISRAEL, AND US

This was an important message for Israel to hear, for the imagery of the once-proud tree that had been reduced to a mere stump spoke to their situation just as much as it did to Nebuchadnezzar's. When the prophet Isaiah was called to preach a message of judgment to the people of his day, two centuries before Nebuchadnezzar, he asked the Lord how long he would labor with so little response. The Lord's reply was as follows:

> Until the cities lie ruined and without inhabitant, until the houses are left deserted and the fields ruined and ravaged, until the LORD has sent everyone far away and the land is utterly forsaken. And though a tenth remains in the land, it will again be laid waste. But as the terebinth and oak leave stumps when they are cut down, so the holy seed will be the stump in the land. (Isa. 6:11–13)

This judgment was exactly what had come upon the people of Israel in Daniel's day. Israel itself was like a tree that had been cut down and destroyed, until only the stump remained. Yet that also meant that Nebuchadnezzar's experience could be a source of hope for them. If Nebuchadnezzar could be forgiven and restored when he humbled himself and looked to the Lord, then Israel too could be forgiven and restored. The Lord's promise in Solomon's day was one in which they could find hope as well: "If my people, who are called by my name, will humble themselves and pray and seek my face and turn from their wicked ways, then will I hear from heaven and will forgive their sin and will heal their land" (2 Chron. 7:14). If, in the midst of the devastating experience of their exile, the Israelites took the lesson to heart and humbled themselves before the Lord, they too could expect to see his favor shown to them once again.

The same reality is also true for us. The gospel is an intrinsically humbling message. The only way for us to enter God's kingdom is with empty hands, lifting our eyes to heaven and confessing our desperate need of a savior. By nature, that is hard for all of us. As we survey our lives and achievements, we want to be able to say with Nebuchadnezzar, "See the beautiful empire that my hands have wrought." We are all inclined to believe that the world revolves around us as its center. Humanly speaking, some of us have many attainments in which to trust. Compared to others around us, we may have lives that look virtuous and noble. But we can receive the gospel only when we stop comparing ourselves with other human beings and recognize that before a perfectly holy God even our very best achievements simply increase our condemnation.

When we stand in front of God, our problem is not just our weaknesses and failures, it is our successes and our strengths, insofar as these lead us to take pride in ourselves. Our goodness itself can be an obstacle to receiving the message of the gospel, because in our pride we don't see our need for God. To cure us of our deadly pride, God may graciously bring us down to disaster. Like the prodigal son, we may find that our need of God finally becomes real to us when our money is all spent and our friends have all departed, leaving us wallowing with the pigs. We may find that it is only when we commit a sin that we thought would never tempt us that God shows us what depths of depravity are really in our hearts. Painful as this experience is for us, it is nonetheless truly a work of God's grace. The worst thing that can happen to us would be for the Lord to leave us comfortable and at ease in our pride. Without the episode in the pigsty, the prodigal would never have gone home. So too, giving us over to a deeply humbling experience of failure or sin can be the means by which God brings about a profound transformation in our hearts and a fresh understanding of the gospel.

As an example of this, I think of a man who used to be an elder in a nearby church and a personal friend, who committed adultery with a woman he was counseling. He then abandoned his family and married this woman and had a child with her. It was an intensely painful episode in his life and the life of the church, as he persisted in his rebellion for many months. Yet at the end of that time the Lord brought him back to himself, a broken and humbled man. I wouldn't wish his experience on anyone, for the devastation wrought in his life and the lives of his family members was severe and its scars are deep and permanent. He will reap the consequences of what he has sown every day for the rest of his life. Nonetheless, the fruit in this man's life was an entirely new appreciation of the grace of the gospel. Had he never fallen so profoundly, he would likely never have seen the pride in his own heart of which the Lord wanted to cure him. The only way for him to learn his own depravity and weakness was through painful personal experience. The Lord is still able to humble the proud and in due season also to restore the humbled to his favor.

SUFFERING AND REDEMPTION

How, though, is it possible for the humble to be restored through these trials? Is there something inherently redemptive about Nebuchadnezzar's suffering and ours that earns God's favor? Is restoration achieved through a kind of penance, a work of suffering that we must learn how to do to atone for our pride and thus get to heaven? If we think that, we haven't understood true humility at all. Remember, Nebuchadnezzar's restoration did not come when he looked at himself but rather when he lifted his eyes to heaven. He looked simply to God's grace to restore him, not based on anything that was in him—not even his newfound humility. His hope was simply in God's mercy.

Yet that still leaves the question, "Why should God exalt the humble?" We may certainly see why God should humble the proud and show them that they are not as great and powerful as they think they are. The Lamplighters of this world need to be taken down a peg or five. Wicked kings like Nebuchadnezzar deserve their comeuppance. But why should God exalt the humble? Why do they receive his favor?

The answer to that question takes us to the consideration of another king who was brought down from the heights to the depths. This king could truly have looked out over all creation and said, "Is not this the world I have created for my royal residence, by my mighty power and for the glory of my majesty?" He didn't simply create one of the wonders of the ancient world; he created the world itself out of nothing. Yet instead of exalting himself, this king voluntarily humbled himself. Even though he was in very nature God, this king humbled himself and became a man. He left the comforts and glories of heaven and came to dwell on earth amongst humanity, a step downwards at least as large as when Nebuchadnezzar went to dwell with the beasts of the field and the birds of the air. Yet he took his humbling even further than that. This king took on himself the form of a servant: he healed the sick and preached to the poor and even washed the feet of his disciples. He carried this servant's form all the way to a criminal's death on the cross, even though he had done nothing wrong (Phil. 2:6–8). What greater humbling experience could there possibly be than for the living God to die? Yet this king's humbling was not forced upon him because of his pride. On the contrary, it was a voluntary choice on his part so that he might redeem us from *our* pride. The one who by rights could legitimately have exalted himself made himself lower than the angels in order to redeem a people for himself.

This humble King is named Jesus. However, his time of humiliation is over and now he is once again exalted in glory. Now he has accomplished our salvation and returned to the Father's side. Now this Jesus is the one to whom our doxology and worship is directed, the one in heaven to whom our eyes are lifted in adoration and praise. This is why the humble are exalted: not because their humility is meritorious, but because they fix their eyes on their Lord, who was once humbled and is now glorified, instead of looking at themselves. They are united to him, so that his glorification means their glorification also.

What is more, this vision of the crucified and exalted Jesus is itself the cure for our overweening pride. How can we exalt ourselves and continue to sing our own praises when our eyes are fixed on Jesus? The glory of his majesty as the uncreated Creator reminds us of our smallness as created beings. He is the real tree of life, the true center of the universe, the one in whom and for whom all things exist, the one in whom all must come to find refuge. What have we accomplished compared to him? What is more, the scars that remain visible even now in his hands and feet as the Lamb that was slain remind us constantly of their cause: our own depravity. In view of the incredible mercy we have received, how can we ever boast in anything except the cross of Christ? As we contemplate Christ, once humbled and now exalted, we are reminded over and over of the profound fact that the only thing we contribute to our salvation is our utter depravity. Yet at the same time we are also reminded that, foul as we are, we are far more loved than we ever dared to hope.

So take your eyes off yourself and your accomplishments. Take your eyes even off your failures and disasters. Stop comparing yourself with others. Instead, lift your eyes heavenward and look to Christ, the humbled and exalted King. His death and resurrection are the means by which you are restored to your senses and made welcome in the most exalted company, heaven itself. Put away your pride in your successes, be humbled by all of your sins and failures, and revel in the extraordinary riches of God's mercy and grace to you. Lift up your eyes to heaven and praise God that though he humbles the proud, he also redeems and exalts the humble and through his grace makes them fit to stand in his presence forever.

6

WEIGHED AND FOUND WANTING

Daniel 5:1–31

Suddenly the fingers of a human hand appeared and wrote on
the plaster of the wall, near the lampstand in the royal palace.
The king watched the hand as it wrote. His face turned pale and
he was so frightened that his knees knocked together and his legs
gave way. The king called out for the enchanters, astrologers, and
diviners to be brought and said to these wise men of Babylon,
"Whoever reads this writing and tells me what it means will be
clothed in purple and have a gold chain placed around his neck,
and he will be made the third highest ruler in the kingdom."
(Dan. 5:5–7)

King Hiero of Syracuse had a problem. He had entrusted a certain weight of gold to a craftsman to make a crown for him, but he didn't really trust the man. The finished crown weighed the right amount, but had the craftsman really used all of the gold to make the crown or had he substituted much cheaper silver for part of it? How could the king test the crown's composition and integrity without destroying it?

King Hiero entrusted the problem to his friend Archimedes, the famous scientist. For a long time, Archimedes puzzled over the problem. At last, he decided to take a bath to clear his head. But he had filled the bathtub too full, and when he sat down in it, the water splashed over the top. In a flash, Archimedes saw the answer to the problem. A body immersed in water displaces its own volume of water. Once he knew the volume and the weight of the crown, he could then calculate its density and determine whether it was pure gold or not. "Eureka!" he cried (which in Greek means "I've found it"), reportedly so excited about his discovery that he proceeded to run through the streets of Syracuse naked. The rest is history, and ever since then the word "Eureka" has indicated the moment of discovery: the point at which the true nature of something is made clear.

Daniel 5 is a "Eureka" moment, in which the true nature of the young Babylonian king, Belshazzar, is exposed, along with the emptiness of his gods. For all their boasted pomp and show and in spite of all of their gold and glory, Belshazzar and his gods are found wanting and exposed as empty and insubstantial when they are weighed in God's balance. They can offer nothing that we should envy, nor can they threaten anything by which we should be intimidated. Rather, we should pity those whose hope and glory are built on such insubstantial foundations.

BELSHAZZAR'S FEAST

The story starts with Belshazzar's feast:

> King Belshazzar gave a great banquet for a thousand of his nobles and drank wine with them. While Belshazzar was drinking his wine, he gave orders to bring in the gold and silver goblets that Nebuchadnezzar his father had taken from the temple in Jerusalem, so that the king and his nobles, his wives and his concubines might drink from them. So they brought in the gold goblets that had been taken from the temple of God in Jerusalem, and the king and his nobles, his wives and his concubines drank from them. As they drank the wine, they praised the gods of gold and silver, of bronze, iron, wood and stone. (Dan. 5:1–4)

Outwardly, this was a glorious event, full of pomp and circumstance, in which a thousand nobles were invited to drink wine with the king (Dan.

5:1). Greek historians like Herodotus recorded many such lavish feasts on the part of the Babylonians, and this was one of the best. Everyone was dressed in his finest clothes and the tables were set with the most ornate silverware. Yet by focusing our attention on this elaborate feast as the sole event worth mentioning in his account, the narrator subtly underlines for us the emptiness of the remainder of Belshazzar's life. Unlike his illustrious predecessor, King Nebuchadnezzar, who destroyed cities and carried off plunder (Dan. 1:2), made mighty statues (Dan. 3), and built the wonders of royal Babylon (4:30), the only thing that Belshazzar could make was a feast.[1] The former built an empire, while the latter planned a party. Even the centerpiece of Belshazzar's feast—the golden vessels that had been taken from the Jerusalem temple—had been carried off by Nebuchadnezzar, not Belshazzar (1:2). Belshazzar's only contribution was to profane those sacred and precious vessels from the Lord's house by using them for a feast at which he praised his own gods—gods made out of gold, silver, bronze, iron, wood, and stone (5:3–4).

A HAND FROM HEAVEN

Belshazzar didn't have long to enjoy his feast, however. Even while he and his nobles were praising their man-made gods, a revelation from God disturbed his revelry:

> Suddenly the fingers of a human hand appeared and wrote on the plaster of the wall, near the lampstand in the royal palace. The king watched the hand as it wrote. His face turned pale and he was so frightened that his knees knocked together and his legs gave way.
>
> The king called out for the enchanters, astrologers and diviners to be brought and said to these wise men of Babylon, "Whoever reads this writing and tells me what it means will be clothed in purple and have a gold chain placed around his neck, and he will be made the third highest ruler in the kingdom."
>
> Then all the king's wise men came in, but they could not read the writing or tell the king what it meant. So King Belshazzar became even more terrified and his face grew more pale. His nobles were baffled. (Dan. 5:5–9)

1. Danna Nolan Fewell, *Circle of Sovereignty: Plotting Politics in the Book of Daniel* (Nashville: Abingdon, 1991), 83.

Belshazzar's response to this hand writing on the wall once again under-lined the difference between him and his predecessor, Nebuchadnezzar. When Nebuchadnezzar had dreams, they "troubled" and "frightened" him (Dan. 2:1; 4:5); Belshazzar, however, was totally undone by the experience of a revelation from God. In fact, the Aramaic literally says that the "knots of his joints were loosened" (5:6); most probably, this does not mean that "his legs gave way," as most English translations render it, but rather that he lost control of his bodily functions, with a wet patch appearing under his chair.[2] When his wise men couldn't interpret the dream, Belshazzar was left pale-faced and indecisive, at a loss to know how to proceed.

It was left to a woman, the queen mother,[3] to solve King Belshazzar's dilemma, a scenario which would have been humiliating in an ancient cul-tural context. She reminded Belshazzar of the existence of Daniel, whose ability to interpret knotty problems[4] had been repeatedly demonstrated during the time of his illustrious predecessor, Nebuchadnezzar:

> The queen, hearing the voices of the king and his nobles, came into the ban-quet hall. "O king, live forever!" she said. "Don't be alarmed! Don't look so pale! There is a man in your kingdom who has the spirit of the holy gods in him. In the time of your father he was found to have insight and intelligence and wisdom like that of the gods. King Nebuchadnezzar your father—your father the king, I say—appointed him chief of the magicians, enchanters, astrologers and diviners. This man Daniel, whom the king called Belteshazzar, was found to have a keen mind and knowledge and understanding, and also the ability to interpret dreams, explain riddles and solve difficult problems. Call for Daniel, and he will tell you what the writing means." (Dan. 5:10–12)

The implication of her speech is that Belshazzar ought to have known to whom he should turn when in need of divine illumination—and he would

---

2. See A. Wolters, "Untying the King's Knots: Physiology and Wordplay in Daniel 5," *JBL* 110 (1991) 117–22. So also Tremper Longman III, *Daniel*, New International Version Application Com-mentary (Grand Rapids: Zondervan, 1999), 138.

3. Literally, "the queen," but since the wives of the king were already present (Dan. 5:2), it seems that another person is indicated. The queen mother held a position of some importance in the Baby-lonian court and would naturally remember events that Belshazzar has forgotten (repressed?). See E. J. Young, *The Prophecy of Daniel: An Introduction and Commentary* (Grand Rapids: Eerdmans, 1949), 122.

4. There is a pun here which reflects Belshazzar's earlier embarrassing problem. Instead of divine revelations "loosening his knots," Daniel is the one who loosens the knots of these problems.

have known, if only he were more like Nebuchadnezzar. In the event, the king decided to follow the woman's advice:

> So Daniel was brought before the king, and the king said to him, "Are you Daniel, one of the exiles my father the king brought from Judah? I have heard that the spirit of the gods is in you and that you have insight, intelligence and outstanding wisdom. The wise men and enchanters were brought before me to read this writing and tell me what it means, but they could not explain it. Now I have heard that you are able to give interpretations and to solve difficult problems. If you can read this writing and tell me what it means, you will be clothed in purple and have a gold chain placed around your neck, and you will be made the third highest ruler in the kingdom."
>
> Then Daniel answered the king, "You may keep your gifts for yourself and give your rewards to someone else. Nevertheless, I will read the writing for the king and tell him what it means." (Dan. 5:13–17)

The queen mother's implicit rebuke perhaps explains the defensive tone in King Belshazzar's voice when Daniel was finally summoned before him. He addressed him not as the Daniel whom his father made chief of his wise men, but as the Daniel whom his father brought in exile from Jerusalem. He wanted to put Daniel firmly in his place at the outset.[5] What is more, he placed a question mark over the claims of Daniel's ability to interpret dreams by prefacing them with "I have heard . . . " (Dan. 5:14, 16). It is as if Belshazzar was putting on the record his skepticism about Daniel by affirming that there was a difference between hearing and believing.

In return, Daniel's response omitted the usual deferential politeness of the Babylonian court. He told King Belshazzar bluntly that he might keep his rewards: Daniel's services were not for sale to the highest bidder, giving a favorable interpretation of a dream only if the price was right (Dan. 5:17). However, before he interpreted the mysterious writing for Belshazzar, Daniel first put the oracle into its context, a context that once again compared and contrasted Belshazzar and his father, Nebuchadnezzar. Indeed, the contrast is highlighted by the structure of the opening sentence. Daniel began, "O king, the Most High God gave your father Nebuchadnezzar

5. Longman, *Daniel*, 140.

sovereignty and greatness and glory and splendor" (5:18). By implication, Daniel was suggesting that the Lord had given no similar sovereignty or glory to Belshazzar. Yet even though Nebuchadnezzar had received from the Lord true greatness and majesty, with godlike powers to raise up and to humble, to kill and to keep alive, when he became arrogant, the Lord had humbled him and brought him down from his lofty perch:

> Because of the high position he gave him, all the peoples and nations and men of every language dreaded and feared him. Those the king wanted to put to death, he put to death; those he wanted to spare, he spared; those he wanted to promote, he promoted; and those he wanted to humble, he humbled. But when his heart became arrogant and hardened with pride, he was deposed from his royal throne and stripped of his glory. He was driven away from people and given the mind of an animal; he lived with the wild donkeys and ate grass like cattle; and his body was drenched with the dew of heaven, until he acknowledged that the Most High God is sovereign over the kingdoms of men and sets over them anyone he wishes. (Dan. 5:19–21)

The point of Daniel's speech is clear: King Nebuchadnezzar had had something to be proud about, yet the Lord had humbled him. Belshazzar, who certainly fell far short of Nebuchadnezzar's achievements, should have learned from this experience and humbled himself as well. Instead, although Belshazzar knew what had happened to Nebuchadnezzar, he had still exalted himself against the Lord, sacrilegiously profaning the temple vessels from Jerusalem by using them in an idolatrous act of worship. He had praised his powerless idols, while neglecting the one true God who gave him his very life-breath. Daniel brought this charge against him, explaining why God was warning him in this way:

> But you his son, O Belshazzar, have not humbled yourself, though you knew all this. Instead, you have set yourself up against the Lord of heaven. You had the goblets from his temple brought to you, and you and your nobles, your wives and your concubines drank wine from them. You praised the gods of silver and gold, of bronze, iron, wood and stone, which cannot see or hear or understand. But you did not honor the God who holds in his hand your life and all your ways. Therefore he sent the hand that wrote the inscription. (Dan. 5:22–24)

WEIGHED AND FOUND WANTING

Daniel then read and interpreted the oracle: "This is the inscription that was written: MENE, MENE, TEKEL, PARSIN. This is what these words mean: *Mene*: God has numbered the days of your reign and brought it to an end. *Tekel*: You have been weighed on the scales and found wanting. *Peres*: Your kingdom is divided and given to the Medes and Persians" (Dan. 5:25–28). If read as they stand, "Mene, mene, tekel, parsin" form a sequence of weights, decreasing from a mina ("mene"), to a shekel (in Aramaic, "tekel": 1/60th of a mina), to a half shekel ("peres").[6] Read as verbs (with a different vocalization of the Aramaic letters), however, the sequence becomes a series of verbs: "Numbered, numbered, weighed, divided." As Daniel himself explained it, the Lord had numbered the days of Belshazzar's kingdom and brought it to an end because King Belshazzar had been weighed in the balance and found wanting. As a result, his former kingdom would be divided and given to the Medes and the Persians ("Peres," the singular of "parsin," sounds like the word for Persia).

Did King Belshazzar believe Daniel's interpretation of the inscription? We will never know for sure. Certainly he gave Daniel the promised reward, for Daniel was "clothed in purple, a gold chain was placed around his neck, and he was proclaimed the third highest ruler in the kingdom" (Dan. 5:29). Yet even this was an empty gift, for that very night, the Medes and the Persians entered Babylon; "Belshazzar, king of the Babylonians, was slain, and Darius the Mede took over the kingdom, at the age of sixty-two" (Dan. 5:30–31). Belshazzar's party is thus exposed as the ultimate act of folly: he was feasting on the brink of the grave and celebrating on the edge of extinction, and he never even knew it. With Belshazzar's death, Babylon's empire was itself brought crashing to the ground, its feet of clay revealed. The sequence of decay that the vision of Daniel 2 anticipated for world history—moving from gold to silver to bronze to fragile feet of iron and clay—found a foreshadowing within the history of the Babylonian empire. Like the sequence of weights in the oracle, the once mighty kingdom became insubstantial and was ultimately blown away by the judgment of God. Or, picking up other biblical echoes, the New Babel ended its days under the

---

6. John Goldingay, *Daniel*, Word Biblical Commentary (Dallas: Word, 1989), 110–11.

judgment of God, under a curse of incomprehensible speech and a divinely imposed division, just like the first Tower of Babel in Genesis 11.[7]

BELSHAZZAR'S MODERN COUNTERPARTS

What lessons does this ancient narrative have for us, who live in an altogether different time and place in history? In the first place, the story of Belshazzar's feast reminds us not to be awed and impressed by earthly power and wealth. God has weighed it in the balance and found it wanting; he will soon bring it to an end. God's power to bring down those who are truly mighty was a central theme in Daniel 4. If God is thus able to humble the mighty, how much more is he able to bring down an empty windbag like Belshazzar! Yet in our culture we are apt to elevate and adulate not only those who have real accomplishments, but even those with empty pretensions. We are much too easily impressed by all that glitters, whether or not it is truly gold. For evidence of this, all you have to do is look at the celebrities who are pictured on the covers of magazines at the local supermarket. Their ranks may include some who have genuine achievements, yet the vast majority have contributed little substantive in which to boast. In our culture we idolize those who are physically attractive, those who have acquired great wealth, and even those who are famous simply for being famous. Belshazzar's feast is set before us every day, and many around us are mortgaging their futures for an invitation to the ball.

It is not just the rich and the famous that we idolize, either. Our envy operates at a far more mundane level as well. We covet not only the assets and the lifestyle of multimillionaires, but those of our neighbors as well. We envy our neighbor's car, or good looks, or successful career, or obedient children. Alternatively, if we have some small successes of our own, we boast in our petty assets and lifestyle, perhaps glorying in our fine house, or thriving reputation in our field of business, or trim figure. The reality is that we are all tinpot Belshazzars, puffed up by our miniscule achievements, even though they may not amount to much on an earthly scale, let alone a heavenly one. God's judgment on our empty pride is severe: our

7. M. Hilton, "Babel Revisited—Daniel Chapter 5," *Journal for the Study of the Old Testament* 66 (1995): 99–112.

deeds and accomplishments have been weighed in the balance and found wanting. When we stand in God's presence, we have nothing of which to boast.

Belshazzar's ability to close his eyes to reality has a contemporary ring to it in every age. Just as Belshazzar feasted even while the armies of his Median and Persian adversaries were encamped outside his gates, so too rebellious humanity actively suppresses the truth about God that bombards their senses on every side (Rom. 1:18). Many around us eat and drink and busily pursue an actively sinful lifestyle, all the while deliberately ignoring God's revelation of himself in the Scriptures, in their consciences, and in the world. Just as Belshazzar used the temple vessels to praise his false gods, so too we take the things that belong to God and use them to feed our lusts and idolatries. Should we continue along that path, our fate is as deserved as it is certain.

THE JUDGMENT OF BELSHAZZAR'S GODS

Yet it is not only Belshazzar who has been weighed in the balance and found wanting; his gods too have failed the test. Belshazzar praised his gods of wood and stone and gold and silver, ascribing to them glory and honor, yet his gods couldn't keep the Lord's messenger from disturbing the peace of his feast. Nor could they keep him safe from the Medes and the Persians. It may have seemed to the Babylonians that when they defeated Judah and destroyed their temple, they were thereby triumphing over Israel's god as well. However, as the story of the Book of Daniel unfolded, it became clear that the reality was that Israel's God could effectively defend the honor of his sacred vessels and the lives of his faithful servants, while Babylon's gods were impotent. The Lord was able to save Shadrach, Meshach, and Abednego from the fiery furnace, but Bel and Marduk had no power to save Belshazzar from the coming of the Persians. Whatever power Nebuchadnezzar possessed to conquer and kill had been granted to him by the Lord, the Most High God, and not by his idols (Dan. 5:19). Through his own profound experience of humbling, King Nebuchadnezzar eventually came to understand that truth and bow his knee before Israel's God. In contrast, Belshazzar didn't live long enough to find it out. He was humbled and crushed rather than being humbled and restored.

Have you learned yet that this world's idols are empty and powerless? Fame and fortune promise great rewards, but they are fickle masters. Wealth may seem to hold the key to an easy life, yet those who attain it discover that their lives become more complicated than ever. Beauty is fleeting and power is deceptive: none of these things can deliver true satisfaction and meaning in life. In the West, we are tempted to idolize freedom and democracy, as if these virtues had the power within themselves to transform our world. Yet, in the last analysis, all of these things are no more substantial than Belshazzar's idols of gold and silver and bronze and stone. They are all great blessings when they come to us from the hand of the Most High God, who made the heavens and the earth, and all that they contain. Yet if we make these created things into our gods and forget our Creator, then we are just as foolish and blind as Belshazzar was, and we stand under the same judgment that he did.

The Lord is the one before whom you should truly stand in awe. He holds your life in his hand, just as he held sway over Belshazzar's life. He could bring you down to poverty in an instant, through ill health or misfortune, or he could snuff you out like a candle in death. The same is true of our vaunted political institutions: the Lord is the one who invested our country with its present strength and influence, and the Lord could humble us and bring us down in a moment, if he chose to do so. His faithful servants are the only ones who will truly endure, and his kingdom is the only one that will never come to an end.

God's Sovereign Mercy

As Christians, we may say that we believe these truths, but in practice we often act as if they were not true. Why is it that we are completely undone by far less threatening scenarios than that which faced Belshazzar? Our hearts are wracked with worry if our job is merely threatened or if the car refuses to start; we are overwhelmed and despairing if our health breaks down or a treasured relationship ends; we respond angrily to people who insult us and damage our pride. These responses reveal our hearts every bit as clearly as Belshazzar's feast revealed his pride and the idols in which his trust was placed. We are all functional Belshazzars. Our excessively strong negative emotions show that we have invested these things—our jobs and our health, our relationships and our comfort, our status and achievements—with divine importance, even while at the same time we confess with our lips that Jesus Christ is our Lord. We take the very things that God has given us—our bodies, our talents, our spouses, our children, our positions of influence and leadership, and our achievements of varying kinds—and we use them to offer worship to our empty idols. If we were to be weighed in God's balance, we would all be found wanting, profoundly guilty of Belshazzar's sin; we are, at best, "half-shekel" believers who deserve to be blown away by God in his wrath.

We should therefore be astonished that God continues to show us his mercy. Taken together, Daniel 4 and 5 show us God's utter sovereignty in salvation. He showed mercy to King Nebuchadnezzar in spite of his earlier persecution of God's people. He humbled him and brought him to the point where he truly understood the reality of God's power over him and bowed the knee before him. Yet there was no such mercy for Belshazzar. His humbling did not bring him to the point of repentance, but only to the point of death.

So also God will bring down all of the proud. Some he will humble redemptively, opening their eyes to see their true need for God and bringing them to bow their knees to him. Others will merely be brought down to death, shown ultimately in a final moment of terror that their whole life has been an empty sham and that now they are doomed to destruction and eternal separation from God. We cannot presume on God's mercy. It is a serious and solemn truth when God says, "I will have mercy on whom I will have mercy, and I will harden whom I will harden" (Rom. 9:15–18). God sovereignly bestows his grace where and when he sees fit.

Perhaps you have never been humbled before God and come to kneel before his throne. Like King Belshazzar, you may have heard stories from your friends and relations about God's power but have never put much stock in them. Since you haven't yet experienced that power personally, you are apt to discount it. If so, then today is the day for you to learn from Belshazzar what a dangerous situation you are in. The Lord could demand your life from you this very night, as he did with Belshazzar: then where would all of your little accomplishments leave you? Every day of your life, you are feasting on the edge of the grave. As long as you stubbornly refuse to open your heart to Christ, the handwriting is on the wall as far as your final destiny is concerned.

But why should you choose death? How much better to learn the lesson that Belshazzar should have learned from King Nebuchadnezzar's experience and be humbled now, before it is too late. God brings down the proud, but he also exalts the humble (James 4:6). Individuals who come to God now, recognizing that they have nothing to offer him in return, crying out to him for the mercy and grace that they need will find it, just as surely as those who remain unhumbled in this life will go on to eternal destruction.

THE DEPTH OF GOD'S MERCY

For those of us who have had our eyes opened by God's grace to see our emptiness, this story should act as yet another reminder of the depth of his mercy. Why should I have been chosen as a recipient of his grace, while he passed over others who have accomplished far more with their gifts and have led much more moral lives than I? Who am I that I should receive an invitation to his feast, while others are left unsummoned? There is nothing in me that makes me worthy of such a great inheritance. The only explanation is God's sovereign mercy that chose me in spite of my stubborn pride and self-centeredness, and then opened my eyes to the depth of my lostness without Christ. How high and how wide and how deep and how long is the love that the Lord has shown to me!

In contrast to the kingdom of Belshazzar, which is weighed in the balance and found insubstantial and wanting to be divided among his enemies, there is the kingdom which God has established in Jesus Christ. Ironically, Jesus had none of the outward glitz and glitter for which this world clamors so loudly. He had virtually no possessions and relatively few followers. He had no outward beauty or majesty to commend him, appearing on earth as a humble carpenter, not as a mighty emperor. Jesus never had the resources to throw a star-studded party for a thousand of his closest friends, though he did brighten up a banquet that he attended by turning water into rich wine (John 2). His kingdom is not of this world.

Yet when Jesus' life was weighed in God's balance, it was found to be perfect and complete, able to satisfy fully the demands of God's holiness, not just for himself but for all those who come to God through him. His great banquet awaits us in the future, at the end of time; on that day, in place of Belshazzar's nobles, there will be thousands upon thousands of Christ's saints in attendance upon him—all those who have washed their robes and made them clean in the blood of the Lamb. At that banquet there will be no place for our pride or for toasting our achievements: rather, every single person who is there will confess freely that they have been saved by God's grace and purified by God's mercy. On that day, there will be no unseemly interruptions of the banquet: God's rule will be established forever and ever. His kingdom will not be divided and given to his enemies: on the contrary, it is formed of a people who are made one in Christ.

So where are your eyes fixed? Is your heart set on an invitation to Belshazzar's feast, the banquet that this world offers: a tawdry affair that is empty and meaningless when weighed on the scale of eternal things? Are you using the gifts that God has given you as offerings to the idols of your own heart? Are you hoping that your own goodness will enable you to stand unhumbled before God? There is no future for that feast. Instead, you and I need to look onward and upward to the true banquet to which Jesus Christ invites us, a feast that can be entered only by grace, by those who are clothed in the garments that God provides (Matt. 22:11–13). This banquet will more than compensate for any pains that we suffer in the short term. God's simple "Well done!" has more weight than all of Belshazzar's gold and honors. Those who have weighed their lives on God's balance scales and see things in eternal perspective will never lose their awe that sinners like them should be invited to share in that table. As the hymnwriter Isaac Watts put it:

> How sweet and awful is the place with Christ within the doors,
>   While everlasting love displays the choicest of her stores.
> While all our hearts and all our songs join to admire the feast,
>   Each of us cry, with thankful tongues, "Lord, why was I a guest?"
> "Why was I made to hear Thy voice, and enter while there's room,
>   When thousands make a wretched choice, and rather starve than come?"
> 'Twas the same love that spread the feast that sweetly drew us in;
>   Else we had still refused to taste, and perished in our sin.

7

IN THE ANGEL'S DEN

Daniel 6:1—28

At the first light of dawn, the king got up and hurried to the lions' den. When he came near the den, he called to Daniel in an anguished voice, "Daniel, servant of the living God, has your God, whom you serve continually, been able to rescue you from the lions?" Daniel answered, "O king, live forever! My God sent his angel, and he shut the mouths of the lions. They have not hurt me, because I was found innocent in his sight. Nor have I ever done any wrong before you, O king." (Dan. 6:19–22)

In the movie *Conspiracy Theory*, Mel Gibson plays a cab driver who is convinced that the world is full of bizarre conspiracies and that he is the personal target of an elaborate government plot. As the movie unfolds, we discover the truth of the old saying, "Just because you're paranoid, it doesn't mean they aren't out to get you." Yet the movie also casts some light on the true mental illness of paranoia. People who suffer from this disease do not necessarily see delusions or hear voices: their perceptions of what is happening may be perfectly normal. The disorder stems rather from a mistaken understanding of *why* these particular events are happening. They see a helicopter fly overhead and conclude that it is part of a secret government plot to monitor their movements; or they see a man in a restaurant look their way and believe that he is planning to murder them. The helicopter and the man are real, but their significance is misunderstood: the paranoid person wrongly thinks that people are plotting to harm him and that there are dangers lurking behind every bush. As a result, his life is wracked with debilitating fear and worry.

Daniel's mind-set, however, could properly be described as the reverse of paranoia. In a world in which there really were people conspiring against him and dangers on all sides, he nonetheless exhibited a peace that is truly remarkable. It is not as though he failed to understand what was happening around him. He knew that we live in an exceedingly dangerous world, a world filled with lions, not all of whom are caged in pits. Yet at the same time Daniel also had a proper understanding of *why* these things were happening and, most importantly, who was in control. He knew that his God was sovereign over even the most fearsome dangers that roam this world. As a result, he was able to experience a profound peace in the midst of his trials and tribulations, just as much as when life was going rather more smoothly. If we want to have peace like the peace that Daniel possessed and to trust that everything will work out for good in the end in the midst of adversities and disappointments, then we need to learn the lessons that this chapter of God's Word has for us.

LIVING AS A PILGRIM

The first point to observe in this chapter is that Daniel had learned how to live as a pilgrim. From the outset of his career in Babylon, Daniel was *in* his culture but not *of* his culture. On the one hand, he didn't withdraw from Babylonian culture as far as he could in order to avoid being stained by it. On the contrary, he had now served the empire faithfully for almost seventy years. Far from using his age as an excuse to retire, he continued to serve the new administration. Belshazzar had been replaced as king by Darius, and the Babylonian empire had been replaced by that of the Medes and the Persians, but Daniel kept on serving:

It pleased Darius to appoint 120 satraps to rule throughout the kingdom, with three administrators over them, one of whom was Daniel. The satraps were made accountable to them so that the king might not suffer loss. Now Daniel so distinguished himself among the administrators and the satraps by his exceptional qualities that the king planned to set him over the whole kingdom. At this, the administrators and the satraps tried to find grounds for charges against Daniel in his conduct of government affairs, but they were unable to do so. They could find no corruption in him, because he was trustworthy and neither corrupt nor negligent. Finally these men said, "We will never find any basis for charges against this man Daniel unless it has something to do with the law of his God." (Dan. 6:1–5)

In fact, Daniel served the empire so well that he continued to get promoted. When King Darius decided to diversify authority in his new kingdom by appointing three administrators over the 120 satraps, or provincial rulers, of his kingdom, Daniel was one of these three (Dan. 6:1–2). There is a certain irony in Daniel's appointment as one of the three *de facto* rulers of the kingdom, given Belshazzar's promise to make Daniel third ruler of Babylon (5:29).[1] In effect, Daniel received Belshazzar's reward in spite of his death. Yet Daniel did such an excellent job in this role that Darius planned to set him in an even higher position, over the whole kingdom (6:3).

Even while Daniel served the Babylonian and Persian empires well, though, he was not shaped by their values. Graft and corruption were widespread in the ancient world, as they are in much of the modern world; how easy it would have been for Daniel to justify taking a little back of everything the empire had stolen from himself and from his people. Yet Daniel's life was so completely free from corruption and negligence that his enemies could find nothing to use against him, even when they searched diligently for it.

We are familiar in our own system with the kind of scrutiny and dirt-digging that take place whenever someone is nominated for high office. Not infrequently, some carefully concealed skeleton comes to light and the person is then disqualified from consideration. Indeed, how many of us have lives that could bear that kind of scrutiny? If we were the ones under the

---

1. Danna Nolan Fewell, *Circle of Sovereignty: Plotting Politics in the Book of Daniel* (Nashville: Abingdon, 1991), 107.

microscope, would the private investigators come back with empty hands and say, "Sorry. You might as well stop digging for dirt on this person. His life is utterly above reproach"? Yet that was his enemies' assessment of Daniel. They recognized that they would never find fault with him unless it was in regard to the law of his God. What an incredible testimonial from the enemies of Daniel and of his God! He embodied the words of Jesus: "Let your light shine before men, that they may see your good deeds and praise your Father in heaven" (Matt. 5:16).

Yet Daniel's goodness did not win him friends on all sides. Instead, his faithfulness to his duty to God and man made him powerful enemies. Some sought to bring him down, probably both because they were jealous of his success and because his incorruptibility was restricting their ability to use the system for their own personal benefit. Isn't that always the way it is? Ever since Cain killed Abel, there has been hostility between God's people and those around them, a hostility that sometimes comes to violent expression. The truth is that we live in a hostile world and we need to be prepared for that reality. Paul warned the Thessalonians ahead of time that they would surely suffer persecution (1 Thess. 3:4), and he told Timothy, "Everyone who wants to live a godly life in Christ Jesus will be persecuted" (2 Tim. 3:12). We should expect persecution as a routine fact of life.

Believers around the world know this from experience, yet here in the prosperous and supposedly tolerant West we have come to expect our lives as Christians to run smoothly and successfully, at least if we are faithfully following the Lord. We think that the slogan "God loves you and has a wonderful plan for your life" means that our lives should be protected by God from any form of unpleasantness. This is a false belief, however. Persecution comes to us in a variety of forms and from a variety of directions, yet it is something that we should expect constantly to mark out our lives in a fallen world. It may come in the form of mockery and isolation at school, or conflict and trouble at work, or simply being regarded as peculiar and strange people, but one way or another we should expect to suffer abuse for the sake of Christ.

Pilgrims remember these things. Pilgrims understand that this world is not our home, and that therefore we shouldn't be surprised if our welcome here is less than warm (1 Peter 2:11). When Daniel's enemies brought the charge against him before the king, they called him "Daniel, the exile from Judah" (Dan. 6:13). They meant it as an insult, a slur that after all these years of living in Babylon, he was still essentially foreign and therefore untrustworthy. His deepest loyalties lay elsewhere. In fact, this was the highest commendation they could have given him. After all these years, even though Daniel served the empire faithfully, Babylon was not his home. He was nothing more and nothing less than a pilgrim there. His citizenship was elsewhere (cf. Phil. 3:20).

Persisting in Prayer

The second point we need to see in this chapter is that Daniel had learned how to be persistent in prayer. Daniel's enemies knew that in order to bring a charge against him they would have to engineer a clash between the law of his God and the law of the state. They knew that if Daniel had to choose between obedience to his God and obedience to the Persian authorities, loyalty to his God would come first. Once again, this observation should be both challenging and convicting to us. Daniel's enemies were totally confident that he would rather die than disobey his God. They knew that he would sooner go to the lions than give up his practice of daily prayer. Would our friends and acquaintances, never mind our enemies, say that about us with equal confidence? Is our commitment to constant prayer so obvious to everyone we meet? In view of Daniel's commitment to prayer, the administrators and the satraps conspired together and went to King Darius with a proposal for a new law.[2]

> So the administrators and the satraps went as a group [conspired] to the king and said: "O King Darius, live forever! The royal administrators, prefects, satraps, advisers and governors have all agreed that the king should issue an edict and enforce the decree that anyone who prays to any god or man during the next thirty days, except to you, O king, shall be thrown into the lions' den. Now, O king, issue the decree and put it in writing so that it cannot be altered—in accordance with the laws of the Medes and Persians, which cannot be repealed." So King Darius put the decree in writing. (Dan. 6:6–9)

2. It is suggestive that the word for "conspired" (*rgs*) comes from the same root as the verb used to describe the gathering of the kings of the earth against the Lord and his Anointed in Psalm 2:1.

Daniel's enemies suggested that the king should issue a decree that for the next thirty days no one was to petition any god or man except the king himself, on pain of being thrown into the lions' den (Dan. 6:7). The intended significance of the new law is not entirely clear. Presumably, Darius was not declaring himself to be divine for a one-month period, nor is there any indication that this was a trial period that would be extended if the scheme proved popular. Most likely, Darius viewed this law as a political rather than a religious edict, a means of uniting the realm by identifying himself as the sole mediator between the people and the gods, the source of their every blessing.[3] This edict thus functioned similarly to Nebuchadnezzar's enormous golden statue. Doubtless Darius was also flattered by the thought that all of his officials wanted to introduce this new edict—so flattered that he didn't notice that Daniel wasn't among them. Whatever the king's motives, he quickly signed the edict into effect as a law of the Medes and Persians which could not be changed (6:8–9).

There are a number of different ways in which Daniel could have responded to this edict. You or I might have rushed before the king to protest the unfairness of the new law or gone home in tears to complain to our friends about it. When Daniel heard about the new law, however, he continued to do exactly what he had always done. Three times a day, it was his habit to go to his upper room to pray, bowing down with his face towards Jerusalem, giving thanks, petitioning and imploring his God: "Now when Daniel learned that the decree had been published, he went home to his upstairs room where the windows opened toward Jerusalem. Three times a day he got down on his knees and prayed, giving thanks to his God, just as he had done before" (Dan. 6:10). There was no biblical command that required Daniel to seek God in this way, but he had made a habit of doing so. As a result, what is remarkable in his behavior is not so much that the crisis drove him to his knees, but rather that it didn't break his regular routine of prayer. He didn't hide himself away in an inner room to pray, in the hopes of remaining undiscovered. When prayer becomes fashionable, praying in secret may be a good thing, but when prayer is proscribed, to pray in private becomes an act of cowardice.[4] It would mean pretending that we are

3. See John Walton, "The Decree of Darius the Mede in Daniel 6," *JETS* 31 (1988): 280.
4. John Goldingay, *Daniel*, Word Biblical Commentary (Dallas: Word, 1989), 131.

complying with a decree that seeks to write God out of our lives, and this was something Daniel was not willing to do.

Nor did Daniel immediately cry out to God for deliverance from this unjust edict. Rather, he began by giving thanks, just like normal. Isn't that remarkable? As he faced imminent death, knowing that his enemies would certainly see him and use his prayers against him, Daniel was on his knees, giving thanks to God. How amazing is his faith! Here is a good test of the depth of your prayer life: how much of your time and energy in prayer is spent complaining about the circumstances of your life and asking for things to be different, and how much is spent in giving thanks for God's overwhelming goodness? The more clearly we see who God is and the great things that he has done for us, the more consistently our hearts will be moved to praise and thank him, whatever our external circumstances. What is more, by beginning with thankfulness, we tune our hearts to remember God's past faithfulness to us, which will render us better able to trust his wisdom and power to answer our petitions for the future.

SEEKING GOD'S FAVOR

What was Daniel praying and pleading for with such consistency that he was on his knees three times every day? The focus of his regular prayers, as we will see when we get to Daniel 9, was pleading that God would show mercy on his land and his temple, which now lay desolate. This explains why Daniel always prayed facing towards Jerusalem. It wasn't merely a superstitious ritual on his part. Rather, he was consciously fulfilling the scenario described in Solomon's prayer at the dedication of the temple in Jerusalem. On that great occasion, Solomon anticipated the day, hundreds of years hence, when God's people would have sinned so greatly against the Lord that they would be deported from the Promised Land for their sins. In his prayer, Solomon asked that when that tragedy occurred and they then turned back to the Lord in the land of their enemies, praying towards the temple, the Lord would hear their prayer and show them favor in the eyes of their captors (1 Kings 8:46–50). In line with this request, Daniel faced Jerusalem three times daily and asked for mercy for his people and for himself from God, the great King. He sought the restoration of the Lord's people to the Lord's land and, doubtless, on this particular occasion he also asked for mercy for himself in his hour of need. He trusted in God's Word and placed his confidence in God's promises.

In view of what followed, it must have appeared to Daniel at first that his prayer had not been answered. The plotters came and found him praying and petitioning his God (Dan. 6:11). Since Daniel prayed publicly three times a day, it probably didn't take a great deal of skill on their part to catch him in the act. Yet surely God could have closed their eyes as easily as he later closed the mouths of the lions, so that Daniel could have prayed unhindered. Could he not in this way have spared Daniel from the whole ordeal? Certainly, he could have done that, but his purpose was not to save Daniel *from* trials but to save Daniel *through* trials. Just as was earlier the case with Shadrach, Meshach, and Abednego, there were lessons that Daniel and those around him would learn, that could be learned only by Daniel going into the den of lions.

This too is an important point for us to understand. God is not committed to our comfort. He is not committed to making our path through life smooth. He *is* committed to sanctifying us and demonstrating his own glory in and through us; and, very often, that commitment means he will subject our earthen vessels to pressures that would certainly shatter us, were his grace not sufficient for us. The Lord will take you into the eye of the storm, to show that he is the storm's master and that he can make your fragile vessel float safely through to the other side. His wonderful plan for your life is to sanctify you through trials and tribulations (1 Peter 1:6–7).

The Law of the Medes and the Persians

When the conspirators approached King Darius, they didn't immediately denounce Daniel but first asked the king to reaffirm the unchangeability of the decree, in order to make it hard for him to circumvent it. Only after he had affirmed that this was indeed a law of the Medes and Persians that could not be changed did they announce the fact that the edict convicted Daniel:

> So they went to the king and spoke to him about his royal decree: "Did you
> not publish a decree that during the next thirty days anyone who prays to any
> god or man except to you, O king, would be thrown into the lions' den?"
>
> The king answered, "The decree stands—in accordance with the laws of
> the Medes and Persians, which cannot be repealed."
>
> Then they said to the king, "Daniel, who is one of the exiles from Judah,
> pays no attention to you, O king, or to the decree you put in writing. He still
> prays three times a day." (Dan. 6:12–13)

This news distressed the king, for he was sorry to lose a faithful and honest servant, and he sought for a way to rescue Daniel from the fate the law
dictated. Yet when the conspirators came at sunset and reminded the king
that the laws of the Medes and the Persians could not be changed, he con-
ceded and made arrangements to throw Daniel into the lions' den: "Then
the men went as a group to the king and said to him, 'Remember, O king,
that according to the law of the Medes and Persians no decree or edict that
the king issues can be changed'" (Dan. 6:15).

Of course, it was not strictly true that there was no other way out for
King Darius. Both here and in the Book of Esther, where we also see the
idea of "a law of the Medes and Persians that cannot be changed," the edict
ended up eventually being voided simply by issuing a counteredict. Presumably Darius could have issued a counteredict at this point, confessing
that he had erred in issuing the first decree. However, after earlier reaf-
firming the edict's validity, such a counteredict would have resulted in an
enormous loss of face for Darius and would have cast the validity of all his
future edicts into question. That is why, at the end of the day, he chose to
sacrifice Daniel rather than undermine the status of his word as inflexible
and unchanging law.

So Darius abandoned Daniel to his fate in the lions' den. To make sure
that no outside help was given to Daniel, the mouth of the den was covered
with a stone, which was then sealed with the signet rings of the king and
his nobles. Humanly speaking, Daniel was left all alone to face his fate. Yet
Darius's last words to Daniel point to a higher source of help: "So the king
gave the order, and they brought Daniel and threw him into the lions' den.
The king said to Daniel, 'May your God, whom you serve continually, rescue you!'" (Dan. 6:16).

DANIEL'S PRESERVATION

That brings us on to the third point that we need to see in this chapter, which is Daniel's preservation in the lions' den:

A stone was brought and placed over the mouth of the den, and the king sealed it with his own signet ring and with the rings of his nobles, so that Daniel's situation might not be changed. Then the king returned to his palace and spent the night without eating and without any entertainment being brought to him. And he could not sleep.

At the first light of dawn, the king got up and hurried to the lions' den. When he came near the den, he called to Daniel in an anguished voice, "Daniel, servant of the living God, has your God, whom you serve continually, been able to rescue you from the lions?"

Daniel answered, "O king, live forever! My God sent his angel, and he shut the mouths of the lions. They have not hurt me, because I was found innocent in his sight. Nor have I ever done any wrong before you, O king."

The king was overjoyed and gave orders to lift Daniel out of the den. And when Daniel was lifted from the den, no wound was found on him, because he had trusted in his God. (Dan. 6:17–23)

The story contrasts with sharp irony the experience of Daniel and Darius during the night. King Darius returned to his palace, where he spent a harried and sleepless night, unable to enjoy his usual comforts of food and entertainment. At dawn, he arose and hurried to the lions' den, crying out as he went, deeply concerned for Daniel. Meanwhile, in his response to the king's anguished cry, Daniel sounds as calm and untroubled as if he had spent the night in his own bed rather than with the lions: "O king, live forever! My God sent his angel, and he shut the mouths of the lions" (Dan. 6:21–22). It is clear that, contrary to all expectations, Daniel actually spent a far more comfortable night in the stinking pit than Darius did in his royal luxury. We may almost imagine the prophet leaning back on a warm, furry lion, conversing for hours with the angel about heavenly things, until he was so rudely interrupted by Darius's question. His fearsome lodging turned out to be a den of angels rather than a den of lions: the angel shut the mouths of the lions and kept God's servant safe.

What a stark contrast this provides! King Darius had at his disposal every pleasure that the ancient world had to offer, yet he could not enjoy any of them, while Daniel had nothing except the presence of his God with him in his trials and yet enjoyed a peaceful night's rest. This shows us that true peace does not come from the possessions that we accumulate but from the presence and favor of God in our lives. What was meant to be a terrifying and deadly trial for Daniel with the lions instead became a strengthening encounter with the angel. God was with him and preserved him safely through the ordeal.

Yet it is not as if the lions had been defanged by the angel and turned into purring tabby cats. After Daniel's release, "at the king's command, the men who had falsely accused Daniel were brought in and thrown into the lions' den, along with their wives and children" (Dan. 6:24), in accord with the common principle in the ancient Near East that anyone who made a false charge against someone else should be punished by receiving the same fate they had sought for their victim (see Deut. 19:16–21). The experience of the conspirators in the den was the exact opposite of Daniel's: "before they reached the floor of the den, the lions overpowered them and crushed all their bones" (Dan. 6:24).

What made the difference in their fate? Why was Daniel spared by the lions, while the conspirators were consumed by them? Daniel explained to King Darius that the lions were unable to hurt him because he was found innocent in God's sight, for he had never done anything to harm the king: "My God sent his angel, and he shut the mouths of the lions. They have not hurt me, because I was found innocent in his sight. Nor have I ever done any wrong before you, O king" (Dan. 6:22). The heavenly tribunal was the one whose decision truly counted: the Most High God holds the true power of life and death, not any earthly king. In making this statement, Daniel was simply living up to his name, which means "My God is the judge." His experience in the lions' den confirmed that basic truth. God had judged him "not guilty" and so he emerged from the lions' den without a scratch. God had indeed answered his earlier prayers and showed him his mercy. Equally, the conspirators' fate demonstrated that they had been judged and found guilty by God, not just the earthly king, confirming the justice of their sentence of death. This contrast is ironically highlighted when we compare Daniel's address to the king from the pit with the king's later edict. Using the forms of conventional politeness, Daniel began, "O king, live forever . . . " Yet Darius himself was forced to confess that the king who truly lives forever is the God of heaven, not the rulers of the earth:

> Then King Darius wrote to all the peoples, nations and men of every language throughout the land: "May you prosper greatly! I issue a decree that in every part of my kingdom people must fear and reverence the God of Daniel. For he is the living God and he endures forever; his kingdom will not be destroyed, his dominion will never end. He rescues and he saves; he performs signs and wonders in the heavens and on the earth. He has rescued Daniel from the power of the lions." (Dan. 6:25–27)

In response to Daniel's deliverance, King Darius issued a counterdecree nullifying his original edict. In this decree he commanded fear and reverence for the God of Daniel, the living God who rescues and saves (Dan. 6:26–27). Of course, no one can enforce devotion to God by decree, anymore than anyone can crush it by decree, but the edict was nevertheless a tangible testimony of God's work in convincing Darius of his existence and power. The Lord had once again brought the ruler of the mightiest of empires to acknowledge his greatness and power, as well as the fact that his kingdom would truly last forever.

PROSPERING IN EXILE

Don't miss the significance of the closing note of the chapter: "So Daniel prospered during the reign of Darius and the reign of Cyrus the Persian" (Dan. 6:28).[5] This rounds off the story of Daniel's life, and puts

---

5. The nature of the relationship between Darius and Cyrus has been much debated. It is clear that Cyrus was already king of Persia at the time when Babylonia fell to the Persians, and to date no reference to "Darius" has been found in the surviving contemporary documents. However, our knowledge of the history of this period, while substantial, is arguably incomplete. Until fairly recently, there was no cuneiform evidence to prove the existence of Belshazzar either. Some evangelical commentators suggest that Darius was a Babylonian throne name adopted by Cyrus himself, so that this sentence should be understood "during the reign of Darius the Mede, *that is*, the reign of Cyrus the Persian" (see D. J. Wiseman, *Notes on Some Problems in the Book of Daniel* [London: Tyndale, 1965], 12–16). Others argue that Darius was actually Cyrus's general, elsewhere named Gubaru or Ugbaru and credited in the Nabonidus Chronicle with the capture of Babylon (see W. H. Shea, "An Unrecognized Vassal King in the Early Achaemenid Period," *Andrews University Seminary Studies* 9 [1971]: 51–67, 99–128; 10 [1972]: 88–117).

his experience in the lions' den into a broader context. It reminds us that Daniel's entire life was spent in exile, in the metaphorical lions' den. Yet as the closing note of chapter 6 reminds us, God preserved him alive and unharmed throughout the whole of that time, enabling him to prosper under successive kings, until the time of King Cyrus, when his prayers for Jerusalem finally began to be answered. Cyrus was God's chosen instrument to bring about the return from the exile, when he issued a decree that the Jews could return to their homeland and rebuild Jerusalem (see 2 Chron. 36:22–23; Isa. 45:1–4).

As far as we know, Daniel never returned home to his beloved Judah. His reward would have to wait until the Jerusalem that is above. In the experiences of Daniel and his three friends, God demonstrated that he could keep his people safe in the midst of their enemies. Life in exile would never be easy, nor would it ever be home. However, through God's faithfulness, it was possible for his people to survive the exile as strangers and aliens, serving the earthly empire in which they found themselves, even while they looked for another city that was yet to come (Heb. 13:14).

This is how Daniel 6 addresses us as well, for we too are strangers and aliens in this world. We should learn from Daniel's experience that the world in which we live is a dangerous place. This world is not our home and never will be. Yet at the same time, we must also recognize that the enmity of the world can never hurt us beyond what the Lord permits. The Lord is our true judge: his verdict on us is the one that really counts. Therefore, in the midst of the greatest of trials and suffering, even when we are persecuted for the faith, we can have a peace that will astound the world, for the Lord holds even our oppressors in his hand, and says, "Thus far and no farther."

THE LIONS' DEN AND THE WAY OF THE CROSS

But does Daniel 6 really give us a realistic perspective on persecution and suffering? Isn't it true that for every Daniel, whom God delivers from the lions' den, there have been hundreds of nameless martyrs whom God did not deliver? Haven't God's faithful ones suffered terribly over the centuries, sometimes at the mouths of lions, or being burned alive in the fire? Aren't believers still suffering terribly around the world today? Where is God in these situations? Were these believers less faithful to God or less important to him than Daniel was?

To answer these questions, we need to see that Daniel 6 provides something more than simply a model of how God deals with suffering believers, or how, like Daniel, we are supposed to stand firm under trials. Rather, Daniel 6 is a foreshadowing in history of the verdict that will be delivered on all believers on the final judgment day. Daniel endured the test of the lions' den, emerging safely out the other side, because God judged him and found him not guilty; as a result, the lions, which acted as God's agents of judgment, did not harm him. However, the unbelievers who plotted against Daniel were found guilty and crushed by God's judgment. They and their families were sentenced to death in a foreshadowing of that final covenantal judgment, like the destruction of Sodom and Gomorrah (Gen. 19), the swallowing alive of the families of Korah, Dathan, and Abiram (Num. 16), and the extermination of the inhabitants of certain Canaanite cities (e.g., Josh. 6). On the last day, all those who are in Adam will be declared guilty and will share their fate of destruction, while all those who are in Christ will be found not guilty and will share Christ's glory and exaltation.

This also points us to the way in which Jesus fulfilled Daniel 6. Like Daniel, Jesus was falsely accused by his enemies and brought before a ruler, Pontius Pilate, who sought unsuccessfully to deliver him from his fate, before handing him over to a violent death. Like Daniel, Jesus was condemned to die, and his body was placed into a sealed pit so that his situation could not be changed by human intervention. Jesus' trial went even deeper than Daniel's, however: he did not merely suffer the threat of death, he went down into death itself. Although Jesus was innocent, he suffered the fate of the guilty ones. There was no angel to comfort him with the presence of God in his pit; on the contrary, he was left in the blackness utterly alone and abandoned by God, suffering the fate that we, the guilty ones, deserved. His body was left entombed in the icy grip of death for three days before the angel finally came to roll away his stone.

Yet Jesus' experience was itself a foreshadowing of the final judgment, a declaration ahead of time of the verdict of the heavenly tribunal. Jesus died for our sins, not his own, and so death had no ultimate power over him, as a truly innocent man. Jesus did not remain in the grip of the tomb: God raised him from the dead, precisely because the heavenly tribunal found him not guilty.

What is more, when Jesus emerged alive from the tomb at daybreak on that first Easter Sunday, he brought with him God's stamp of acquittal not only on himself but on all those who are joined to him by faith. When Daniel came forth from the lions' den, he came out alone. No one else was saved by God's deliverance of him. But when Jesus came forth from the tomb, he came out as the head of a mighty company of people who have been redeemed from the pit through his death. Whoever believes in Jesus will receive the same verdict from the heavenly court as he did, for his righteousness is counted as theirs. Because of the work of Christ on behalf of his people, the divine judge says: "Not guilty! You may go free!" Now we too can find favor with God through the cross of Christ.

The people that Jesus redeemed through his death and resurrection are not all superbelievers like Daniel. Most of us are ordinary sinners, people who cave in constantly to the unrighteous demands of the empire. From our earthly perspective, it may not seem to us that the motley assortment of deeply flawed humanity that makes up the church has much to commend it. What kind of a reward is this for Christ's suffering? Yet Jesus does not hesitate to call us beautiful! Even someone deeply sinful can be found beautiful before the perfect and holy God because he sees the end of the process, the glorious church that he will present to himself without flaw or wrinkle. My salvation rests not on my ability to "Dare to be a Daniel," but solely on Christ's perfect obedience in my place. In the midst of a world of trials and tribulation, that is where my peace and comfort rest. In the world to come, that will be all of my glory: the righteousness of Christ, given to me.

8

THE TRIUMPH OF THE SON OF MAN

Daniel 7:1–28

In my vision at night I looked, and there before me was one like a son of man, coming with the clouds of heaven. He approached the Ancient of Days and was led into his presence. He was given authority, glory and sovereign power; all peoples, nations and men of every language worshiped him. His dominion is an ever-lasting dominion that will not pass away, and his kingdom is one that will never be destroyed. (Dan. 7:13–14)

*T*he end of the world is a remarkably popular subject these days. Hollywood movies, always a useful cultural barometer, are a clear witness to this fact. Over recent years we have seen the release of films in which the future of life on our planet is threatened by aliens, asteroids, floods, frost, killer viruses, lethal machines, mutant creatures, and nuclear holocaust, to name just a few. This interest may stem from the existential angst that comes from the threat of a terrorist attack, or a growing awareness of humanity's ability to make this planet uninhabitable, or from some quite different root cause. Wherever it comes from, however, it is undeniable that there is more interest in the end of the world these days than there has been for a while.

105

This phenomenon should make this a good time to study the apocalyptic portions of the Bible, for they too are interested in the end of the world. If people want to know how the world will end—whether with a bang or with a whimper—what better place to turn than to the Word of the sovereign God, who controls all history? Daniel 7–12, which contains just such apocalyptic literature, should therefore be intensely relevant for all of us.

Yet for many Christians the apocalyptic sections of the Bible, such as the end of the Book of Daniel and the Book of Revelation, are sealed: they are nervous about entering them for fear that they will not be able to understand what they find there. It doesn't help that some preachers who do tackle these portions of Scripture expound in lurid terms the way in which the current configuration of European or Middle Eastern states exactly fits the end-times scenario they have constructed. This scenario, which is made up of a cocktail of two parts Daniel, three parts Revelation, and a dash of Ezekiel, rather resembles one of the composite beasts of Daniel 7: it is part lion, part bear, part man, but not exactly any of these. These complicated end-times scenarios tend to combine disparate elements of the biblical text into a single piece, ignoring the fact that the end result cannot be harmonized with a plain reading of any one of the individual parts. It leaves you wondering, "Is there another way to understand these biblical passages, a way that through sane and sensible interpretation uncovers the message of these passages for believers in all times and places?"

If we understand the central purpose of these passages and focus our attention on what is clear and straightforward rather than on what is complicated and obscure, then we will find blessing and encouragement in the apocalyptic portions of the Bible. What is more, Christians who hold to a variety of different end-times scenarios can agree on these central truths, which will minister to all believers, whether the Lord returns sooner or later.

Understanding Apocalyptic

First, though, a word about method. To understand any kind of writing, we need to understand its purpose. We often make such judgments intuitively. We instinctively know that a sentence that begins "The stars will fall from heaven, the sun will cease its shining and the moon will drip blood" will not end "and the rest of the country will be partly cloudy with scattered showers."[1] The reason is that we immediately perceive a mismatch between the genres of the two phrases: one is apocalyptic, while the other is a more conventional weather forecast.

This means that to understand these chapters we first need to understand what apocalyptic literature is, and what it is trying to do to us and for us. In simple terms, biblical apocalyptic can be defined in the following way:

> Biblical apocalyptic is a revelation of the ending of this present age, which is an age characterized by conflict, and its replacement by the final age of peace. It shows us ahead of time the end of the kingdoms of this world and their replacement by the kingdom of our God and of his Christ. This revelation is unfolded in complex and mysterious imagery, and has the purpose of comforting and exhorting the faithful.[2]

Apocalyptic literature thus proclaims a theology of hope to those whom the world has marginalized: it reminds us that God is presently on the throne and that he will ultimately triumph. In the meantime, whatever the present cost may be in terms of suffering, obedience to God is the only way. Though the propagandists for the present world order proclaim that our resistance is futile, the apocalyptic writer refuses to be assimilated to this world's way of thinking. He has seen heaven opened and he knows how the story ends. As a result, to paraphrase the words of Winston Churchill's great speech, he will fight them on the beaches; he will fight them in the streets; he will fight them in the hedgerows, on the land and on the sea. He expects nothing other than blood, sweat, and tears, but he will *never* surrender. Rather, he looks forward with unshakable hope to his final vindication, when the day at last comes for God to act decisively to bring in his new and final age of salvation.

1. John Barton, *Reading the Old Testament: Method in Biblical Study* (Philadelphia: Westminster, 1984), 17.

2. The definition of apocalyptic given here is synthesized (and substantially simplified) from the following standard sources: John J. Collins, "Introduction: Towards the Morphology of a Genre," *Semeia* 14 (1979): 1–20; John J. Collins, *The Apocalyptic Imagination* (New York: Crossroad, 1984), 1–32; Paul D. Hanson, *Old Testament Apocalyptic* (Nashville: Abingdon, 1987), 25–43; Adela Yarbro Collins, "Apocalyptic Themes in Biblical Literature" *Interpretation* 53 (1999): 117–30.

A Vision of Monsters

This chapter tells how "in the first year of Belshazzar king of Babylon, Daniel had a dream, and visions passed through his mind as he was lying on his bed" (Dan. 7:1). In other words, we have moved backwards in time from the reign of the Medes and Persians, Darius and Cyrus, to the time when the Babylonians ruled the world. Daniel "wrote down the substance of his dream," as follows:

> In my vision at night I looked, and there before me were the four winds of heaven churning up the great sea. Four great beasts, each different from the others, came up out of the sea.
>
> The first was like a lion, and it had the wings of an eagle. I watched until its wings were torn off and it was lifted from the ground so that it stood on two feet like a man, and the heart of a man was given to it.
>
> And there before me was a second beast, which looked like a bear. It was raised up on one of its sides, and it had three ribs in its mouth between its teeth. It was told, "Get up and eat your fill of flesh!"
>
> After that, I looked, and there before me was another beast, one that looked like a leopard. And on its back it had four wings like those of a bird. This beast had four heads, and it was given authority to rule. After that, in my vision at night I looked, and there before me was a fourth beast—terrifying and frightening and very powerful. It had large iron teeth; it crushed and devoured its victims and trampled underfoot whatever was left. It was different from all the former beasts, and it had ten horns. (Dan. 7:1–7)

In his vision Daniel saw the four winds of heaven stirring up the great sea. Immediately we should recognize that we are in the realm of visionary metaphor and imagery rather than that of straightforward description. In the Bible, as elsewhere in the ancient Near East, the sea was the symbol of chaos and rebellion against God (see Ps. 89:9; 93:3–4).[3] For that reason, the sea was considered to be the natural home of monsters such as Leviathan, the multiheaded monster of ancient mythology (see Ps. 74:13–14). What is more, these monsters were terrifying not merely because they were large and dangerous, as we might find the thought of crocodiles or a Tyran-

3. See the evidence adduced by John J. Collins, *Daniel*, Hermeneia (Minneapolis: Fortress, 1993), 286–89.

nosaurus Rex terrifying. Rather, they are terrifying because they are evil, opposed to God, the agents of chaos and destruction. Such creatures are therefore not merely "PG-13," like the dinosaurs out of Stephen Spielberg's movie *Jurassic Park*; they are "R" rated, like the vampires and evil zombies of the most chilling and disturbing horror movie.

Here in Daniel's vision the stirred-up sea is producing horrific creatures, one after the other—four in all, each one more frightening than the one that came before it. These enormous, composite, misshapen animals were like nothing you have ever encountered in your worst nightmares. The first of these beasts was a lion with eagle's wings, an unclean mixture of animal and bird. While Daniel watched, though, the beast was transformed: its wings were stripped off, it was raised to its feet like a man, and it was given a human mind. The second beast was like a bear, but it was raised on one side—either because it was poised and ready to spring or because it was grotesquely deformed, like the Hunchback of Notre Dame.[4] It already had a mouth full of the ribs of its previous victim, but it was told to arise and devour even more. The third beast was another composite animal, part leopard, part bird, with four heads. Such a flying leopard would combine both ferocity and speed, so that no one could run from it, while its four heads would render it capable of seeing in all four directions at once, making it impossible to hide from.[5] This beast was also given authority to rule.

Frightening though the first three animals were, the most hideous creature was yet to come. The fourth beast could not even be described in terms of earthly animals. It was frightening and dreadful, incredibly strong, with large iron teeth that devoured and crushed, and it trampled down whatever it didn't eat. Its head had ten horns, and since horns are symbols of strength in the Bible, ten of them symbolizes massively multiplied strength. To envision this beast, we would need to borrow from the monsters dreamed up by the world of science fiction, such as the terrifying machines that the Martians constructed in H. G. Wells's *War of the Worlds*. In an even more bizarre twist, another small horn came up among the horns while Daniel watched,

---

4. For the former, see J. A. Montgomery, *The Book of Daniel*, International Critical Commentary (Edinburgh: T&T Clark, 1926), 288; for the latter, see Paul Porter, *Metaphors and Monsters: A Literary-Critical Study of Daniel 7 and 8* (Lund: Gleerup, 1983), 17.

5. In that respect, it is reminiscent of the cherubim in Ezekiel 1.

uprooting three others: "While I was thinking about the horns, there before me was another horn, a little one, which came up among them; and three of the first horns were uprooted before it. This horn had eyes like the eyes of a man and a mouth that spoke boastfully" (Dan. 7:8). This horn had eyes and a mouth that spoke arrogantly.

By this point, we should certainly be feeling scared. Spending a night in a den of lions would be a comfortable prospect compared to the prospect of confronting these outlandish and dangerous beasts! Daniel himself admitted that he was "troubled in spirit, and the visions that passed through my mind disturbed me" (Dan. 7:15). These beasts represent kings, the authorities that are in control of the world in which we live (Dan. 7:17), and so the vision declares that our world is being run by a succession of fearsome monsters that will go from bad to worse, each one more frightening than the one before.

THE MEANING OF THE BEASTS

The temptation for readers is to want to identify *which* four earthly kingdoms match up with the beasts, especially since the first beast, the winged lion that became a man, seems to represent Babylon. Its humbling and humanizing transformation makes us think of Nebuchadnezzar's humbling and (re)humanizing in Daniel 4. Meanwhile, in the parallel vision of four kingdoms in Daniel 2, the first kingdom, the head of gold, was explicitly identified as Nebuchadnezzar (Dan. 2:38). Starting from that generally agreed point, commentators debate whether the four kingdoms are Babylon, Media, Persia, and Greece, or Babylon, Medo-Persia, Greece, and Rome.[6] They will never resolve the discussion, however, since the data the vision provides are not sufficiently precise for that purpose. For example, the Greek empire was certainly fast and ferocious, like the winged leopard, but so too were the Persians (Isa. 41:3); both kingdoms aspired to dominate the four corners of the world (Dan. 8:4–5). These attributes of speed and ferocity apply equally well to Nazi Germany, though, and to many other warlike nations before and after them that have attempted world domination.

6. See the references footnoted in Daniel 2.

Even more importantly, however, when the angelic interpreter explains to Daniel what the dream means in 7:17–18, he does not clarify the identity of the kingdoms. This suggests that a proper understanding of the vision does not rest on resolving this question. In fact, the attempt to identify the various beasts actually directs us *away* from the proper interpretation of the vision. Such approaches assume that the rule of the beasts describes the way the world *used to be* up until the time of Antiochus Epiphanes, or until the Romans, depending on the viewpoint adopted. In the present, however, things are supposedly different and less beastly.[7]

The identification of the beasts as four past empires is the exact opposite of the message of apocalyptic literature. For apocalyptic, nothing less than the beginning of the new age can change this world. Until the coming of this new age, the darkness will not lift significantly. It is therefore better to take the number of the beasts as representing a symbol of completeness rather than a particular number of world empires.[8] On such a view, the message of Daniel 7 is that life in this present age will *always* be this way until the end of this age. It is striking that the superpowers of our own age still customarily represent themselves by predatory animals, such as the Russian bear, the Chinese dragon, and the American eagle.[9] The beasts of the present world order may change their shape as the centuries pass, but their violence and lust for power continues. Nebuchadnezzar turns into a Darius, who becomes an Alexander the Great and then an Antiochus Epiphanes, the Seleucid king who brutally oppressed the Jews in the mid-second century B.C. These fierce rulers are in turn followed by

7. To be sure, some premillennial interpretations do leave room for a kind of revival of the reign of the fourth beast in a period of great tribulation at the end of time. This revived Roman empire supposedly resumes an antagonistic persecuting stance toward the people of God. Yet on this hypothesis too, there is a lengthy period during which less beastly attitudes prevail on the part of the authorities of this world towards the church, before the onset of a final period of persecution. In contrast, the focus of apocalyptic literature is on the constant continuation of trials and persecution until the return of the King.

8. Tremper Longman III, *Daniel*, New International Version Application Commentary (Grand Rapids: Zondervan, 1999), 190. On the symbolic use of four to represent completeness, see *The Dictionary of Biblical Imagery* (Downers Grove, IL: InterVarsity, 1998), 307–8. Specific examples of such a symbolic use in prophetic and apocalyptic contexts include four horns (Zech. 1:18), four craftsmen (Zech. 1:20), four winds (Zech. 2:6), four chariots (Zech. 6:1), four spirits (Zech. 6:5), four living creatures (Rev. 4:6), four horsemen (Rev. 6), and four angels (Rev. 7).

9. I am indebted to a sermon by Geoff Thomas for this observation. See "The Dream in the First Year of Belshazzar. Daniel Chapter 7," <http://www.alfredplacechurch.org.uk/sermons/dan5.htm>. Accessed September 11, 2006.

a Nero and a Domitian. Their fires of persecution continued to be stoked centuries later by the Inquisition. In the last century, we have seen further manifestations of the beast in the persons of Hitler, Stalin, and Kim Il Jung. The frightening beasts of this age were present at the gas chambers of Belsen, and on the killing fields of Cambodia and Rwanda, and they are still tormenting the saints in Sudan and China, and in other parts of our modern world.

This continual presence of the beasts in our world ought not to surprise us because every human manifestation of evil is simply a reflection of the work of the Great Dragon, Satan himself. In Revelation 13, we see a beast rising from the sea representing the persecuting power of the antichrist, a beast that combines aspects of each of Daniel's creatures into one, a lion-bear-leopard with ten horns. Whatever our location in space and time, frightening monsters array themselves against the Lord and his anointed. We inhabit a world in which there is good reason to have trouble sleeping at night. As Paul reminds us in Ephesians 6, we wrestle not with flesh and blood but against the rulers, the authorities, the powers of this dark world and against the spiritual forces of evil in the heavenly realms.

THE END OF THE BEASTS

Yet it is essential for us to notice that the focus of the chapter as a whole is not on the monsters themselves. After all, the purpose of the passage is not to give us nightmares but to calm our nightmares. The focus of Daniel 7 is rather on the coming day of divine judgment, when these monsters will finally receive justice and God will win the final victory. This is one of the ways in which the viewpoint of the Scriptures and the viewpoint of ancient mythology diverge. The Bible can and does use mythological imagery in its apocalyptic passages, yet these mythological elements are now incorporated into a fundamentally historical view of the world. In ancient mythology there is no end to the conflict between the two equally ultimate realities, chaos and order. The struggle must continue forever. However, the Bible repeatedly declares that God alone is ultimate and that in the end his order will prevail.[10] This is precisely how the interpreting angel sums up the

10. See R. S. Wallace, *The Message of Daniel*, The Bible Speaks Today (Downers Grove, IL: InterVarsity, 1979), 123–24.

message of the chapter. When Daniel "approached one of those standing there and asked him the true meaning of all this," the angel gave him an "interpretation of these things: 'The four great beasts are four kingdoms that will rise from the earth. But the saints of the Most High will receive the kingdom and will possess it for ever—yes, for ever and ever'" (Dan. 7:16–18). The angel is not fixated on the identity of the beasts; rather, the central point is the certainty of the final victory of the saints, a triumph whose fruits will last forever.

Daniel presses the angel with a question about the identity of the fourth beast and the ten horns:

> Then I wanted to know the true meaning of the fourth beast, which was different from all the others and most terrifying, with its iron teeth and bronze claws—the beast that crushed and devoured its victims and trampled underfoot whatever was left. I also wanted to know about the ten horns on its head and about the other horn that came up, before which three of them fell—the horn that looked more imposing than the others and that had eyes and a mouth that spoke boastfully. As I watched, this horn was waging war against the saints and defeating them, until the Ancient of Days came and pronounced judgment in favor of the saints of the Most High, and the time came when they possessed the kingdom. (Dan. 7:19–22)

Yet the angel's explanation adds little to what Daniel already knows. Nor are there sufficient details given for us to identify the beast:

> The fourth beast is a fourth kingdom that will appear on earth. It will be different from all the other kingdoms and will devour the whole earth, trampling it down and crushing it. The ten horns are ten kings who will come from this kingdom. After them another king will arise, different from the earlier ones; he will subdue three kings. He will speak against the Most High and oppress his saints and try to change the set times and the laws. The saints will be handed over to him for a time, times and half a time.
>
> But the court will sit, and his power will be taken away and completely destroyed forever. Then the sovereignty, power and greatness of the kingdoms under the whole heaven will be handed over to the saints, the people of the Most High. His kingdom will be an everlasting kingdom, and all rulers will worship and obey him. (Dan. 7:23–27)

The description of the time of trial and judgment under the fourth kingdom is vague enough to describe plausibly several historical tyrants, including Antiochus Epiphanes, yet at the same time nonspecific enough to leave the identity of this horn ultimately uncertain.[11] The reason for this vagueness on the angel's part lies in the fact that his primary interest is not in the boastful horn. The angel's answer therefore went beyond Daniel's question about the horn to reiterate his earlier point about the judgment to come and the triumph of the saints. It is as if the angel was saying, "Daniel, you're missing the point. Yes, the horn will assault God's people and it will be a trying time for the saints, but look beyond the horn. The point of this vision is that the time when the beasts will oppress the saints is limited by God. Beyond it lies the scene of the heavenly court, where the beasts will finally be tamed and destroyed. Then the sovereignty, power, and greatness will be handed over to the saints, to the people of the Most High. And his kingdom will never end." At this point, however, it is clear that Daniel did not understand the angel's message, for he says, "This is the end of the matter. I, Daniel, was deeply troubled by my thoughts, and my face turned pale, but I kept the matter to myself" (Dan. 7:28).

A VISION OF THE HEAVENLY COURT

Following the angel's interpretative guide, let us turn our attention to the heavenly court:

> As I looked, thrones were set in place, and the Ancient of Days took his seat. His clothing was as white as snow; the hair of his head was white like wool. His throne was flaming with fire, and its wheels were all ablaze. A river of fire was flowing, coming out from before him. Thousands upon thousands attended him; ten thousand times ten thousand stood before him. The court was seated, and the books were opened. (Dan. 7:9–10)

At the center of Daniel's vision, thrones were set up for judgment (Dan. 7:9; see Ps. 122:5). The Ancient of Days, God himself, sat upon the central

---

11. That is not to say that some future climactic tyrant will not perfectly fit this description. Yet it will be possible to be sure that this was the person indicated only by looking backwards from the perspective of fulfillment.

throne. His clothing was as white as snow, an image of uncompromising and radiant purity (Isa. 1:18); his hair was as white as wool, also a symbol of purity and perhaps of the wisdom that comes with great age. His chariot-throne flamed with fire and its wheels blazed, representing the divine warrior's fearsome power to destroy his enemies. A river of fire flowed out from the throne, and he was surrounded by myriads upon myriads of angelic attendants. Here we see a judge who has the wisdom to sort out right from wrong, the purity to choose the right, and the power to enforce his judgments. It didn't take long for the judge to get to work, either: the court was immediately convened and the books that recorded the deeds of humanity were opened. Though the beast with the boastful horn continued to mouth defiance at the heavenly court, the agents of the Most High slew it and threw its body into the fire: "Then I continued to watch because of the boastful words the horn was speaking. I kept looking until the beast was slain and its body destroyed and thrown into the blazing fire. (The other beasts had been stripped of their authority, but were allowed to live for a period of time)" (Dan. 7:11–12).

This vision forms a remarkable picture, especially when we remember how reluctant the Bible is elsewhere to describe God. In Exodus 34 Moses encountered God on the mountaintop, but he saw little and heard only God's description of himself in terms of his attributes (Ex. 34:6–7). In Isaiah 6 the prophet saw the Lord seated in the temple, yet few details apart from the immensity of God can be discerned from Isaiah's description. We hear of flying seraphim, but the smoke almost totally obscures the vision of the divine throne itself. That vision forms a dramatic contrast with Daniel's vision of the heavenly court and the one like a son of man, where everything is clearly perceived.

Why do we have such a detailed picture here? Daniel is painting the real world—that is, the world to come—in glowing color images to counter the insistent propaganda that bombards our senses in this present age. Every day our eyes see this world in all of its glory and our ears hear its siren songs. Our lips taste its delightful fruits and our noses are bewitched by its sweet perfumes, while our fingers revel in its soft caresses. Alternatively, when life goes badly, as it often does for those for whom apocalypses are written, our eyes are filled with horrific images of saints burning at the stake, while our ears cannot shut out their screams. Our lips pucker at this world's bitter taste, and our nostrils are filled with the stench of burning flesh, while our fingers now flinch from its harshness. Every time we close our eyes, the monsters haunt us. For better or worse, for good or evil, this world is terribly real, and incredibly "in your face."

How is Daniel to convey to us the greater reality of the world to come? The answer lies in his graphic descriptions of the true nature of this world and the world to come. The rewards that this age offers to us are empty prizes, the golden baubles of a Belshazzar whose time is already up. The horrors of this age are equally empty of power to do us real harm, though. The monsters that we so dread are as toothless as the lions in Daniel's den, for God is our judge. It is his tribunal before which we must ultimately stand, and it is what is written about us in his book that will determine whether we reign with his saints forever, or spend eternity in the fire with the beast. It is that black and white. The stakes are high, but when we weigh life in this world against life in the world to come, it becomes evident that faithfulness to the Lord is the only way, no matter what the cost. The earthly tribunals may have the power to condemn us to burn at the stake or to die in the gas chamber, or to suffer some other beastly fate, but they have no power over the soul. When the beasts have done their worst to our physical body and we take our leave of them, we are simply going from them to God. As Jesus himself said, "Do not be afraid of those who kill the body but cannot kill the soul. Rather, be afraid of the One who can destroy both soul and body in hell" (Matt. 10:28).

A VISION OF THE COMING SON OF MAN

Yet the Ancient of Days on the throne is not the only character in the judgment scene. With him is one like a son of man, coming with the clouds of heaven:

> In my vision at night I looked, and there before me was one like a son of man, coming with the clouds of heaven. He approached the Ancient of Days and was led into his presence. He was given authority, glory and sovereign power; all peoples, nations and men of every language worshiped him. His dominion is an everlasting dominion that will not pass away, and his kingdom is one that will never be destroyed. (Dan. 7:13–14)

116

For Daniel, this must have been a puzzling picture, because this being seems to combine in one person both human and divine traits. He is "one like a son of man," that is, he appeared to be simply a mortal human being. Elsewhere in the Old Testament, this phrase "son of man" often distinguishes mere mortals from God (e.g., Ezek. 2:1). This is a particularly striking choice of description here because earlier in Daniel's vision the Ancient of Days was also described in anthropomorphic form: he sits on a throne, wears clothing, and has white hair. Yet it is this second figure that is described as "one like a son of man," which suggests that there is something more to his humanity than merely God appearing in human shape.

At the same time, however, to "come on the clouds" is a clear symbol of divine authority. In the Old Testament God alone rides on the cloud chariot (see Ps. 68:4; Isa. 19:1).[12] What is more, when this son of man comes into the presence of the Ancient of Days, he is given authority, glory, and sovereign power. These attributes are not simply the authority and sovereignty that God gives to human kings such as Nebuchadnezzar (see Dan. 5:18), for this son of man also receives the *worship* of all peoples, nations, and languages (see Dan. 7:14). Thus, he cannot merely be an angel or personified representative of Israel.[13] This son of man is given an everlasting and indestructible dominion, a sovereignty that belongs to God himself.

So what are we to make of this vision of a God-man—one who shares our humanity, yet at the same time endows it with the fullness of undiminished deity? It is far easier for us to understand it than it was for Daniel, for we have the benefit of the hindsight of the prophecy's fulfillment. "The son of man" was the perfect title for Jesus to bear on his incongruous mission precisely because it combined in itself the incongruous ideas of "mere humanity" with the unparalleled glory of God himself.[14] In his earthly ministry, it was the "human" aspect of the son of man that was prominent. In Eugene Peterson's words: "This Son of Man has dinner with a prostitute, stops off for lunch with a tax-collector, wastes time blessing children when there were Roman legions to be chased from the land, heals unimportant

12. Longman, *Daniel*, 187.
13. The Aramaic word for "worship" (*pelach*) used here always has reference to deities (apart from Dan. 7:14, 27, it is also used in Dan. 3:28; 6:16 [17], 20 [21]). See Stephen R. Miller, *Daniel*, New American Commentary (Nashville: Broadman, 1994), 208.
14. Bruce Chilton, "The Son of Man—Who Was He?" *Bible Review* 12 (1996): 34–45.

losers and ignores high-achieving Pharisees and influential Sadducees."[15] Ultimately, he hung pierced and bleeding upon a cross; he died and was buried in a tomb, surely the most ungodlike of acts. But his majesty, even though veiled while he was on earth, was still present. He taught as one with unparalleled authority (Matt. 7:29), he forgave people their sins (Luke 5:24), and he spoke of possessing a kingdom (John 18:36). Both divine and human aspects are present because Jesus is son of man and Son of Man, very man and Very God.

For the first disciples, the lesson that Jesus was the son of man focused upon the humanity of Jesus. They had to learn that salvation does not come through the advent of a triumphal heavenly figure bearing a sword, blasting his opponents with fire from heaven. Rather, it comes through the advent of a baby in a manger, who grew up to bear a crown of thorns and carry a cross. The Son of Man had come not to be served (as one might have expected from Daniel) but rather to serve and to give his life as a ransom for many (Mark 10:45).

However, for the hearers of the Book of Revelation, the lesson of the Son of Man was reversed. They were in the situation of Daniel's hearers, suffering intense persecution for their faith, and so needed to be reminded of the central lesson of Daniel 7. The return of our Lord will not be the same as his first advent. Christ is not eternally suffering upon the cross, but when the time is ripe, he will return (as the Son of Man!) in glory on the clouds, bearing a sharp sickle to bring final judgment on his enemies (Rev. 14:14–20).

THE MESSAGE OF THE VISION

The message of Daniel 7 for us is that the human Christ of the crucifix is not the end of the story. For now, we live in the day of the monstrous beasts. They have authority to rule and to kill and to eat: they are even permitted to triumph over the saints for a while. Some of those beasts have human faces: they are the persecutors of the faithful in Sudan and in China, in Saudi Arabia and in North Korea; they are the terrorists who fly planes into buildings and blow up innocent people on buses and underground trains. Some of those beasts take the more institutionalized

---

15. *Reversed Thunder: The Revelation of John and the Praying Imagination* (San Francisco: Harper & Row, 1988), 30.

form of economic systems. Communism treats human beings as if they were raw materials that exist merely to further the interests of the State. Meanwhile, capitalism too can show an oppressive, beastly face. Companies that treat their employees as commodities to be used and then carelessly discarded when they are no longer needed are furthering the beasts' agenda. Likewise, those who exploit the political weakness of developing countries in order to maximize their own profits are doing the beasts' work. Still other beasts are impersonal manifestations of the brokenness of the world in which we live, such as AIDS, cancer, child poverty, slavery, warfare, and hunger.

Today, we live in a world of terrifying beasts, but we shall not live in their world forever. There will come a day when all wrongs will be set right, when all tyrants will be dethroned, when all that is broken will be fixed. There will come a day when all hunger will come to an end, when all sickness will be cured, when every sorrowing heart will be comforted. There will come a day when even death, the last weapon of the beast, will have its power broken once and for all. On that day, the Great Beast, Satan himself, will be bound and brought before the throne; he will answer for his crimes and be cast into the lake of fire forever (Rev. 20:10).

The challenge of Daniel 7 for us is therefore not to work out the specific identity of the different beasts, in case ours should be the final hour. Rather, in the midst of this beastly world, our challenge is to live our lives with our eyes firmly fixed on the heavenly throneroom. Instead of being terrified by the beasts, we must daily live remembering the one who will deliver the final and decisive judgment.

If it is true that God is our judge, are we ready to meet with him? Are we ready to have the book of life opened and its contents put on public display, with all of our lust, jealousy, anger, pride, and self-centeredness made visible for all to see? On that day of judgment, our only hope will be that Jesus Christ, the Son of Man, has taken the judgment we deserve for all of those sins and many more. He was bruised for our transgressions and mauled for our iniquities, so that in the coming day we could be exalted with him and reign with him forever. He has faced the Great Beast in all of his fearsomeness in our place. Unlike the experience of God's saints, the time of his trial on the cross was *not* cut short in God's mercy. On the contrary, Jesus felt the full measure of the fiery agonies of hell, distilled into six hours of exquisite agony. The debt for every sin that I ever committed or ever will commit was laid on his shoulders, and he bore it all.

The result of his sacrifice, though, is that whatever now faces me in this life—whether death or life, angels or monsters, dictators or demons—nothing in all creation can separate me from the love of God in Jesus Christ (Rom. 8:38–39). If God is my judge and the Son of Man is my savior, then let the world do its worst. Ultimately, the world has no power to hurt me, and I know that after the world has done its worst, God will welcome me into his very best. The Lord has a glorious inheritance stored up for me, along with all of the saints, a kingdom that is mine by grace alone, through faith in Christ alone. There is a day coming when the beasts will all be gone and only the saints will remain.

So when you feel the beasts surrounding you and their hot breath closing in upon you, look upward and onward. Look up to your Judge; look up to your Savior; look onward to your glorious inheritance. Sing with the hymnwriter,

> The King there in His beauty, without a veil is seen:
> It were a well spent journey, though seven deaths lay between:
> The Lamb with His fair army, doth on Mount Zion stand,
> And glory—glory dwelleth in Immanuel's land.
>
> The Bride eyes not her garment, but her dear Bridegroom's face;
> I will not gaze at glory but on my King of grace.
> Not at the crown He giveth but on His pierced hand;
> The Lamb is all the glory of Immanuel's land.[16]

Samuel Rutherford, the seventeenth-century Scottish pastor whose words lie behind that hymn, was no stranger to suffering and persecution. As a young man, he was exiled by the church authorities from his beloved parish of Anwoth in Southern Scotland for writing in defense of the doctrines of grace. As an old man, when the monarchy was reinstated under Charles II, he was charged with high treason for his book in which he argued that even monarchs were subject to the law. When the summons came, however,

---

16. The words come from "The Sands of Time Are Sinking," Anne Cousin's reflection on the letters and final words of Samuel Rutherford.

he responded from his deathbed, "Tell them I have got a summons already before a superior Judge and judicatory, and I behove to answer my first summons, and ere your day come I will be where few kings and great folks come." His hope was placed in the knowledge that there would soon come a time when this present world would have run its course, to be replaced by a better one. The day is indeed hastening on when the sands of time will run out and the beasts will face their judgment, but for the saints, glory will dwell forever in Immanuel's land!

9

LIVING IN THE VALLEY
OF DARKNESS

Daniel 8:1–26

*While I, Daniel, was watching the vision and trying to under-
stand it, there before me stood one who looked like a man. And I
heard a man's voice from the Ulai calling, "Gabriel, tell this man
the meaning of the vision." As he came near the place where I was
standing, I was terrified and fell prostrate. "Son of man," he said
to me, "understand that the vision concerns the time of the end."
While he was speaking to me, I was in a deep sleep, with my face
to the ground. Then he touched me and raised me to my feet.*
(Dan. 8:15–17)

*H*ave you ever noticed how many preachers read apocalyptic books like Daniel and Revelation and conclude, "The
end is near"? Of course, this is not a new trend: people
have been identifying world leaders as the antichrist and setting a date for
the end of the world for a long time. From Roman emperors like Nero and
Caligula to modern leaders like Ronald Reagan and Mikhail Gorbachev,

the list of potential candidates is long and still growing. While browsing through the Christianity section of a local bookstore, I discovered a book that confidently predicted that the end of the world would come in 2011. But this same author had also predicted that the world would end in 1994, which made me more than a little skeptical of his new claims.

Oddly enough, I didn't find any books in my survey of that store telling me that the end of the world was *not* nigh. At some point, the end of the world will indeed come. Jesus Christ will come back to draw all of history to its conclusion and to usher in the new heavens and the new earth. Few truths of Scripture could be clearer than that. Yet statistically speaking, even if Christ returns soon, for most readers of the Book of Daniel and Revelation, the end of the world was not just around the corner. So why do preachers keep telling us that the primary message of these books is that it is?

The answer lies in a dynamic that is familiar to many parents who have endured long car journeys with small children. On these trips, it seems that you have hardly pulled out of the driveway before the children start squirming around in their car seats, asking, "Are we there yet?" To which, some of us have responded at one time or another, "We're almost there"— even if we know that we still have four hundred miles to go. It would be more honest for us to acknowledge to our children that we have a long and potentially tedious journey in front of us, but frankly we'd rather pretend than face reality.

Daniel 8 encourages us to face up to reality: we may have a long way yet to go before the resolution of life's pains and injustices, and there is no promise from God that he will rapture us out of this world before our tribulations get too bad. The prophet is explicitly told to seal up the vision because it refers to a distant time (Dan. 8:26); it must be sealed, not so much in order to keep it secret but to keep it safe in the midst of turbulent times.[1] Yet if the promised new world of Daniel 7 may still be a long way away, in the interim God's people will need help to keep their faith fresh over the long haul. How do you persist in faith and obedience to God when you live under constant pressure and intense persecution, and it seems that there is no imminent end in sight? That is the issue that faces many of us from day to day, and it is the question with which Daniel 8 deals.

1. Stephen R. Miller, *Daniel*, New American Commentary (Nashville: Broadman, 1994), 236.

A VISION OF A RAM AND A GOAT

Daniel had another vision—this one occurring "in the third year of King Belshazzar's reign ... after the one that had already appeared to me" (Dan. 8:1). In this vision, Daniel found himself "in the citadel of Susa in the province of Elam ... beside the Ulai canal" (Dan. 8:2). The location prepares us for the fact that this vision is going to be different from that in chapter 7. The earlier vision expressed universal and ultimate realities in the language of symbolism rather than history, and therefore appropriately took place in an undefined location, beside the great Sea (Dan. 7:2). In the vision of chapter 8, however, we focus on the particularities of specific and easily identifiable historical figures and kingdoms, and so the vision is located in a specific geographical location. The vision is recounted as follows:

> I looked up, and there before me was a ram with two horns, standing beside the canal, and the horns were long. One of the horns was longer than the other but grew up later. I watched the ram as he charged toward the west and the north and the south. No animal could stand against him, and none could rescue from his power. He did as he pleased and became great.
>
> As I was thinking about this, suddenly a goat with a prominent horn between his eyes came from the west, crossing the whole earth without touching the ground. He came toward the two-horned ram I had seen standing beside the canal and charged at him in great rage. I saw him attack the ram furiously, striking the ram and shattering his two horns. The ram was powerless to stand against him; the goat knocked him to the ground and trampled on him, and none could rescue the ram from his power. The goat became very great, but at the height of his power his large horn was broken off, and in its place four prominent horns grew up toward the four winds of heaven. (Dan. 8:3–8)

The first object that Daniel saw in his vision was a ram with two horns, one of which was longer than the other. The ram charged to the west, north, and south, and none could stand against him. But then a male goat appeared from the west, with a single conspicuous horn. The goat engaged the ram in battle and destroyed him, shattering both of the horns and trampling him to the ground. The male goat thus grew in power,

124

replacing the ram in greatness. However, at the pinnacle of his power, the single horn was shattered and four others came to replace it, pointing in all four directions.

Daniel needed the angel to interpret the meaning of this vision for him, though later readers could have unpacked it for themselves with the benefit of historical hindsight. Even as Daniel was having the vision, the angels began to discuss the fulfillment of what he was seeing and how important it was for him to understand its significance:

> Then I heard a holy one speaking, and another holy one said to him, "How long will it take for the vision to be fulfilled—the vision concerning the daily sacrifice, the rebellion that causes desolation, and the surrender of the sanctuary and of the host that will be trampled underfoot?"
>
> He said to me, "It will take 2,300 evenings and mornings; then the sanctuary will be reconsecrated."
>
> While I, Daniel, was watching the vision and trying to understand it, there before me stood one who looked like a man. And I heard a man's voice from the Ulai calling, "Gabriel, tell this man the meaning of the vision."
>
> As he came near the place where I was standing, I was terrified and fell prostrate. "Son of man," he said to me, "understand that the vision concerns the time of the end."
>
> While he was speaking to me, I was in a deep sleep, with my face to the ground. Then he touched me and raised me to my feet. He said: "I am going to tell you what will happen later in the time of wrath, because the vision concerns the appointed time of the end." (Dan. 8:13–19)

As the angel explicitly states, the ram with the two horns is the Medo-Persian kingdom (Dan. 8:20), an unequal alliance in which the more powerful member (the larger horn) was the Persians. The male "shaggy goat is the king of Greece, and the large horn between his eyes is the first king" (Dan. 8:21). In retrospect, we can also identify the goat's large horn as Alexander the Great, who succeeded in toppling the mighty Persian empire from its position of power. Alexander conquered virtually the whole of the known world by the age of thirty-three, after which he died, leaving his empire to be divided among his four generals. These generals, and the four parts of Alexander's empire that they ruled, are the subsequent four horns of the goat: "The four horns that replaced the one that was broken

125

off represent four kingdoms that will emerge from his nation but will not have the same power" (Dan. 8:22).

Here, then, is the first part of the vision's message. Like the vision in Daniel 7, this vision describes a series of kingdoms in the form of animals that exalt themselves, with one kingdom rising after another, aspiring to greatness and achieving it, but then being shattered. The ram seems invincible until the goat arises, but then he is swiftly destroyed. The first horn of the goat throws the ram to the ground and no one can rescue the ram from the horn's power, but at the height of his power, the large horn too is shattered. In other words, no matter how great and menacing an empire may appear to be, it is simply an actor in a play written by someone else. It plays out the role assigned to it by God on the revolving stage of world history, and then, when its lines are over, it slinks off ignominiously into the wings. The rise and fall of these real historical nations, predicted accurately centuries ahead of time by the Lord through his prophets, remind us clearly who is directing the course of history. Earthly thrones and dominions come and go in a ceaseless round; only the kingdom of God is forever.

THE MESSAGE OF THE RAM AND THE GOAT

The message of the vision was thus good news to generations of saints who suffer at the hands of earthly kingdoms, whether the Babylonians, or the subsequent Persians and Greeks, or present-day persecutors. These empires that to human eyes looked so powerful, that seemed to have no weaknesses or chinks in their armor, were actually merely sheep and goats whose destiny lay in the hands of the divine shepherd, the Lord himself. They weren't even the cosmically frightening monsters of Daniel 7, but only overgrown domestic animals. Like any good shepherd, the Lord is easily able to judge mere sheep and goats who step out of line and to put them back in their place (see Ezek. 34).

The same lesson is valid for us as well. The monsters that fill our nightmares, depriving us of sleep, are most commonly not the rise and fall of world empires but threats to our own present or future safety and security. Perhaps your health outlook is threatened by the discovery of a lump that might be cancerous, or your children are about to leave home and you fear that your life will be empty. Perhaps you have to care daily for a loved one and you don't know how to cope with today, let alone tomorrow. Perhaps you wrestle with depression and despair, to the point that you have contemplated suicide. Perhaps you are already experiencing intense pain and suffering from a sickness that is only likely to grow worse.

Let this vision of Daniel 8 cut your monsters down to size: these monsters that seek to hurt you and trample you are nothing more than big sheep in the Lord's eyes. If the divine shepherd is with you, he will not let them trample you utterly into the dust. The menacing world that is out of your control is never beyond his control. The one who raises up world conquerors and then consigns them in turn to the pages of ancient history books is the same one who controls your personal story as well. If you belong to Christ, the whole world revolves in the hand of the one who cares for you far more deeply than you can imagine. As a result, nothing in the present or in the future can ever separate you from his love (see Rom. 8:38–39).

THE VISION OF A LITTLE HORN

Yet the ram and the goat are merely the curtain raiser in Daniel's vision, not the main action. They largely reiterate the lesson of Daniel 7, that God is sovereign over the kingdoms of men. Daniel's second vision has more to communicate:

> The goat became very great, but at the height of his power his large horn was broken off, and in its place four prominent horns grew up toward the four winds of heaven.
> Out of one of them came another horn, which started small but grew in power to the south and to the east and toward the Beautiful Land. It grew until it reached the host of the heavens, and it threw some of the starry host down to the earth and trampled on them. It set itself up to be as great as the Prince of the host; it took away the daily sacrifice from him, and the place of his sanctuary was brought low. Because of rebellion, the host of the saints and the daily sacrifice were given over to it. It prospered in everything it did, and truth was thrown to the ground. (Dan. 8:8–12)

After the one-horned goat's kingdom had split into four parts, another little horn emerged from one of these kingdoms and expanded his realm

127

towards the south and the east, towards the Beautiful Land (that is, Israel). In his aggression, this little horn took on the heavenly realm as well as the earthly. In visionary language, the horn fought against the stars, God's heavenly host, as well as the people of God's land, and he experienced triumphs on both fronts.[2] On the heavenly battlefront, he cast down some of the stars to the earth—the soldiers of God's heavenly host[3]—and reached up to make himself as great as the Prince of the heavenly host, God himself.[4] On the earthly side, the horn brought an end to the regular daily sacrifices in the temple and overthrew the sanctuary itself. Because of rebellion, the saints and the regular daily temple sacrifices were handed over into his power. Truth was overthrown, and evil seemed to triumph. Yet the little horn too would be judged by God, his power brought to an end: "He will cause deceit to prosper, and he will consider himself superior. When they feel secure, he will destroy many and take his stand against the Prince of princes. Yet he will be destroyed, but not by human power. The vision of the evenings and mornings that has been given you is true, but seal up the vision, for it concerns the distant future" (Dan. 8:25–26).

Here we move beyond "wars and rumors of wars," beyond the general trials and tribulations of life that mark out every era of history, to focus on one of the specific assaults of Satan against God's people. God is sovereign over all of the events of world history, but his greatest concern is with the fate of his own people. Alexander the Great was one of the greatest military strategists, one of the pivotal men in world history. Yet in Daniel 8 he is a mere footnote, meriting barely a mention before the vision moves on to the more important matter of the little horn and his assault on God's people, and even on God himself.

Once again, with the benefit of historical hindsight, we can clearly identify the little horn of Daniel 8 as a historical figure, Antiochus Epiphanes IV (175–164 B.C.). Antiochus, whose nickname "Epiphanes" means "God made manifest," was king of the Seleucid empire, one of the four kingdoms that emerged from Alexander the Great's former territory. Initially he was not first in line for the throne, but he seized it from his nephew through

2. John Goldingay, *Daniel*, Word Biblical Commentary (Dallas: Word, 1989), 209.
3. Understanding the conjunction as an explicative *waw* (see J. A. Montgomery, *The Book of Daniel*, International Critical Commentary [Edinburgh: T&T Clark, 1926], 340).
4. Goldingay, *Daniel*, 210.

intrigue and then enlarged his kingdom through substantial military successes. Antiochus was a tyrant who tried to unify his kingdom by forcing all of his subjects to adopt Greek cultural and religious practices. He banned circumcision, brought an end to sacrifice at the temple in Jerusalem in 167 B.C., and then deliberately defiled it by burning pig's flesh on the altar and placing an object sacred to Zeus in the Holy of Holies. He also burned copies of the Scriptures and slaughtered those who remained true to their faith in God, fitting perfectly the description of a stern-faced king who was completely wicked. This king was part of the fulfillment of the dream, for the angel had prophesied that "in the latter part of their reign, when rebels have become completely wicked, a stern-faced king, a master of intrigue, will arise. He will become very strong, but not by his own power. He will cause astounding devastation and will succeed in whatever he does. He will destroy the mighty men and the holy people" (Dan. 8:23–24).

These acts of gross sacrilege by Antiochus triggered a rebellion on the part of faithful Jews, who were led in their revolt by the Maccabees. After a lengthy struggle, their rebellion culminated in the Seleucid forces being driven out of Judah and the temple being cleansed and rededicated in 164 B.C. Antiochus himself died in somewhat obscure circumstances during a campaign in the eastern part of his empire in 164 B.C. These events of real history faithfully reflect the events described in Daniel 8, reinforcing once again the message of God's control of all of history.

Daniel 8 opens a window onto the bigger picture of the struggle against Antiochus, though. Antiochus was not simply at war against the earthly saints, but against the heavenly host as well. We are told that he made himself as great as God, the Prince of the heavenly host, and swept some of the stars from the sky. This is a visionary way of describing the cosmic struggle that will come to the fore in Daniel 10. It is as if the curtain is drawn back, and behind Antiochus we see the ominous power of the spiritual forces of darkness arrayed against our God.

THE SIGNIFICANCE OF THE LITTLE HORN

As we face a world in which the end may or may not be near, it is important for us to remember the spiritual dimension of our warfare. When we fail to take this into account, we are unprepared for the intensity of our conflict. Sometimes we are isolated from the struggle by our comfortable circumstances. If we have a pleasant situation in life with a comfortable house, attractive spouse, beautiful children, a fulfilling career, and a generous retirement package, we are unlikely to cry out "How long, O Lord?" We would be quite happy for God to wait a while, thank you. When life is good for us, we forget to pray. We forget that we are wrestling with powers that are far more than merely human adversaries, powers that we can never conquer in our own strength. Yet in our attempts to share the gospel with our neighbors and our community, or to build godly marriages and families in our church, or to win the victory against our own sinful natures, we are always profoundly overmatched by the forces ranged against us. Unless the Lord intervenes on our side, we can never stand up against the gathering darkness. We should therefore constantly be fighting on our knees, committing our struggles to God in prayer daily, and even hourly.

At the same time, however, the cosmic dimension of the warfare reminds us that we are not alone in our struggle. In a song made famous by Bette Middler, "From a Distance,"[5] the singer imagines a benevolent God watching the world serenely from far, far away, from a vantage point from which all of the conflicts of earth disappear into a haze of inconsequentiality. From a distance, supposedly, everyone has enough to eat and no one is in need; in fact, from that far away, even people who are at war with each other look like friends and no one can work out what the fighting is all about.

Daniel 8 gives us exactly the opposite picture of our universe. In Daniel's vision, God is not depicted as passively surveying the conflict from the comfort of heaven, wondering, "Why can't they all just get along?" On the contrary, his forces are actively engaged in the same struggles that we have, fighting side by side with us. Daniel's God is not smugly watching from a distance: he is involved in our daily warfare against evil right alongside us. Those who assault us are at the same time assaulting our God. Like the disciples in the boat in the middle of the storm, when we cry out, "Teacher, don't you care if we drown?" (Mark 4:38), we may know that our God does notice and he does care. He is not remote or absent, but present in the midst of his people, in the midst of their sufferings. Our fight is his fight too.

5. "From a Distance," copyright Julie Gold (1986).

Yet if God is not remote from the struggle against evil, how is it that the battle sometimes seems to be moving in a negative direction? If the all-powerful God who controls history is for us, why don't we march on from victory to victory, crushing all of the forces of evil underfoot? If the God of creation is our God, why is the storm not stilled for us? How is the little horn able to rise to power and oppress the saints of the Most High?

This question too has an answer in Daniel 8. The problem is not merely Satan's enmity; rather, it is transgression (*pesha'*; 8:12). It is "because of rebellion" that the army of God's people and the daily sacrifices and the sanctuary were handed over into the power of the little horn.

Whose transgression is in view here? Most commentators take this transgression as the rebellion of the little horn.[6] However, it makes far more sense to understand this transgression as the rebellion of God's own people, a theme that anticipates Daniel's prayer of repentance in Daniel 9.[7] After all, the outcome of this rebellion is that the host and the sanctuary are "given over" into the power of the little horn (Dan. 8:12). It is certainly true that at times the sovereign Lord may bring an enemy against his people in order to display his own glory, when they have not sinned against him (e.g., 2 Chron. 20; Ezek. 38). Yet he would hardly give his people and sanctuary over into the hand of his enemy, except on account of their own sin (see Deut. 28:45–48). This was the case in Daniel's own day (see Dan. 1:2), and what Daniel saw was a future repetition of the sin and judgment of God's people that had led to the fall of Jerusalem to Nebuchadnezzar. The holocaust of the exile was not the end of the cycle of sin and judgment for Israel.[8]

Yet even in this coming outpouring of judgment upon Israel's sin, evil would not triumph forever. The Lord's people and his sanctuary would be

6. So, e.g., Tremper Longman III, *Daniel*, New International Version Application Commentary (Grand Rapids: Zondervan, 1999), 204; Goldingay, *Daniel*, 211.

7. So John Calvin, *Daniel*, trans. T. Myers (Grand Rapids: Baker, 2003 reprint), 2.102. Miller notes the statements in 1 and 2 Maccabees concerning unfaithfulness in Israel at the time of Antiochus (*Daniel*, 227).

8. This interpretation also best fits the parallels between Daniel's vision and the opening vision of Ezekiel. Both visions took place beside a canal (Ezek. 1:1; Dan. 8:2). Both men were left prostrate in the presence of God, and they were restored to their feet by the Lord so that they could hear the interpretation of the vision (Ezek. 1:28; 2:2; Dan. 8:17–18). In his vision, Ezekiel heard the announcement of the judgment that was coming on his people because of their continual history of transgressing (*pasha'*; Ezek. 2:3), an announcement that left him "devastated" (*mashmim*; 3:15). So too Daniel heard about a forthcoming disaster because of transgression (*pesha'*; Dan. 8:12) and ended up "devastated" (*'eshtomem*; Dan. 8:27; both verbs coming from the root *shamem*).

given over into the power of evil, but only for a limited time: 2,300 evenings and mornings (Dan. 8:14). "Evenings and mornings" immediately recalls the language of the days of creation in Genesis 1 and suggests that, like the attempts to sweep the stars from the sky (Dan. 8:10) and to change the religious festivals (7:25), what the little horn is seeking to achieve is nothing less than the dissolution of creation. In that attempt he will certainly fail, because the Lord has already set the number of these days.[9] Yet why 2,300 days? This period is just short of seven years, which might be considered a full period of judgment, as in Daniel 4. However, the number doesn't exactly fit any pairing of events in the Maccabean period, although many attempts have been made to do so. It may be, therefore, that we are simply intended to see this number as a figurative representation of a significant but limited period of suffering on the part of the people of God.[10] What is particularly striking about the figure, though, when compared to the less precise "three and a half times" of Daniel 7, is the fact that this period is measured in *days*. The most important point may be that God has a precise calendar for the events of world history, a calendar that is accurate to the day, yet at the same time utterly inscrutable to all human efforts to decode it.

HOPE IN THE BLACKEST NIGHT

We will explore that idea more fully in our next study, when we look at Daniel's response to the vision. Yet for now we need to see clearly how Daniel 8 gives us hope in the blackest of nights, in the face of the worst of our own failures and the worst assaults of Satan against us. The church still struggles because of our own unfaithfulness and the assaults of Satan. As the hymn writer described it, the church's normal condition in this age is "By schisms rent asunder, by heresies distressed."[11] Like the apostle Paul, we often find ourselves hard pressed from every direction, persecuted and buffeted on all sides, to the point that we may be tempted to despair of the

---

9. See Jacques B. Doukhan, "Allusions à création dans le livre de Daniel" in A. S. van der Woude, ed., *The Book of Daniel in the Light of New Findings* (Leuven: Leuven University Press, 1993), 285–94.

10. Goldingay notes that twenty-three is one third of sixty-nine, which is the number of a period of weeks in Daniel 9 (*Daniel*, 213). The number twenty-three also appears in 1 Enoch to designate groupings of gentile kings (Paul Porter, *Metaphors and Monsters: A Literary-Critical Study of Daniel 7 and 8* [Lund: Gleerup, 1983], 44).

11. Samuel J. Stone, "The Church's One Foundation."

future (2 Cor. 1:8–9). Nor is that simply an issue in the church. In the midst of our own personal failures in the ongoing struggle against sin, we may be tempted to question whether God can really sanctify people like us. How can God's purposes to save and sanctify stand in the face of man's continual rebellion and Satan's constant assaults?

The answer to that question comes as we see how Daniel 8 affirms God's victory even in the face of the coming darkness of the days of Antiochus Epiphanes. If God's purposes were not thwarted by that period of rebellion and defilement, then they will certainly never be thwarted by our personal experience of unfaithfulness or persecution.

Yet from our standpoint in redemptive history, we can now see the same lesson demonstrated on an even larger scale. We can look beyond the darkness and restoration of the days of Antiochus to an even greater act of rebellion and defilement—the climactic act of rebellion and defilement that, in God's grace, itself became the source of our hope. The defilement that Daniel foresaw in the time of Antiochus was certainly horrific, with the temple being desecrated and truth cast to the ground, but there was even worse yet to come.

Even though Antiochus desecrated the temple, at least at that time no one laid hands on God himself. But nearly two hundred years later, in the person of Jesus Christ, the dwelling place of God was once again desecrated because of man's sin and rebellion, and Satan's enmity. God's own people rejected the Messiah that he had sent; as John put it in his Gospel, "he came to that which was his own, but his own did not receive him" (John 1:11). Instead, the leaders of God's chosen people actually allied themselves with the forces of evil against the prince of the Lord's army and handed him over to death, crying out, "Crucify him!" (Matt. 27:22). What worse abomination or act of betrayal could there ever be than crucifying God? No wonder it was dark on that day: it was not just that a few of the stars had been swept from the sky; rather, the sun itself refused to shine on such an outrage! It seemed that the darkness had completely triumphed and God's "Let there be light" had been swallowed up by night.

The cross is surely the ultimate expression of the rebellion of God's people and the enmity of the kingdoms of this world against him. Nor should we think that we Christians are any better than those first-century Jews. We too were once God's enemies: by nature, all of us are rebels against God, who if left to ourselves would also have been found among those crying out, "Crucify him! Crucify him!" We too loved darkness rather than light because our deeds were evil (John 3:19). Our own hearts testify to the profound truth of that judgment. By our comfortable coexistence with our cherished sins, we daily bear witness to the darkness that still remains in our hearts.

Yet even such abominable rebellion and enmity could not thwart God's purposes. At the cross Satan did his worst to Jesus, and as a result simply brought about precisely what God had planned from the beginning. The light shines in the darkness, and the darkness has not overcome it (John 1:5). A mere three days later, God rebuilt the temple that the Jews had desecrated, by restoring the body of his Son from the grave. God raised up this Jesus, whom men had rejected, and he exalted him in glory to the Father's right hand in heaven. Now, through the power of the cross, the Lord is building Jews and Gentiles together as living stones into his new temple, the church, turning former rebels and enemies into God's friends through the gospel, cleansing us from our sin and rebellion (see Eph. 2:14–22).

The cross is thus the place where God gave his final answer to our rebellion and transgression, as well as to Satan's enmity. At the cross, Jesus took upon himself the full weight of all of our transgression and rebellion, dealing once and for all with our sin. If ever there was a "time of wrath," it was during those six hours when Jesus hung on the cross, bearing the wrath of God against our wickedness and idolatry. His devastation there brought God's wrath against our sin to a final end. There at the cross he broke the sting of death, which is the power of sin, and so guaranteed the ultimate happy ending to our story. Just as Christ was raised from the dead in glory, so also all those who are in him will one day rise in glory, on the day when God's timetable is complete.

The cross is therefore the guarantee that God's plan will always prevail in the face of our weakness, rebellion, and sin, and in spite of the fierce enmity of Satan and all of his hosts. Because of the victory won on the cross, the gates of hell can never prevail against Christ's flock. To be sure, evil remains awful and powerful in this world. Sin still has devastating effects, whether it comes from outside or inside the church, and it will not simply pass away as our world matures. Our path to heaven often takes us through the valley of deep darkness, through horrible realities in the here and now that may be the fruits of our own sin, or of the sins of others, or of the enmity of powerful spiritual forces.

Yet in the midst of that sobering reflection, we must never lose sight of the glories of heaven and the fact that God's timetable is the one that directs events. His timetable will eventually draw our time on this earthly stage to a close and usher in God's victory. We don't know when that end will be, either for us as individuals, or for the world as a whole. The end may indeed be nigh, or it may still be some time away, but either way we can still live in its radiant light and long for the coming of the dawn. On that final day, the question that God will ask each one of us will be, "What have you done with the gift of my Son, Jesus Christ? Have you submitted your heart to him? Have you received him as Savior and Lord, looking to his righteousness to atone for your rebellion? Or have you rebelliously thought to justify yourself through your own efforts?"

What is more, in the time that remains before that final day comes, our God remains in control of this world that he has made, even when we pass through the valley of darkness. In spite of our own worst failures and the enemy's best efforts, God will bring all things to their proper end at the time he has determined. He will bring the nations to himself and sanctify each one of us through the slow but persistent work of his Spirit. In the meantime, we are called to be faithful and obedient, trusting in Christ alone and giving thanks daily for the cross, the place of his triumph over our sin. As we wait, we are to look forward with longing eyes to the day of his return, crying out, "How long will it take for the vision to be fulfilled?" How long will it be until the darkness will finally be over and the daylight will come? How long until the sun of righteousness will rise, and his saints will shine with him forever and ever? How long until we are sanctified through and through and cleansed of all of our remaining sin? How long, O Lord? Come quickly, Lord Jesus, and bring your great work to its completion in us.

10

HOW TO WAIT FOR GOD

Daniel 8:27

*I, Daniel, was exhausted and lay ill for several days. Then I got up
and went about the king's business. I was appalled by the vision;
it was beyond understanding.* (Dan. 8:27)

*I*n Samuel Beckett's two-act play, *Waiting for Godot*, five
actors spend the entire time by a tree, waiting, as the play's
title suggests, for the key character to appear. In the end,
though, he never comes, and it is never explained who Godot is, or why
it might be important to meet him. In fact, there is very little action in
the play, leading one reviewer to describe it as a play in which "nothing happens, twice." Another critic used stronger language, borrowing a
line from the play itself to convey the plot: "Nothing happens, nobody
comes, nobody goes, it's awful!"[1] Beckett himself strenuously denied
that the play had any reference to Christianity, yet insofar as the play
accurately reflects his existentialist philosophy, it could hardly avoid a
clash of worldviews with the gospel. For Beckett, life itself can effectively
be summed up as an absurd play in which "Nothing happens, nobody

---

1. Cited in "Waiting for Godot," *Wikipedia*, November 5, 2005. <http://en.wikipedia.org/wiki/
Waiting_for_Godot>. Accessed November 7, 2005.

comes, nobody goes, it's awful!" Godot, whoever he or she might be, will never come and nothing in life makes sense.

As we saw in our last study, Daniel 8 is a vision about waiting. It is a vision of an end that is not nigh, at least not for Daniel and not for many generations of readers since then. Yet unlike the characters in Beckett's play, their lives are not rendered absurd by the fact that they have spent their whole lives waiting for someone who has not yet come. On the contrary, the very act of waiting is given its meaning by the certainty that at the right time—the time of God's own choosing—the Son of Man will come on the clouds to bring history to its conclusion (Dan. 7:13). Every earthly kingdom, in spite of its apparent invincibility, has an "after this," a time when its power will be vanquished and it will be trampled into the dust. Yet the Book of Daniel urges its readers on to a faithfulness that is meaningful precisely because we wait for the kingdom that will come after all these earthly kingdoms have run their course, a kingdom that will have no "after this" but rather will endure forever.[2] Like Daniel, we too are believers waiting for the end of all things, an end that may or may not be nigh. In the meantime, we have important lessons to learn from Daniel regarding how we should live while we wait.

DIFFERENT WAYS OF WAITING

Believers have a variety of attitudes towards the period of waiting for Christ's return, based on their different expectations of how that return will take place. The most common views are premillennialism, postmillennialism, and amillennialism, names which are drawn from the different understandings each view has of the millennium, or thousand years, mentioned in Revelation 20:1–6.[3]

Premillennialism believes that Christ will return to earth before ("pre") the millennium, which will be a one-thousand-year-long time of peace during which the kingdom of God will be consummated and Jesus will reign on the earth with his saints. Since this view usually anticipates a period of

2. See Jacques Doukhan, *Daniel: The Vision of the End*, (Berrien Springs, MI: Andrews University Press, 1989), 47.
3. For a fuller description and evaluation of the major millennial views, see Anthony Hoekema, *The Bible and the Future* (Grand Rapids: Eerdmans, 1979), 173–222.

great apostasy and tribulation before the return of Christ, many (though not all) premillennialists are pessimistic about the value of engagement with society and culture. On this view, the focus of our calling as we await the return of Christ is often seen as rescuing as many souls as possible. It hardly seems coincidental that the people most interested in identifying the Lord's return as imminent are typically premillennial. Using the analogy developed in the previous study, those who believe most strongly that the journey itself is secondary and that only the destination really counts are likely to shout the loudest, "Are we there yet?"

Postmillennialism, by contrast, is the view that Christ will return after (post) the millennium, a lengthy period during which the world will become increasingly Christianized and the kingdom of God will be manifested on the earth. Because this view holds a positive expectation for the future, Christians who hold it are often very involved in society and optimistic about what may be accomplished for God here on earth. In fact, they tend to stress the point that our primary calling while we await the return of Christ is to redeem culture, seeking to claim every square inch of it for the Lord. They affirm clearly the value of the journey.

Amillennialism, which literally means "no millennium," might better be termed "present millennialism" or "realized millennialism," for it stresses a more symbolic interpretation of the prophecies in Revelation, and sees the millennium as a pictorial way of speaking of the "now" and "not yet" of the heavenly reign of God. For these believers, the kingdom of God is even now experienced in the church, where Christ's reign has been manifested since his resurrection and ascension. Even now, Christians are seated with Christ in the heavenly realm, where we are blessed with all spiritual blessings. Even now, Satan is bound and his power to deceive the saints is restricted by God. Christians who hold the amillennial view anticipate with confidence the spread of Christ's reign through the nations by means of the gospel, yet at the same time they do not anticipate the "Christianization" of the world. Rather, they believe that while the gospel will increase, so too will apostasy and tribulation before the coming of the end.

To sum up the attitudes of these views towards the present and the future, then, we may say that premillennialism tends to be generally pessimistic about the future of church and society, postmillennialism tends to be generally optimistic about church and society, while amillennialism tends to be optimistic about the future of the church but pessimistic about society. A full evaluation of the merits of these various views would take us far afield from the Book of Daniel, in which a millennium is not even mentioned. However, Daniel's response to the vision of chapter 8 affirms and challenges aspects of each of these views with respect to how we should wait for the end.

Daniel gives us his response in a single verse at the conclusion of the chapter: "I, Daniel, was exhausted and lay ill for several days. Then I got up and went about the king's business. I was appalled by the vision; it was beyond understanding" (Dan. 8:27). Daniel tells us that he could not understand the vision, that he was overpowered and devastated by the vision, and that at the end of his time of devastation he got up and went about the king's business. Each of these three aspects of his response to his vision should lend shape to our waiting for the time of the end.

LIVING WITH PARTIAL UNDERSTANDING

First, Daniel tells us that he could not understand the vision. At first sight, this statement might not seem very surprising. After all, the historical events described in the dream were many years in the future in Daniel's day, and interpreters still struggle to comprehend the intricacies of what he saw. Certainly a lack of comprehension is what most readers experience when they first encounter these visions.

Yet when we think more deeply about it, it should strike us as noteworthy that Daniel is unable to comprehend the meaning of his own vision. This is the same Daniel who alone was able to interpret Nebuchadnezzar's dreams in Daniel 2 and 4, of whom Nebuchadnezzar said, "I know that the spirit of the holy gods [or God] is in you, and no mystery is too difficult for you" (Dan. 4:9). In chapter 5, when no one else could read the handwriting on the wall, the queen mother said confidently of Daniel, "[He] was found to have a keen mind and knowledge and understanding, and also the ability to interpret dreams, explain riddles and solve difficult problems. Call for Daniel, and he will tell you what the writing means" (5:12). Daniel then read and interpreted without difficulty the mysterious writing that had troubled Belshazzar and his nobles. If anyone could understand these apocalyptic visions, surely it would have been Daniel!

Yet in these latter chapters of the Book of Daniel, we are told twice that Daniel was unable to understand the visions (Dan. 8:27; 12:8). This is particularly remarkable since the visions and their interpretations are explicitly given to enable Daniel to understand (7:16–17; 8:15; 9:22; 10:14). Indeed, we are told that what distinguishes between the wicked and the wise is precisely the fact that the wicked will not understand the visions but the wise will understand them (12:10). Since Daniel is the wisest of the wise, how could he not have understood them? What is more, we are told at one point that Daniel *did* understand the vision (10:1).

So which is it? Did Daniel understand the visions or did he not understand them? I think the answer is "both." Clearly, there were aspects of the visions that he understood. The visions were given to him by God so that he might understand something, and God's purposes are never thwarted. The central message of these visions was surely clear to Daniel even centuries before the specific events alluded to in the visions began to unfold. That is why, for example, in response to the revelation of a coming time of rebellion and judgment, we find him on his knees before the Lord in a prayer of corporate confession and repentance (Dan. 9). He certainly understood the central thrust of that vision.

Yet at the same time there were also aspects of the vision that Daniel did not understand. Even such a great interpreter of mysteries as Daniel could not fathom exactly what the Spirit of God was pointing forward to in these visions, no matter how hard he tried. As the apostle Peter put it,

> The prophets . . . searched intently . . . trying to find out the time and circumstances to which the Spirit of Christ in them was pointing when he predicted the sufferings of Christ and the glories that would follow. It was revealed to them that they were not serving themselves but you, when they spoke of the things that have now been told you by those who have preached the gospel to you by the Holy Spirit sent from heaven. Even angels long to look into these things. (1 Peter 1:10–12)

As Peter suggests, some of those things that were mysterious to Daniel are now clearer to us. We can now see who some of the historical characters in his visions were, and in the light of fulfillment, we can see more clearly how his visions pointed forward to Christ. Yet at the same time, there are other aspects of his visions that we should expect to remain mysterious to us still. When we look back on history from the perspective of glory, we may understand more than we yet do, but even then our knowledge may not be comprehensive. If, as Peter says, some of these things are mysterious even to angels, perhaps it should not be surprising if they never become transparently clear to ordinary mortals like us.

This is an important point to make in the face of continuing efforts by well-intentioned believers to fix, if not the day, then at least the month and the year of the Lord's return. There are those, especially in the premillennial camp, who seem sure that they understand exactly how the prophetic timetable will work itself out and who the main characters will be in that final conflict. In the 1970s, Hal Lindsey's book *The Late Great Planet Earth* convinced many that we were living on the eve of destruction and that an invasion of Israel by Russia was imminent. The ten nations that then made up the European Common Market were declared to have a key role to play. More than thirty years later the scenarios have been revised and updated, but the same message continues to be widely and confidently proclaimed. It seems to me, however, that the proper answer to the question "When and how will the end of the world come?" is "God knows"—in both senses of that phrase. We may affirm "God *knows*" in the sense that he knows exactly when the end will come, down to the exact day. However, we should also affirm "*God* knows," in the sense that no human being will ever know ahead of time that information. The mysterious 2,300-day period of Daniel 8:14—a time period that resists easy explanation yet affirms the preciseness of God's control over history—is a good example of this kind of uncertainty.

This balance between what may confidently be understood and what must remain for now somewhat hazy is important to maintain. There are some things that God has revealed clearly in his Word, and other things that remain concealed from us (Deut. 29:29). We may take comfort in God's sure and certain control of each day of history—both global history and our own personal history—all the way to the bitter end. We may be sure of Christ's personal, bodily return to claim his people and usher in the new creation. Yet at the same time we should also learn a proper humility concerning our ability to predict the time and the precise outworking of such important events.

This humility should even extend to those of us who are confident that the complex scenarios envisaged by some of our premillennial brethren are mistaken. It may be that some prophecies that we believe are not intended to be literally fulfilled will actually be fulfilled more precisely than we anticipate, just as some that they expect to be literally fulfilled will likely be fulfilled in a spiritual sense: the essential features of the prophecies will come true, though the details are not precisely literal.

This variety in form of fulfillment is exactly what the fulfillment of prophecies in the first coming of Jesus should have taught us to anticipate. Some of those prophecies were fulfilled literally, just as everyone expected—for example, his birth in Bethlehem in accord with Micah 5:2. Other prophecies were fulfilled, but not so literally: John the Baptist was not literally Elijah, but he came in the spirit of Elijah, clad in Elijah's distinctive style of clothing and bearing Elijah's message of judgment and repentance (Mark 1:6; 2 Kings 1:8). The Day of Pentecost was a fulfillment of Joel's prophecy of the coming Day of the Lord, even though the heavenly signs of judgment were not yet manifest (Acts 2:17–21; Joel 2:28–32). There are still other Old Testament prophecies of the coming of Christ that would probably have sparked debate ahead of time as to whether they were to be understood literally. Did Isaiah 7:14 require the coming Messiah literally to be born of a virgin and to be God in human flesh? Did Psalm 16 require the physical resurrection of the Messiah? Did Zechariah 9:9 literally expect the Messiah to ride into Jerusalem on a donkey? There might well have been lively discussion and debate about the interpretation of these verses, and some would perhaps have been surprised by just how literal their fulfillment turned out to be. So too, all of us should be humble in our convictions about the way Jesus' second coming will work itself out, holding firmly to that which is clear and being gracious in responding to varying opinions about that which is less clear.

OVERWHELMED BY COMING JUDGMENT

The second aspect of Daniel's response to the vision was that he was sickened and overwhelmed by the vision for some days (Dan. 8:27). This is similar to his response to the other visions he received (7:15, 28; 10:16). Why did he feel so overwhelmed by these visions that he received? It wasn't simply their breathtaking scope and dizzying scale; rather, it was their message of forthcoming judgment and destruction on God's own people.

Here the parallels between what Daniel experienced and the effects of the prophet Ezekiel's initial vision are helpful.[4] Like Ezekiel (see Ezek. 3:15), Daniel was overwhelmed by his vision because he felt within his own body a foreshadowing of the effects of the judgment of God on the community.[5] The prophet identified with his people as well as with God, and so even though the judgment Daniel saw lay many years in the future, he could not simply pronounce it upon them from a comfortable distance. On the contrary, he physically identified with his people in their forthcoming suffering, to the point of feeling their pains in his body.

The prophet's identification with those for whom his message was intended is an important model for us as we wait for the end. In view of our expectation of the second coming, it can be easy for us to become isolated from the society around us. The more convinced we are of the imminence of Christ's return, the more isolated we may become. This tendency is perhaps particularly common among premillennialists, but is by no means restricted to them. Other believers too can be tempted to form a safe enclave and preach from its walls a message of judgment on the world around us, without any empathy for, or involvement with, those our words condemn. Daniel's personal involvement with the message of his vision calls us not merely to condemn the lost world around us but to weep for it, just as Jesus wept over lost Jerusalem (Matt. 23:37). We are called to care deeply and passionately for our lost neighbors, to be personally devastated by the prospect that they may spend all eternity in hell. Compassion for their souls demands nothing less from us. The extent to which the lostness of the world around us touches our hearts is the extent to which we will be motivated to bring our neighbors the good news of the gospel—and to go on bringing it to them, even when they don't want to hear it.

I am personally convicted that as I search my own heart, I find so little compassion and concern for those around me. In consequence, I am rarely driven to pursue opportunities to share the gospel with my neighbors and

4. For the parallels between Daniel 8 and Ezekiel 1–3, see note 8 in ch. 9: "Living in the Valley of Darkness."
5. See Iain Duguid, *Ezekiel*, New International Version Application Commentary (Grand Rapids: Zondervan, 1999), 70.

friends, and even when they raise the topic, I can easily view it as a burden rather than an opportunity to meet their deepest need. This is especially true if the people in question are evidently "rebels" against God (Dan. 8:12), living an outwardly defiant lifestyle. Yet those rebels—the "tax collectors and sinners"—were precisely the people that Jesus targeted as most deserving of the good news of the gospel (Matt. 9:11–13). I need to hear Daniel's call to empathy and compassion towards those whose lifestyle most clearly places them under the judgment of God. If we have Daniel's heart for his people, we can never be content with the fact that we and our immediate family are saved. Instead, we will have a passion that our neighbors, our friends, the prodigals and the wanderers, and indeed the whole world should come to know and worship our God and King.

Busy about the King's Business

Yet Daniel wasn't simply devastated at the prospect of forthcoming judgment on his people. At the end of his time of sickness, he got up and "went about the king's business" (Dan. 8:27). This is a remarkable statement, given the fact that the king at this time was Belshazzar (Dan. 8:1). In spite of the folly and wickedness of the civil authorities of the day, Daniel did not isolate himself from the culture around him, but continued faithfully in his service of the (pagan!) Babylonian society. His vision that the future belonged to the kingdom of God did not send him off to hide in a corner but continued to drive him out in service of his community.

Daniel's quiet commitment to do the work of the king, even in a pagan culture, shows the value of the work that we do in the meantime, while we wait. We need to recognize the value and meaning of the penultimate as well as of the ultimate, of doing the will of the Father here on earth, just as we shall one day in heaven (Matt. 25:14–30). Here on earth we find ourselves perpetually in exile, yet this is nonetheless the culture in which God has placed us, so that we can be salt and light. Our daily work for the king—for the good of our secular employer and the benefit of our pagan culture—is itself meaningful and valuable. Indeed, the very phrase "[Daniel] went about the king's business" (Dan. 8:27) is ambiguous, for this chapter is full of kings and it follows a vision in which the Lord himself was enthroned as King. Perhaps we should recognize that even as Daniel served his earthly master, King Belshazzar, he understood that at the same time he was about the business of the heavenly King, God himself.

So too, we need to learn to recognize that our daily labors are not meaningless as we wait for our King's return. Martin Luther was once asked what he would do if he knew that the world would come to an end tomorrow. His response was that he would plant a tree. Luther understood that the imminence of the end does not diminish the value of faithful labors for God here and now. So too, whether our calling is changing diapers or cleaning the kitchen, filing reports or designing aircraft, painting pictures or making music, teaching students or tending the sick, we should be about whatever business the Great King has assigned us. Whenever our master returns, whether soon or at a distant time, he should find us obediently and productively at work when he comes. It is no coincidence that having warned his disciples that the day and hour of his return were unknown, Jesus went on to tell a parable about the master who went away for a long time and then returned unexpectedly, only to find his servants lax in their duties (Matt. 24:45–50). We need to be busy about the King's business, which means serving our culture with all of the gifts and abilities that God has given us.

Yet even while premillennialists may sometimes be too focused on the prospect of being snatched away to heaven to be as much earthly good as they should be, postmillennialists are sometimes overly optimistic about the impact they can have on society. Postmillennialists are often very involved in society and culture, seeking to claim every square inch of it for Christ. In the process, they accomplish many good things. Yet if the penultimate "end" in the days of Antiochus that is described in Daniel 8 tells us anything at all about the ultimate end of all things, it gives us little expectation of a gradual "Christianization" of the world. Rather, it leads us to expect continued (and perhaps increased) trials and tribulations towards the time of the end, compounded by a deep unfaithfulness on the part of God's own people. This is precisely what Paul warned Timothy about:

> But mark this: There will be terrible times in the last days. People will be lovers of themselves, lovers of money, boastful, proud, abusive, disobedient to their parents, ungrateful, unholy, without love, unforgiving, slanderous, without self-control, brutal, not lovers of the good, treacherous, rash,

conceited, lovers of pleasure rather than lovers of God—having a form of godliness but denying its power. (2 Tim. 3:1–5)

So then, as we await the end of all things, we should be fully involved in the community in which we live, working to bring about its betterment in whatever ways we can. As Christians, we can and should be involved in the political process, in business and the arts, according to our gifts and calling, bringing glory to God in these areas as well as in more mundane tasks such as sweeping the floor and doing the dishes. What we do here and now really matters to God, not just what we will do for him when we reach heaven.

CRYING OUT FOR THE SON

Even while we are busy about the business of our Father and King, we should still be longing and crying out for his Son's return. Until that day comes, our deepest problems will remain a reality. Through the efforts of committed Christians of earlier generations, slavery was abolished and the lives of the working poor transformed, yet racism and economic exploitation still continue to plague modern society. Even if we were able to pass legislation that would defend the biblical concept of marriage and protect the lives of the unborn—and these would undoubtedly be good things— we cannot abolish tears, or pain, or death itself. Only the return of Christ will accomplish this renovation of the world.

In all of this, Jesus himself is our model of how we should live as we wait. He modeled true Christian activism, cleansing the temple and driving out the moneychangers (Matt. 21:12–13), even though he knew that in a few short years the Jerusalem temple would be destroyed forever (Matt. 24:21–22). He modeled passionate concern for the souls of the lost, weeping over Jerusalem and lamenting the white harvest that lacked harvesters. While on earth, Jesus acknowledged that in his human nature he did not know the date of the end of the world, information that was reserved for the Father alone (Matt. 24:26). Yet he also showed us the perfect life of waiting and longing, a life of constant dependence on the Lord and spiritual warfare through prayer, crying out for the consummation. His perfection in this waiting substitutes for us, who are so far from perfect in our waiting and longing. His perfect obedience was accomplished for us and is presented to the Father in our place, just as his death on the cross paid for all our sin.

So learn from Jesus how to wait. As you wait, your life has real value and meaning, unlike the lives of those characters in the Beckett play. A cup of cold water, given in Jesus' name, has worth (Matt. 10:42). Serving your neighbor has value; sharing the gospel is important; creating something beautiful has significance; caring for your loved ones has meaning. But these penultimate acts have meaning precisely because of the ultimate act of redemption that God accomplished for us in Jesus Christ. Because he took the sting of our sin and rebellion, and reconciled us to God, now even our smallest acts of obedience have profound meaning. They have value because the day will come when the penultimate gives way to the ultimate, and on that day we shall be waiting for God no longer. Instead, we shall be standing in his presence. On that day we shall hear him graciously affirm the value and meaning of all of the good deeds that he enabled us to do by his Spirit, and we shall hear him forgive all of our vast transgression and rebellion for Christ's sake.

Live richly, therefore, while you wait: serve the King, weep for the lost, love your neighbor, fellowship with the saints, and as you do these things, long for the day when all of these penultimate acts of obedience will be done and the ultimate, eternal service of praise and worship will begin.

11

Praying in the Darkness

Daniel 9:1–19

*In the first year of Darius son of Xerxes (a Mede by descent), who
was made ruler over the Babylonian kingdom—in the first year
of his reign, I, Daniel, understood from the Scriptures, according
to the word of the LORD given to Jeremiah the prophet, that the
desolation of Jerusalem would last seventy years. So I turned to
the Lord God and pleaded with him in prayer and petition, in
fasting, and in sackcloth and ashes.* (Dan. 9:1–3)

If God is a sovereign God, why should we pray? In other words,
if God has everything planned out ahead of time and knows
already what he will do tomorrow and the next day, what is the
point in getting down on our knees and asking for something? Aren't we
wasting our time and breath pleading with God, when the outcome of the
case has already been settled?

Of course, one answer to those questions would be to confess that there
are certain times when we can hardly help praying. It has been said that
there are no atheists in foxholes, and most of us know from our own personal experience that when life gets particularly hard, we are more likely

148

than usual to be found on our knees. When the sun is shining, we may think that we can get by with nothing more than a mumbled "Thank you" to God at mealtimes, but in the valley of the deepest shadow, our souls cry out to him in earnest.

That is why people who ask the question about the connection between God's sovereignty and prayer do not normally intend to cast doubt on whether we should pray—the necessity for that is evident enough from Scripture and our own hearts. Rather, the question is posed as an implicit challenge to God's sovereignty, or at least to certain formulations of that doctrine. Pray we must—but can we really pray as we ought, if we believe that God has predetermined the future? And how exactly ought we to pray, when we find ourselves in the valley of deepest shadow? These are questions with which Daniel 9 will help us.

Prayer and God's Word

The first thing to notice about our passage is that Daniel's prayer was prompted by reading God's Word: "In the first year of Darius son of Xerxes (a Mede by descent), who was made ruler over the Babylonian kingdom—in the first year of his reign, I, Daniel, understood from the Scriptures, according to the word of the LORD given to Jeremiah the prophet, that the desolation of Jerusalem would last seventy years. So I turned to the Lord God and pleaded with him in prayer and petition, in fasting, and in sackcloth and ashes" (Dan. 9:1–3). Daniel had been reading the words of the prophet Jeremiah, words that he described as "the Scriptures" (*hasseparim*), the "word of the Lord given to Jeremiah" (Dan. 9:2). Here we see Daniel acknowledging the inspiration and authority of the writings of a fellow prophet as part of a wider canon of inspired writings, the Scriptures, little more than a generation after they were written. In doing this, Daniel models for us the attitude we are to have to his own visions: they themselves are the inspired Scriptures, the written word of the Lord given through his prophets, to be studied, searched, and submitted to as the living oracles of God. This passage is not simply an interesting and informative ancient text, a source of miscellaneous information about the culture and beliefs of antiquity. It is nothing less than the Word of God, the only authoritative and infallible rule for our life and doctrine.

As Daniel read the Scriptures of the Book of Jeremiah, he found in them a reference to the fact that the desolation of Jerusalem would last seventy years. The passages that he was pondering were probably Jeremiah 25:11–12 and Jeremiah 29:10:

> "This whole country will become a desolate wasteland, and these nations will serve the king of Babylon seventy years. But when the seventy years are fulfilled, I will punish the king of Babylon and his nation, the land of the Babylonians, for their guilt," declares the LORD, "and will make it desolate forever." (Jer. 25:11–12)

> This is what the LORD says: "When seventy years are completed for Babylon, I will come to you and fulfill my gracious promise to bring you back to this place." (Jer. 29:10)

In these oracles Jeremiah announced that the Lord's plan was to subject his people to Babylon for seventy years for their sin, but at the end of that time God would act to judge the Babylonians and to bring his people home. What triggered Daniel's interest in this prophecy was likely the overthrow of the Babylonian empire by the Medes and the Persians, and the death of King Belshazzar at the hands of Darius, the new ruler. Evidently, God was now judging the king of Babylon and his nation, just as he had promised. Therefore, even though it wasn't quite seventy years yet since the destruction of Judah, Daniel began to pray with greater intensity for the fulfillment of the second half of this prophecy: the gracious restoration of God's people to his land.[1]

To be sure, this was probably not a new prayer that Daniel began to pray at this time; as Daniel 6 suggested, his practice of praying three times a day

---

1. The date on which to begin counting the seventy years is not clear, nor is the ending date. We may begin in 605 B.C., when Nebuchadnezzar first invaded Judah and brought Jerusalem under his control. That is perhaps a fitting date for the description of "serving the king of Babylon," yet the land was hardly reduced to a wasteland at this point. That description better fits the date of 586 B.C., when Nebuchadnezzar leveled Jerusalem and burned the temple. If the ending point is Cyrus's decree that the Jews may return to Judah, as 2 Chron. 36:22–23 suggests, then the terminus of the prophecy is 538 B.C. However, in Zech. 1:12, which dates to 520 B.C., the seventy years of judgment still seems to be in progress, though nearing an end. This suggests that for Zechariah, the end of the period was found in the rebuilding of the temple in 515 B.C. Whether the dates are 605 to 538 or 586 to 515, or some other combination of dates, the period is close to but not exactly seventy years. This fulfilled prophecy thus further underlines our comments in the previous study that dates in prophecy are not always intended to be taken completely literally; some of the numbers in the Bible may be symbols, not statistics.

towards Jerusalem was a regular and longstanding habit. This habit too was formed by his reading of the Scriptures: he regularly prayed towards the site of the Jerusalem temple in the manner that Solomon had prescribed for future exiles, on the day when the temple was first dedicated (1 Kings 8:48). Yet as Daniel saw God's promises starting to be fulfilled, he increased in the urgency of his prayer, pleading for God's mercy and favor to rest upon his people.

This increased intensity in prayer is marked by Daniel's decision to fast and pray in sackcloth and ashes, signs of intense mourning and repentance for his people's sin. It is worth noting that Daniel's progression from faith in God's sovereignty to passionate prayer is exactly opposite to the question with which we began. To the question "If God is a sovereign God, why should you pray?" Daniel would have responded "It is *because* God is a sovereign God that I pray." It was precisely when Daniel read in the Scriptures the plan of God to judge Babylon and restore his people, and saw that sovereign plan starting to be put into effect in history, that he lifted up his voice in prayer. Daniel didn't turn to prayer because he thought that the prophecy of the seventy years might somehow fail or be delayed if he didn't do so. Rather, it was because he was confident that his sovereign God would do exactly what he had promised to do that he poured out his heart to him in fervent prayer.

This is an important lesson for us as believers. Most of us have probably had the experience of setting aside time to pray but not knowing what to pray for. Even in the midst of trials and difficulties, sometimes we barely know how to pray. In those circumstances, we can take a leaf out of Daniel's book and search the Scriptures, so that we may pray for the things that God has clearly promised. For example, God has promised to complete the good work he began in us (Phil. 1:6). Thus, in the midst of my trials, I can pray that God will use these trials to further his work in my heart and life, humbling me and breaking my pride, showing me how desperately I need him in my weakness and sinfulness. God has promised to give me a peace that transcends the peace that this world gives (John 14:27). As a result, in my confusion and inner turmoil, I can ask him to give me the peace that he alone can bestow. The Lord has promised to be my shepherd and to walk through the valley of the shadow of death with me (Psalm 23). Therefore, I can pray that he will watch over my soul and hold my hand in the blackest hour of the night. God has promised to bring in a new heaven and new earth, where he will wipe away the tears from every eye (Rev. 21:1–4). For that reason, I can pray for the day to come swiftly when the present world will dissolve and be replaced by that ultimate place of refuge and joy. Daniel prayed that God would do what he had promised, and he prayed with confidence *because* he was praying for what God had promised.

PRAYER AND GOD'S KINGDOM

Daniel was not simply praying for his own comfort and protection in the darkness. His concern was to pray for God's people and God's kingdom. It is right and fitting that in the darkness we take our own personal concerns before the Lord, but we should not get so swept up in our own suffering that we forget the wider needs of God's people. It is appropriate for us to pray "Give us this day our daily bread," but we must also remember to pray "Your kingdom come, your will be done, on earth as it is in heaven." Even though Daniel doubtless had many concerns and worries of his own in the first year of Darius (see Dan. 6), the need of God's kingdom was his central concern in his prayer in Daniel 9, that God would do what he had promised with respect to his own people.

In that task of interceding for his people, Daniel was fulfilling his calling as a prophet. We often think of intercession as a priestly task, and certainly the priests did intercede, but in the Old Testament, intercession was a central part of the prophet's role. They did not merely bring God's word to man; they also brought man's response to God by way of intercession. So in Genesis 20:7 it is the fact that Abraham is a prophet that qualifies him to intercede on behalf of Abimelech. For those of us living in the New Testament era, however, the pouring out of the Spirit on all of God's people means that we can now speak of the prophethood of all believers: we are now the ambassadors of Christ, who share in the task of bringing his message of life and death to the world around us (2 Cor. 2:15–16; 5:20). We therefore all share the duty and privilege of interceding for God's people and kingdom, both locally and around the world, lifting up the needs of the church and the wider world before the throne of grace.

If it is true that we have an obligation to pray for God's people and kingdom, how should we pray for them? Here the content of Daniel's long prayer provides us with a model for our own prayers:

O Lord, the great and awesome God, who keeps his covenant of love with all who love him and obey his commands, we have sinned and done wrong. We have been wicked and have rebelled; we have turned away from your commands and laws. We have not listened to your servants the prophets, who spoke in your name to our kings, our princes and our fathers, and to all the people of the land.

Lord, you are righteous, but this day we are covered with shame—the men of Judah and people of Jerusalem and all Israel, both near and far, in all the countries where you have scattered us because of our unfaithfulness to you. O LORD, we and our kings, our princes and our fathers are covered with shame because we have sinned against you. The Lord our God is merciful and forgiving, even though we have rebelled against him; we have not obeyed the LORD our God or kept the laws he gave us through his servants the prophets. All Israel has transgressed your law and turned away, refusing to obey you.

Therefore the curses and sworn judgments written in the Law of Moses, the servant of God, have been poured out on us, because we have sinned against you. You have fulfilled the words spoken against us and against our rulers by bringing upon us great disaster. Under the whole heaven nothing has ever been done like what has been done to Jerusalem. Just as it is written in the Law of Moses, all this disaster has come upon us, yet we have not sought the favor of the LORD our God by turning from our sins and giving attention to your truth. The LORD did not hesitate to bring the disaster upon us, for the LORD our God is righteous in everything he does; yet we have not obeyed him.

Now, O Lord our God, who brought your people out of Egypt with a mighty hand and who made for yourself a name that endures to this day, we have sinned, we have done wrong. O Lord, in keeping with all your righteous acts, turn away your anger and your wrath from Jerusalem, your city, your holy hill. Our sins and the iniquities of our fathers have made Jerusalem and your people an object of scorn to all those around us.

Now, our God, hear the prayers and petitions of your servant. For your sake, O Lord, look with favor on your desolate sanctuary. Give ear, O God, and hear; open your eyes and see the desolation of the city that bears your Name. We do not make requests of you because we are righteous, but

153

because of your great mercy. O Lord, listen! O Lord, forgive! O Lord, hear and act! For your sake, O my God, do not delay, because your city and your people bear your Name. (Dan. 9:4–19)

Daniel's prayer essentially consists of three elements: invocation, confession, and petition. Daniel began by recognizing and acknowledging who God is (invocation); then he confessed the sins of his community and acknowledged the rightness of God's judgment upon them (confession), and finally, he pled with God to fulfill his purposes for his people (petition). We will look at each of these elements in turn.

INVOCATION, CONFESSION, PETITION

First, there is invocation: Daniel recognized and acknowledged at the outset the God to whom his prayer was addressed. The focus of Daniel's acknowledgment was on God's greatness and his grace. The Lord is "the great and awesome God" (Dan. 9:4), "righteous" (9:7,14), the one "who brought your people out of Egypt with a mighty hand and who made for yourself a name that endures to this day" (9:15): he is indeed a mighty God. Yet he is also a God who "keeps his covenant of love" (9:4), faithfully fulfilling his promises to his people. He is a God who is "merciful and forgiving" (9:9). In fact, these words are both plural in Hebrew, suggesting God's repeated acts of mercy and forgiveness to his rebellious people.[2] This abundant mercy formed the basis of Daniel's request in the petition section at the end of the prayer.

Yet if the God to whom Daniel prayed is righteous and faithful to his promises, Daniel's own people had been the exact opposite, and so Daniel confessed his people's sin. Israel had sinned and rebelled against this kind and gracious God, repeatedly turning away from his laws and refusing to listen to his prophets (Dan. 9:5–6, 10–11). The contrast between the Lord and his covenant people is underlined by the pattern of doubling synonyms: the Lord is "great and awesome," "righteous and forgiving," faithful to "all who love him and obey his commands," while Israel has "sinned and done wrong," "been wicked and rebelled," and "has turned away from your commands and laws."

2. Ernest C. Lucas, *Daniel*, Apollos Old Testament Commentary (Downers Grove, IL: InterVarsity, 2002), 238.

The contrast could not be starker between the faithful and holy God, who is true to all of his promises, and the faithless and unholy people, who had broken all of their commitments and rebelled against their overlord. Under the terms of the covenant that God made with his people at Mount Sinai, such a combination could only ever have one result: the destruction and exile of God's people from the land of promise (see Deut. 28). Because the Lord is righteous and faithful, he had to follow through with this threatened judgment, pouring out his fierce wrath on Jerusalem, his chosen city and dwelling place (Dan. 9:16), making his people the object of deserved scorn among the nations all around them. So Daniel confessed the sin of his people and acknowledged the justice of God's judgment, severe though it had been. There was no effort on Daniel's part to make excuses for Israel or to challenge the fairness of God's dealings with them. Israel fully deserved the fate they had experienced for their rebellion against such a holy and kind God.

Yet Deuteronomy spoke not merely of the judgment that was to come on Israel when they sinned and rebelled against the Lord. It also spoke of the promise of a new and gracious beginning for Israel beyond sin and judgment. When they experienced the wrath of God and repented of their sins, turning to God among the exiles where the Lord had scattered them, the Lord would restore their fortunes and gather them once again to the land (Deut. 30:2–3). This is the response from God that Daniel sought in the petition section of his prayer. He asked that God would hear his prayer and show favor to his desolate sanctuary, bringing the exile to an end (Dan. 9:17). He did not ask this because of any righteousness in himself or his people, but simply because of God's commitment to the glory of his own name (9:19).

When God chose Israel and brought them out of Egypt, making them his own people, he irrevocably linked his name with them. As a result, if Israel perished in exile, it might be a fitting and just punishment for them, but it would lead the nations to question God's power. Was the Lord after all unable to deliver his own people and give them the things he had promised? To show the greatness of his grace and vindicate the honor of his name, the Lord must once again redeem his people and restore them to his favor. So Daniel prayed with bold confidence that God would hear his prayer, show favor to his people, and restore his sanctuary.

PRAYING TO THE GOD OF GREATNESS AND GRACE

All three of these aspects of Daniel's prayer—invocation, confession, and petition—can help us learn how to pray for God's kingdom in our world. We too should begin by reminding ourselves of God's greatness and his grace, shown in his faithfulness to his covenant promises. If we forget God's greatness, then our prayers will be too small. Indeed, I find that my own prayers are almost always too small. I don't find myself praying for a great and mighty work of God's Spirit in our community and in our day. I don't very often pray for remarkable demonstrations of God's power in our church. I forget God's greatness: that he is the one who created all things out of nothing, the one who hung the stars in the heavens and assigned the seas their boundaries. I have forgotten that he is the one who raises up kings and world leaders, and brings them down again. If I remembered God's greatness, my prayer life would be radically transformed.

Yet my prayers are also too small because I forget God's grace. I am often tempted to think that I am beyond fixing, and that so too are those around me. The more I see of my own heart, the more I know that I am a rebel and a sinner. I have not listened to God's laws and made them my delight, nor have I taken to heart the admonitions of God's prophets. How great a condemnation that is for someone like me whose whole life is spent in studying God's Word! In view of the privileges and opportunities I have been given, what an unprofitable servant I am! Seeing myself as I really am in this way could easily lead to despair, and to failing to pray, because I start to think God couldn't possibly use someone like me. What is more, seeing the depth of the sins of others around us can have the same result. As we live and work with people, sooner or later the mask slips and we see their sin too. This is true not just of non-Christian friends and workmates, but of Christians as well. People in the church regularly disappoint us and let us down, and we are tempted to believe that God cannot use them either. Why pray at all, for ourselves or for others, if we are all such chipped pots and damaged vessels?

The answer is that we should pray because of God's grace. The solution to our sin is not to brush it under the carpet and pretend that it doesn't exist. There are plenty of people who want to do that in our contemporary context, people who don't even want to mention the word "sin." That was not Daniel's way. The answer to our sin is to remember God's grace and to confess it before him, throwing ourselves on his sovereign mercy. I am indeed a filthy sinner, quite unfit for God's use, and so are you. Yet this same holy God has nonetheless set his name upon us, calling us "Christian," and choosing us to be incorporated into his flock. He has attached his honor to us in this world, so that in large measure, what people think about him is shaped by what they see in us.

Here there is a motivation for passionate prayer. As I ponder God's grace, I can cry out, "Lord, I am utterly unfit to be your ambassador, but you have called me and thrust me out to serve you. I cannot stand for a moment in my strength, and I have no words of my own to say. Lord, give me the strength to stand and the words to say for you. Accomplish your purposes in this world through me, and through other sinners like me. Build this church, and your kingdom in this place, not because we are worthy—far from it. Build your kingdom here because your name is worthy, and the people all around us need to see your glory. They will never see it from our wisdom or strength; they will see your glory only if you demonstrate it through taking flawed and tarnished people like us and making our lives extraordinary demonstrations of your grace." Recognizing God's greatness and grace will regularly drive us to our knees in thanksgiving and confession, and fervent petition for the sake of his name.

PRAYERS WITH POWER

Daniel's prayer was answered in remarkable fashion. Very often, we pray and wonder whether anyone was listening, or whether our prayer simply bounced off the ceiling. In this case, though, the Lord sent an angel to address Daniel's concerns while he was still praying (Dan. 9:20–21). Now there is prayer power! We shall look in detail at the answer that Daniel received in our next study. However, in general terms, we can say that Daniel's prayer received both an immediate and an ultimate answer. God's immediate answer to Daniel's prayer was to raise up Cyrus, the Persian king, who issued the decree that allowed the Jews to return to their home. This decree was issued in 538 B.C., within a year of the fall of the Babylonian empire, so it occurred almost immediately after Daniel's prayer in the first year of Darius.[3] Daniel prayed, and in response God moved the heart of the greatest ruler of the day to bring about a return of his people to their land, where they could once again rebuild the ruined temple.

But as we shall see in the next study, the message that the angel Gabriel brought to Daniel was that this immediate answer to Daniel's prayer was merely a partial fulfillment of God's plans. The problem of Israel's rebellious heart that caused the exile in the first place would not be dealt with merely by bringing them back to the land. That would require a much more awesome demonstration of God's greatness and grace, which would be accomplished in the coming of Jesus.

Jesus is the one in whom God would deal once and for all with our sin, and thus fulfill his original purposes for his people. In Jesus, there is an unparalleled demonstration of God's greatness. With the coming of Jesus, God's glory was revealed on earth in a way never before seen. The Word became flesh: the almighty God who created the universe became incarnate in a little baby. As John says in his Gospel, "We have seen his glory, the glory of the One and Only, who came from the Father, full of grace and truth" (John 1:14). In Jesus was light, the true light that gives light to every man (John 1:9). Yet the coming of the light of God to dwell among man did not in itself transform us. Instead, it simply revealed the ugly truth about us: "This is the verdict: Light has come into the world, but men loved darkness instead of light because their deeds were evil" (John 3:19). The revelation of God's holy greatness did not deal with our sin; it simply made our sin even more visible.

God's holiness by itself would condemn us out of hand. Because of this, many people have denied or ignored God's holiness and imagined for themselves a god of grace alone, who would never judge anyone. It may be comforting to think about such a god, who makes no demands and will easily forgive everything we have ever done, but if he is not the true God, his supposed forgiveness doesn't help us. It is like the comfort of those who imagined that the *Titanic* was unsinkable. That thought was certainly very comforting and reassuring to the passengers—right up until the moment when the ship experienced its disagreement with an iceberg! On the day of judgment, all of us will meet up with the true God, the great and awesome

3. On the relationship between Darius and Cyrus, see note 5 in ch. 7: "In the Angel's Den."

God of righteousness and truth, who will demand of us a reckoning for all of the things we have done and thought and said. On that day, God's holiness will demand our condemnation.

Yet in Jesus, God did not come to condemn the world (John 3:17). Jesus was the expression not merely of God's greatness and holiness, but also of God's grace. The true God is the God of grace and holiness, who has provided the real solution to our sin problem in Jesus. He did so at the cross, the ultimate manifestation of God's righteousness and grace. If God were simply a God of righteousness, then there is no explanation for the cross. He could simply and justly have blotted us out of existence for our sin, as Daniel confessed. In fact, the Bible could have been reduced to three sentences: God created a perfect world for the man and the woman. They sinned. End of story. Similarly, Israel's own story would have ended with their rebellion and exile, never to rise again. Only God's nature as a God of grace explains his patience with his Old Testament people. Only his grace accounts for his extraordinary loving condescension in becoming a man and suffering the shame and agonies of the cross to redeem his people. Only God's grace explains Jesus' willingness to undergo the period of excruciating separation from his Father for the first time in all eternity, so that we, the guilty sinners who deserved to be separated forever from his light, might inherit his promises instead.

But if God were only a God of grace, a God who forgave sin simply and easily because it was part of his nature to do so, then there is also no explanation for the cross. There would be no reason for the Son of God to be so cruelly executed, unless God is also the God of righteousness. The truth is that sin—our sin—had to be paid for. There had to be a day of reckoning for all the wrong things we have done, a day of reckoning that occurred on that first Good Friday. As Jesus hung there and died, he paid in full the deaths that each of us deserved to die. True payment was made for true sin, so that there could be true grace for true sinners.

THE CROSS AND PRAYER

This demonstration of God's greatness and grace at the cross is the true motivation for our prayers. Since God has loved his people so much that he sent his Son to die for us, he will surely also give us the resources and the words to bring that good news to those around us. God has promised our holiness, so we should be much in prayer for the furtherance of that great work in our hearts and lives. God has promised to sanctify his church, so we should be praying earnestly for our brothers and sisters in Christ, that God would sanctify them through and through. God has promised to save his wandering sheep and add them to his flock, so we should be praying passionately for the conversion of neighbors and friends and family members who are not yet believers.

Such fervent prayer should also be our first response when a fellow believer sins against us. Instead of criticizing, or gossiping, pray. Say, "Father, this is your child. I know that their sanctification is your will for them. I'm just as big a sinner as they are, though perhaps in different ways. Please work in their heart and in mine by your Spirit and grant us both repentance and transformation." Husbands should pray for their wives in this way, when they sin. Wives should pray in the same way for their husbands. When parents exasperate their children, the children should pray for them. When children rebel and reveal their wicked hearts, their parents should pray for them. Pray on the basis of God's promise to sanctify a people for himself.

These are prayers that God delights to answer, because we are praying on the basis of what he has himself promised. We may see these prayers answered in part in the present, as God continues to sanctify us and his people around us. Yet we must also expect to keep on praying such prayers until God's final answer to our sin, which will not be delivered until the Lord Jesus returns. On that day, all of our praying will be done, for faith will be replaced by sight, and our aspiration for holiness with its fulfillment. Then we will see the demonstration of God's greatness and grace in an enormous gathering of people from all over the world, drawn from every nation and culture, but united in singing God's praise. The common theme of our songs on that day will be "Amazing grace, how sweet the sound, that saved a wretch like me." Great indeed is God's grace and mercy that people like us should be destined for eternal glory in his presence. Yet this is his promise, and we can be sure that at the end it will indeed be so.

12

HOPE IN THE DARKNESS

Daniel 9:20–27

While I was speaking and praying, confessing my sin and the sin
of my people Israel and making my request to the LORD my God
for his holy hill—while I was still in prayer, Gabriel, the man I
had seen in the earlier vision, came to me in swift flight about the
time of the evening sacrifice. He instructed me and said to me,
"Daniel, I have now come to give you insight and understanding."
(Dan. 9:20–22)

Have you ever asked what you thought was a simple question, only to be utterly baffled by the depth and complexity of the answer? Perhaps you asked a brain surgeon how he knew where to make the incision, or a nuclear physicist to explain to you how atoms are constructed. Once they started to talk, however, you found yourself completely mystified. You were looking for an explanation along the lines of the "Science for Dummies" series, only to discover fairly rapidly that there are some subjects that apparently are not suited for dummies to learn. There may be a reason why "Rocket Science for Dummies" is an oxymoron!

This is the feeling that many of us have when we approach the latter half of Daniel 9. We want someone to explain the meaning of the vision to us on a level that we can understand, but we are tempted to fear that it simply cannot be understood by people like us. High brainpower biblical specialists may perhaps be able to get their minds around Daniel 9, but at first sight it seems that this is one of those passages that is simply not accessible to ordinary people, to "dummies" like us. If that is our concern, then it may be comforting to know that we are not alone. In 400 A.D., one of the most brilliant scholars and linguists in the ancient church, the church father Jerome, wrote: "Because it is unsafe to pass judgment on the opinions of the great teachers of the church and to set one above another, I shall simply repeat the view of each and leave it to the reader's judgment as to whose explanation ought to be followed."[1] He then listed nine conflicting opinions on the meaning of the passage, declaring himself unable to decide which one (if any) was right.

I hope what follows will answer such concerns. This vision too is part of God's Word that is "useful for teaching, rebuking, correcting and training in righteousness" (2 Tim. 3:16). It was given to Daniel in order to make something clear, not in order to confuse things further (see Dan. 9:22). The key to understanding the vision is to focus on what is central and clear, rather than what is challenging and complicated. We shall not unravel every complexity in the passage, but if we follow this rule, the central message of the vision should not be difficult to see.

THE CONTEXT: DANIEL'S PRAYER

First we need to remind ourselves of the central burden of Daniel's prayer in the first half of Daniel 9. This prayer is the context in which the vision comes to Daniel, a context that has often been overlooked in interpreting the vision. As we saw in our last study, Daniel tells us that he had been pondering Jeremiah's prophecy of a seventy-year period of exile and subjection to the Babylonians and to their king, after which God would judge the Babylonians, and his people would return to their land to rebuild the temple. Daniel's prayer took place during the first year of King

1. *Jerome's Commentary on Daniel*, trans. Gleason Archer (Grand Rapids: Baker, 1958), 95.

Darius, immediately after the Babylonian empire had fallen to the Medes and the Persians. He recognized that the Babylonians and their king had been judged by God, fulfilling the first part of Jeremiah's prophecy. So Daniel prayed that God would now fulfill the second part as well, restoring his people to their land in his mercy and grace and showing favor again to the desolate sanctuary in Jerusalem. Daniel acknowledged that God had judged his people and his sanctuary for their sin, just as faithfulness to the Sinai covenant demanded. Yet that same Sinai covenant also held out the prospect of a new beginning after the punishment of exile, a new beginning in which the Lord would circumcise the hearts of his people and give them hearts that long to obey him (see Deut. 30:1–6).

Indeed, as Daniel read the words of Jeremiah, he would also have read more prophecies that spoke of that promised new beginning. Jeremiah announced that God would make a new covenant with his people that would be different from the covenant that they broke through their sin, a covenant that would finally fulfill Deuteronomy's promise of hearts that desired to obey the Lord:

> "The time is coming," declares the LORD, "when I will make a new covenant with the house of Israel and with the house of Judah. It will not be like the covenant I made with their forefathers when I took them by the hand to lead them out of Egypt, because they broke my covenant, though I was a husband to them," declares the LORD. "This is the covenant I will make with the house of Israel after that time," declares the LORD. "I will put my law in their minds and write it on their hearts. I will be their God, and they will be my people." (Jer. 31:31–33)

Daniel was praying for the fulfillment of these promises of the transformation of the people of God. He longed to see them changed from sinners to a holy people with God dwelling in their midst, and to see Jerusalem restored through the coming of the messianic king. In Daniel's day, the covenant relationship between God and his people had been broken by the sin and transgression of Israel and Judah. Yet his hope and prayer was that the ending of Jeremiah's seventy-year period of judgment would usher in the time when that prophet's words of restoration of the covenant relationship would be fulfilled. As the people repented, Daniel hoped to see the renewal of God's favor, the rebuilding of the temple, and the ushering in of the promised new covenant which would transform the people from rebellious sinners who hated God's law and spurned his prophets into a holy people who loved God's law. According to Jeremiah, this change would also be marked by the arrival of the messianic Branch of righteousness, whose reign would issue in a state of justice, righteousness, and peace for Judah and Jerusalem (Jer. 33:15–16).

This hope is the background against which to read Daniel's vision, a context in which each of the various elements of the vision that the angel Gabriel brought to Daniel makes sense:

> While I was speaking and praying, confessing my sin and the sin of my people Israel and making my request to the LORD my God for his holy hill—while I was still in prayer, Gabriel, the man I had seen in the earlier vision, came to me in swift flight about the time of the evening sacrifice. He instructed me and said to me, "Daniel, I have now come to give you insight and understanding. As soon as you began to pray, an answer was given, which I have come to tell you, for you are highly esteemed." (Dan. 9:20–23)

As if to underline the connection between the prayer and the vision, Gabriel's appearing itself provided an immediate and explicit answer to Daniel's petitions. Daniel cried out to the Lord, "Hear!" (Dan. 9:18–19); the presence of the angel is clear proof that his prayer has been heard. Daniel sought God's favor (9:17); Gabriel addressed him as "highly esteemed" (9:23), an assurance that he was indeed favored by God. Daniel pleaded with the Lord not to delay (9:19), and he received a response before he had even finished praying (9:20). In fact, Gabriel told him that a decree was issued from the throne as soon as Daniel began to pray (9:23).

THE GOOD NEWS: DANIEL'S PRAYER ANSWERED

What is more, Gabriel had come to tell him that his requests for a transformation in the state of his people and city would all be answered in the affirmative:

> Seventy "sevens" are decreed for your people and your holy city to finish transgression, to put an end to sin, to atone for wickedness, to bring in

everlasting righteousness, to seal up vision and prophecy and to anoint the most holy.

Know and understand this: From the issuing of the decree to restore and rebuild Jerusalem until the Anointed One, the ruler, comes, there will be seven "sevens," and sixty-two "sevens." It will be rebuilt with streets and a trench, but in times of trouble. After the sixty-two "sevens," the Anointed One will be cut off and will have nothing. The people of the ruler who will come will destroy the city and the sanctuary. The end will come like a flood: War will continue until the end, and desolations have been decreed. He will confirm a covenant with many for one "seven." In the middle of the "seven" he will put an end to sacrifice and offering. And on a wing of the temple he will set up an abomination that causes desolation, until the end that is decreed is poured out on him. (Dan. 9:24–27)

A day was coming when God would act "to finish transgression, to put an end to sin, to atone for wickedness, to bring in everlasting righteousness, to seal up vision and prophecy, and to anoint the most holy" (Dan. 9:24). Transgression, sin, and wickedness on the part of God's people had led to their abandonment by God, but the day would come when those words would no longer be necessary, because their power would be broken and their punishment atoned for. One day, God's sinful people would be justified before God. In the place of wickedness and rebellion, God would bring in everlasting righteousness, sanctifying his flock to make them a holy nation. Instead of the past neglect of the words of the prophets by his people, the Lord would "seal up" their words (9:24). "Sealing" here does not so much indicate closing their books or keeping their words secret, but rather vindicating them, stamping them with God's seal of ownership through their fulfillment, just as a document might be sealed with the mark of its owner (1 Kings 21:8; Neh. 10:1–2).[2] What is more, the sanctuary in Jerusalem, which in Daniel's day lay destroyed and desolate, would once more be reconsecrated. In the context of Daniel's reading in Jeremiah, this is nothing less than a commitment on the Lord's part to bring in the promised new covenant.

We mentioned this point in our previous study, but it is worth reiterating because it is one of the central emphases of this passage: God hears and answers the prayers of his repentant people. There is no conflict

2. Joyce G. Baldwin, *Daniel*, Tyndale Old Testament Commentaries (Downers Grove, IL: Inter-Varsity, 1987), 169.

between divine sovereignty and foreknowledge on the one hand, by which God knows and governs all aspects of the future, and, on the other hand, the truth that the prayers of God's people have a real impact on events. As James puts it in his epistle, "The prayer of a righteous man is powerful and effective" (James 5:16). James cited Elijah as an example to prove his point, but he could just as easily have used Daniel. Daniel prayed and his prayers elicited a response from the divine throne room before he had even finished speaking. This truth is not restricted to the prayers of "super saints," either. We also have the privilege and responsibility of approaching the throne of grace with our petitions and requests. Yet often our response to the darkness around us is either a human activism that places all of our hopes in our own efforts, or a passive despair that assumes that nothing can be done to counter the spread of evil. Daniel 9 challenges us to get on our knees before the Lord and plead with him to bring in the promised new world where sin and rebellion are gone and eternal righteousness is here. Our prayers are far too small.

GOD'S TIMESCALE

Thus far, the message Gabriel has brought to Daniel is good news. However, there is also bad news to come. This promised transformation—the new covenant of which Jeremiah spoke—will not arrive at the end of the seventy years of the exile. In fact, that period of judgment is simply a small part of a much larger plan of God, a plan which will not be completed in a period of seventy years but will take "seventy sevens" to work itself out (Dan. 9:24). God's timescale is far bigger than Daniel had imagined.

Many understand these "seventy sevens" to be a literal period of 490 years. Since seven and seventy are both numbers of completeness in the Bible, others understand the figure that results when they are multiplied together as representing the ultimate in completeness. This is certainly the case in Matthew 18. In that passage, Jesus is responding to Peter's question as to how often he should forgive his brother when he sinned against him. Should he forgive him as many as seven times? In reply, Jesus told him to forgive his brother seventy times seven times (Matt. 18:22). No one interprets this number literally, as if Peter were obligated to forgive his brother

490 times, but not on the 491st occasion. Rather, they recognize that the point Jesus was making was that Peter's perspective on forgiveness was too small and needed to be expanded. So too here, the vision is challenging Daniel's perspective on the timescale needed to do away with transgression and achieve restoration. It would not take a mere seventy years to accomplish a transformation in the hearts and lives of God's people but seventy times seven to accomplish a complete and ultimate victory over sin and evil. However, this bad news is not intended to cause Daniel to despair. Even though its coming will occur after his lifetime, the promised new covenant will arrive in due season and it will accomplish everything that God has designed for it.

We need to hear the challenge that this passage poses to our expectations of the way God works in our lives. We live in the age of the "instant," when we expect everything to come to us now, if not sooner. To satisfy our impatience, we have invented meals that can be prepared rapidly in a microwave, and rice that takes no more than a minute to cook. People can barely remember the days when they had to wait for televisions and radios to warm up before the program came on. How did we ever endure the suspense? The same "instant" attitude also carries over into our relationships, both with God and with our neighbor. We want instant sanctification for ourselves, demanding God to transform our lives in the twinkling of an eye and to remove immediately the sins that so frustrate us. We likewise want our spouses and our children to be made holy at once, or by next Tuesday at the very latest. Since we know that it is God's will for us to be made holy ultimately, we expect it to be accomplished immediately!

Yet Daniel 9 shows us that God's timescale for the sanctification of his people and the renovation of the world is far larger than we typically think. He is not as concerned as we are with fixing us right away, nor is he in the business of transforming our friends and family members into perfect saints immediately. To be sure, he will accomplish the complete transformation and sanctification of our lives eventually. As someone once said, "The mills of God grind slow, but they grind exceeding small." He will not leave the project half-done, like a do-it-yourself project begun with enthusiasm and left to gather dust after our interest in it waned. Yet at the same time his work in us is a long-term project, not a transformation that will be accomplished by the wave of a magic wand. Our sanctification will literally take a lifetime—our lifetime—to be complete. We are all works of renovation in progress, and will be so until the day we die.

It is important that we remember this truth, so that we will be patient with God's work in ourselves and in those around us. This reality is not to be viewed as a license for us to give in to sin or be slack in pursuing holiness. On the contrary, the assurance that God will surely complete the good work he has begun in us should stir us to the diligent pursuit of present obedience to his Word. Yet the knowledge that this work is often slow, and that as long as we are in this world we will continue to be assaulted by besetting sins, should constantly cast us back to depend upon God's mercy and grace, which are sufficient even for sinners like us. As long as we are still in this world, we will never move beyond the need for God's forgiveness and daily empowerment. In fact, the very slowness of God's work of sanctification in our lives demonstrates just how important it must be to God that we should be constantly aware of our own desperate need for his grace in our lives. He is determined to develop our humility and perpetual dependence upon him.[3]

In addition, as we reflect on the slow progress of our own sanctification, it will make us more patient with the continuing sinfulness of others. We are naturally quick to judge others, especially when their besetting sins are transgressions over which we have ourselves gained the victory. We easily think, "I put to death that sin, so why can't they?"—as if our progress in sanctification were simply the result of our own effort. Yet when we struggle in an ongoing way against a particular sin that painfully and persistently keeps on tripping us up, then we learn to show to others the same grace that we receive daily from the Lord. As we discover that his mercy is there for us each time we fail and fall short, we begin to extend that same mercy to others also. The knowledge of our own weakness and sin enables us to stretch out our hands and hearts to others in their sinfulness.

THE CUTTING OFF OF THE MESSIAH

The vision that was given to Daniel also revealed that the completion of this promised restoration of God's people and sanctuary would come

3. The former slave trader turned pastor, John Newton, helpfully develops this point in a letter entitled "The Advantages of Remaining Sin" in *The Letters of John Newton* (Edinburgh: Banner of Truth, 2000), 131–35.

49 yrs. ?

in three stages. The first stage—the first seven sevens—would run from the issuing of the decree to restore and rebuild Jerusalem to the time when that rebuilding is complete. This decree (*dabar*) that went forth to restore and rebuild Jerusalem in verse 25 is not the decree of a human king but rather the decree (*dabar*) that went forth in response to Daniel's prayer in verse 23. That word itself effectuated the decree (*dabar*) of restoration that the Lord promised in Jeremiah 29:10, almost seventy years earlier. The decree of Cyrus in 538 B.C. that allowed the Jews to return to Jerusalem was merely the earthly reflex of that heavenly decision. This distinction between earthly and heavenly decrees underscores the difficulty which attends any attempt to fix a *terminus a quo* from which to measure a literal period of "seventy sevens" of years.

This first seven shows God's immediate response to Daniel's request: the city of Jerusalem will indeed be rebuilt in the short term. Jeremiah's prophecy of a restoration after seventy years will find a partial fulfillment. However, this period of restoration, along with the subsequent sixty-two sevens after the city has been rebuilt, would be a time of trouble. Jerusalem will not yet enjoy the complete safety and security of which Jeremiah 33:16 spoke. The messianic ruler (*mashiach nagid*) will make his appearance only at the end of these sixty-nine sevens, ushering in the climactic seventieth seven. Yet even then, his appearing would not immediately usher in the peace and righteousness that Jeremiah anticipated. Instead, the Messiah will himself be cut off, leaving him with nothing (9:26).

Once again, this turns our expectations of history on their head. We tend to assume that if God is in control of history and of our lives, then they should run fairly smoothly, onward and upward towards glory. There may perhaps be a few hiccups on the way, but on the whole we expect God to make our paths smooth and easy, especially when we are walking in obedience to him. Yet sixty-nine out of Daniel's seventy sevens are marked by difficulties and trials, and the seventieth seven is no easier. The future that Daniel is shown is a future encompassing wars and rumors of wars, along with trials anticipated or experienced. What is more, the future that he describes for God's people reflects our own future throughout our earthly pilgrimage, the arduous path that we tread to glory.

Yet these trials are our path to glory because they were first our Messiah's path to glory. God doesn't demand of us anything he is not willing to undergo himself. His own Anointed One, the Christ, came to a world of suffering and experienced that suffering firsthand, to the point of being cut off and left with nothing. Our health concerns seem smaller when we compare them to the experience of crucifixion to the point of death. Our money troubles are put in context when we compare them with having soldiers gambling for the shirt off Christ's back, the only possession that he owned. Our difficult relationships and feelings of being abandoned and alone are nothing compared to Jesus' experience of having all of his friends flee from him and deny they even knew him in his hour of need. There is no greater abandonment than having the Father turn his face away in repugnance because of the load of sin he bore. The Anointed One was cut off for us and left with nothing: he was wounded for our iniquities, bruised for our transgressions, abandoned for our betrayals. The way to glory for him led through the path of suffering, and we too are called to follow the same trail.

THE DESTRUCTION OF THE SANCTUARY AND THE CONFIRMING OF THE COVENANT

Thus far, it is fairly straightforward to establish the meaning of Daniel's vision and its relationship to history. After all, Jerusalem was eventually rebuilt, and its trials and difficulties certainly continued. When Jesus the Messiah finally arrived, he was indeed cut off, crucified on a cross, and left with nothing. The most difficult part of the vision is what follows the cutting off of the Messiah. At this point, Daniel was told that Jerusalem and its sanctuary will be destroyed by "the people of the ruler who will come." But who are these people and who is their ruler? Also, we read that someone is going to confirm a covenant with many for that final, climactic seventieth seven, and in the middle of that seven, he will put an end to sacrifice and offering. Who is this person? And what is the mysterious desolating abomination in Daniel 9:27? How does this relate to the events described earlier?

According to some believers—those we described as premillennial in an earlier study—these last events represent a jump far into the future from the preceding context. There is, they argue, a parenthesis in between the sixty-ninth and the seventieth weeks, during which the history of the church plays itself out, after which the antichrist will come and destroy

Jerusalem and its rebuilt temple. On this approach, "the covenant" in verse 27 is a political agreement that the antichrist will make in those last days with some of the Jews, and he is the one who puts an end to the renewed sacrifices and offerings in these last days by destroying the Jerusalem temple, which will have been rebuilt by then. On the other hand, amillennial and postmillennial Christians believe that the covenant mentioned here is God's new covenant with his people, inaugurated by the Messiah, Jesus, and that the desolation and destruction of the temple took place in the first century A.D.

We need to recognize that both of these views are advanced by people who love the Lord and take the prophecy of Daniel seriously, and that these verses are certainly difficult to interpret. However, the alternative explanations cannot possibly both be right. So we need to ask, "Which of these views has the stronger claim to be right, and how do we decide between them?" The best method is to let the immediate context guide our interpretation. Remember, Daniel's prayer was deeply concerned with the fate of God's covenant relationship with his people.[4] In response, Gabriel announced to him that the seventy weeks would see the coming fulfillment of all of the promises of Jeremiah's new covenant, with the elimination of rebellion and sin and the vindication of prophecy. It seems to me, therefore, most natural to see the covenant that is mentioned without further description in verse 27 as the new covenant, which will be confirmed in the final, climactic seven of world history.[5] The seventieth seven is a kind of "jubilee" week, in which God restores all things to their proper state.

If that is correct, then clearly it is the Messiah who confirms the covenant with many and brings an end to sacrifice and offering. With the coming of Jesus into the world, and especially with his death and resurrection, the seventieth week has dawned. In Christ, our jubilee trumpet has sounded, and the victory over sin and transgression has been won. What is more, with the death of Jesus on the cross, the sacrifices of the Old Testament became redundant and worthless. The Son of Man gave his life as a ransom

4. On the covenant theme in Daniel's prayer, see Meredith G. Kline, "The Covenant of the Seventieth Week" in John H. Skilton, ed., *The Law and the Prophets: Old Testament Studies Prepared in Honor of O. T. Allis* (Nutley, NJ: Presbyterian and Reformed, 1974), 455–58.

5. This view is further supported by the Hebrew terminology. When a covenant is first "made" or "established" the verb used is *karat*; here, however, the verb is *higdil* ("confirmed" or "made effective"). See Kline, "Seventy Weeks," 463–66.

171

for the many, bringing those whom God had chosen into the new covenant relationship with the Lord (Mark 10:45). The new covenant of which Jeremiah spoke is now here, as our Lord himself taught us on the night before he died, when he called the cup that he shared with his disciples "the new covenant in my blood" (1 Cor. 11:25). With the coming of Christ, all of the things that Daniel 9:24 anticipated have been accomplished in principle: our sins are atoned for, our transgressions have been removed from us, and the words of the prophets have been vindicated. Of course, we still await the end of this seventieth week, the day when God will bring all of these things to final consummation: we still drink the cup of the new covenant time after time, proclaiming the Lord's death until he comes.

Yet since the final sacrifice that atoned for the transgressions of the many had now been offered, there was and is no further need for the temple in Jerusalem. As soon as Jesus died on the cross, the Jerusalem temple was functionally obsolete. That is why when Jesus breathed his last breath, the curtain in the temple was torn in two, symbolizing the final departure of the Lord from his former abode, never to return.[6] Jesus himself declared the temple and the city of Jerusalem doomed by their refusal to come to him and submit to his rule (see Matt. 23:37–24:2), a sentence that was carried out in A.D. 70. This too is exactly what Daniel 9 anticipated: the city and the sanctuary would be destroyed by the people of "the ruler" (*nagid*) who is to come (Dan. 9:26). This ruler is not a new figure at this point in the prophecy but the same "anointed ruler" (*mashiach nagid*) anticipated in verse 25.

This one person who unites the two offices of "Anointed One" and "ruler" in Daniel 9:25 is addressed separately as "Anointed One" in the first part of verse 26, where the focus is on his priestly work of offering himself as a sacrifice for the sins of the many, and as "ruler" later in the same verse, where the focus is on the failure of his own people to submit to his rule.[7] In other words, Daniel was being told that the people of the Messiah would once again destroy Jerusalem and its sanctuary in exactly the same way they had in Daniel's own day, through their disobedience and rebellion. This is precisely what happened. In a profound sense, the destruction of the city and temple of Jerusalem in A.D. 70 was not so much the work of the Roman

6. See Craig S. Keener, *Commentary on the Gospel of Matthew* (Grand Rapids: Eerdmans, 1999), 686.
7. Kline, "Seventy Weeks," 463n31.

soldiers as it was the result of the transgression of God's people in rejecting the Messiah that God had sent to them. The events that Daniel lamented in his own day were going to be repeated in the future.

THE CLIMACTIC ABOMINATION AND THE ULTIMATE HOPE

This brings us to the final words of the chapter, which are more diffi-cult than anything we have addressed so far. The individual Hebrew words are straightforward enough, but putting them together into a sentence that makes sense is quite challenging. My rather wooden translation is as follows: "In the middle of that seven, he will put an end to sacrifice and offering, and on account of[8] the extremity[9] of abominations that cause desolation, until the end that has been decreed, it will be poured out unto desolation." What this verse seems to envisage is a crowning climactic abomination that causes the devastation of final judgment that we were told in the previous verse had been decreed for Jerusalem. In the light of what we have already said, it seems probable that rather than describing some still-future event, this extreme abomination that caused the destruc-tion of Jerusalem and its temple is nothing other than the crucifixion of Christ, the rejection and cutting off of God's appointed Messiah.

If this was to be Jerusalem's ultimate fate, however, was Jeremiah's prophecy of a new covenant in vain? Was Israel locked in an endlessly repeating cycle of transgression and destruction? Not at all. The Lord had already made it clear in Daniel 9:24 that he would indeed bring about everything that Jeremiah had spoken of in the new covenant. Verse 27 affirms that in spite of the continuing wickedness and rebellion of his peo-ple, which would culminate in the rejection of the Messiah and the con-sequent destruction of Jerusalem, the Messiah would nonetheless confirm God's covenant with the many, making effective its provisions. In the face of ultimate abomination, God's grace would find its ultimate triumph.

Herein lies hope for the worst of sinners in the darkest of moments. Even if we have crucified Christ by our lifestyle, taking the Messiah that God sent

8. For this meaning, see BDB, 'al 1.f (b).
9. Literally, the Hebrew *kanaph* means "wing," but the same word can also indicate the extremity of a garment, or of the earth itself (see Isa. 24:16). Similarly, John Calvin, *Daniel*, trans. T. Myers (Grand Rapids: Baker 2003 reprint), 2.228.

173

to be our Savior and using his name as a swear word, God's grace is sufficient for our sin. Even if we have rebelled and transgressed against him in every possible way, there is still hope. Whether our rebellion involves drugs, or sexual sin, or violent crime, or financial scandal, or malicious cruelty, we too can come to the one who was cut off and receive the mercy and forgiveness we need (see 1 Cor. 6:9–11). We can receive effective cleansing from him, a cleansing that will ultimately wash away every single one of our sins. What a wonderful salvation we have in Christ!

Daniel 9 also shows us that Christ is our only hope in the darkness. Sacrifices and offerings were the approved means by which sinful men and women were instructed to approach God in the Old Testament era. Yet with the coming of the Christ, those sacrifices were done away with. It would be a tragedy to turn the clock back, as if the Jerusalem temple could be rebuilt in the present and its offerings made effective once more (see Heb. 10). What is more, if even the ways that God himself ordained under the old covenant are now transcended by the coming of Christ, how much less could we approach God through any means of human devising and wisdom! Christ, and Christ alone, is the one through whom we must have access to God and receive the forgiveness and peace that he offers us. The blood of the new covenant is the blood of Christ, which is the only detergent capable of effectually washing away all of our sins. There is no other way to enter into God's presence and survive.

Finally, Daniel 9 reminds us to keep looking beyond this world for the ultimate fulfillment of God's promises. We can and should work for the improvement of this world in whatever ways we are able to do so, during whatever portion of time remains available to us. Yet our ultimate hope is the trumpet sound of God's jubilee, which will announce the coming of the victory that was won for us by Christ, but is presently still stored up for us in heaven. As one day follows another, our eyes must constantly be straining forward, looking for the time when the new covenant will be consummated in fullness, when we will drink the cup of the new covenant with the Lord Jesus around that heavenly table. On that day, all of our transgression will be finished, our sin ended, our wickedness atoned for, and our eternal righteousness assured forever. Then, the new Jerusalem will come down from heaven and usher in God's final reign of peace and rest, and we shall reign with him in glory.

On that day, the road we will have traveled to reach glory will not seem too long, though seventy sevens of trials and conflicts lie between us and our final home. God's glorious presence is a sufficient encouragement along the way, and it will be an all-satisfying reward at the end of the journey.

Amen!

13

PREPARED FOR BATTLE

Daniel 10:1—11:1

*On the twenty-fourth day of the first month, as I was stand-
ing on the bank of the great river, the Tigris, I looked up and
there before me was a man dressed in linen, with a belt of the
finest gold around his waist. His body was like chrysolite, his
face like lightning, his eyes like flaming torches, his arms and
legs like the gleam of burnished bronze, and his voice like the
sound of a multitude.* (Dan. 10:4–6)

*I*s anything worse than arriving at an event wrongly dressed?
Perhaps everyone else has come to the party clad in suits and
dresses and you came in your jeans and a sweater, or alternatively, everyone else came in jeans and you are dressed up to the nines.
Either way, it can be an awkward feeling. In fact, this is quite literally
the stuff nightmares are made of. When I was a teenager, I sometimes
dreamed that I had accidentally gone to school in only my underwear.
How embarrassing that would be! In real life, of course, when we turn
up for something wrongly dressed, the problem is usually that we didn't
understand what kind of function it was going to be. The concert we

were going to turned out to be polka rather than Puccini, or vice versa. The event was different from our expectation.

Many Christians have a similarly false expectation of life that results in their being improperly dressed. I'm not talking about what people choose to wear to attend church. Rather, I'm talking about being properly clothed to face life. Many of us go through life expecting it to be a picnic. As a result, we are mentally dressed in light clothing and sandals, expecting sunshine, sand, and fun. We are unprepared for things to go wrong, and when they do, we immediately start muttering something about the fact that life shouldn't be this way. All of the children get out of bed in a foul mood, no one can find what they need for school, the dog throws up on the kitchen floor, and when everyone is finally loaded up, this is the day when the car won't start. Immediately our first thought is, "It's not fair! These things shouldn't happen to me! Life shouldn't be this hard!" Where does this thought come from, though? Who says that life shouldn't be hard? All too often, our problem is that we have a false expectation about what life should be like.

Daniel 10 is written to help us understand *that* life is hard and *why* life is hard, but also to remind us that we are not alone in our struggles. It is part of the larger concluding vision to the Book of Daniel, which runs from the beginning of Daniel 10 through to the end of the book. Daniel is informed at the outset that this vision concerns a great conflict (Dan. 10:1). We will see more of the details of that great conflict in chapter 11, but Daniel 10 is also important for preparing us to understand that conflict, especially its spiritual dimensions. In short, it shows us that the conflicts that we experience here on earth are the counterpart of a great spiritual conflict that is presently ongoing in the heavenly realm. An awareness of this great spiritual conflict will help us to be prepared for the challenges of life here on earth, by being clothed in the appropriate spiritual armor.

A GREAT CONFLICT

This vision was received by Daniel in the third year of Cyrus, king of Persia: "In the third year of Cyrus king of Persia, a revelation was given to Daniel (who was called Belteshazzar). Its message was true and it concerned a great war. The understanding of the message came to him in a vision. At that time I, Daniel, mourned for three weeks. I ate no choice food; no meat or wine touched my lips; and I used no lotions at all until the three weeks were over" (Dan. 10:1–3). In the first year of Cyrus, the first party of Jewish exiles had returned to Jerusalem in response to Cyrus's decree, but they had found life there far from plain sailing. They rebuilt the altar of the temple but almost immediately ran into powerful opposition from their new neighbors on all sides (Ezra 3:1–6). This opposition, on top of the difficulties of scratching out a basic living in their new home, caused the returned exiles to cease the work on the temple, a hiatus that would continue for more than fifteen years until the time of Haggai and Zechariah. The third year of Cyrus would therefore have been a time of discouragement for God's people, both in Judah and in Babylon. The euphoria that surrounded the initial return and the rededication of the altar was fading and the challenges of maintaining faithfulness over the long haul in the midst of great opposition would have been on Daniel's mind.

Many of us can think back to an earlier period of the Christian life in which obedience to God seemed somehow easier and more exciting. But now we are in a dry time of life, faced with many challenges and difficulties, in which the joy of earlier service seems a long time ago. What word does God have for us that will help us to maintain our faithfulness over the long haul?

Mourning and Fasting

Daniel's response was to begin that year in an extended period of mourning and fasting. It was not a total fast from all food; rather, Daniel fasted from choice foods such as meat and wine, adopting a deliberately ascetic diet for three weeks, as a sign of his mourning over the situation in Jerusalem. He also abstained from the various lotions that made life more comfortable in a dry, desert climate. The fact that his fast persisted through the Passover festival in the middle of the first month is both a sign of the seriousness of his commitment to mourn and an implicit cry to God to repeat his ancient acts of salvation in Daniel's own day. It was his way of identifying with the difficulties and trials that faced God's people who had returned to their homeland and crying out to God for their ultimate deliverance.

178

Daniel's solidarity with his brothers and sisters in the Lord, even at a great distance, should be a challenge to us. The church around the world is one family of God's people. When one suffers, we should all sorrow; when one rejoices, we should all celebrate (see 1 Cor. 12:26). This obligation requires that we develop an awareness of what is happening elsewhere in the world. Doing this may be as simple as reading prayer letters and emails from one of the missionary families that our church supports, or as complicated as going on a short-term mission trip to encourage believers in another country. None of us can know what is going on everywhere, but each of us can know what God is doing somewhere in the world, and we can play our part in supporting and encouraging those whom God has called. This ministry of prayer and encouragement can be a particularly important support for those of our brothers and sisters in Christ whose path is hard. It may be relatively easy to preach the gospel in a place where our ministry is blessed with much fruit. It is much harder to maintain faithfulness to God in a difficult situation, where there is little to show for our efforts. In such contexts, a simple note that shows that we have not been forgotten and that someone is remembering to pray for us is greatly appreciated.

We should particularly remember the persecuted church. In many parts of the world there are those who suffer severely for their allegiance to Christ. The writer to the Hebrews urges his readers to "Remember those in prison as if you were their fellow prisoners, and those who are mistreated as if you yourselves were suffering" (Heb. 13:3). Of course, in most cases we cannot write to these people personally, to assure them of our support. Nonetheless, we can do what Daniel did, which is to fast for a time from some of the luxuries that are a routine part of our lives, and devote ourselves to praying for these persecuted saints in their time of desperate need. By voluntarily giving up for a period of time some of the joys and pleasures that are so readily available to us, we can identify with those believers who have no prospect of ever experiencing such things. Such an act is also good for us when we are tempted to grumble about the difficulties and challenges of our present situation. It reminds us to be thankful for God's mercies to us in our setting, and to pray for God's people under trials. Abstinence also helps us to keep in mind the fact that this world is not our home. Like the believers under persecution, we too

179

are engaged in a profound spiritual battle against powerful opposition, a battle that rages around us at all times.

A HEAVENLY BEING

This spiritual battle is the focus of the rest of the chapter. At the end of Daniel's time of fasting, he received a dramatic vision as he stood beside the river Tigris: "On the twenty-fourth day of the first month, as I was standing on the bank of the great river, the Tigris, I looked up and there before me was a man dressed in linen, with a belt of the finest gold around his waist. His body was like chrysolite, his face like lightning, his eyes like flaming torches, his arms and legs like the gleam of burnished bronze, and his voice like the sound of a multitude" (Dan. 10:4–6). In his vision, Daniel saw a heavenly being, dressed in linen with a belt of gold around his waist. The body of this being glowed with inner light like chrysolite, a flashing golden gemstone. His face shone like lightning; his eyes were like torches; his arms and legs like polished bronze. His voice echoed like the booming roar of a crowd.

Who is this heavenly being? Many commentators, picking up the parallels with Ezekiel's opening vision and the description of the glorified Christ in Revelation 1, argue that this must be a vision of God.[1] Yet the fact that this figure is sent by someone else to strengthen Daniel and that on this mission he was delayed by the prince of the Persian kingdom until he received the help of Michael, one of the chief princes (or angels; Dan. 10:13), seems to point in a different direction. Other commentators have identified two different figures in the chapter, the divine figure in Daniel 10:5–6 and a separate angelic messenger who appears in Daniel 10:10 to lift Daniel to his feet and give him a message.[2] However, that leaves the divine figure speaking and being heard by Daniel in verse 9, but no record of what he said, while the speech that follows in verse 11 is attributed to an angel whose arrival is not mentioned.

A simpler answer is possible, however. A careful study of the parallels with Ezekiel's vision of God shows that the closest parallels are with the cherubim who pull the divine chariot and the wheels of the chariot itself rather

---

1. E.g., E. J. Young, *The Prophecy of Daniel: An Introduction and Commentary* (Grand Rapids: Eerdmans, 1949), 225.

2. E.g., Stephen R. Miller, *Daniel*, New American Commentary (Nashville: Broadman, 1994), 282.

than with the figure of God. The cherubim had the form of a man (although with a variety of features from other animals; Ezek. 1:5); they had the appearance of torches (1:14) and their limbs gleamed like burnished bronze (1:7); they moved about like flashes of lightning (1:14) and their wings produced a mighty sound, "like the voice of the Almighty" (1:24). The wheels of the divine chariot sparkled like chrysolite (1:16). Meanwhile, the man clothed in linen also closely resembles the angelic mediator in Ezekiel who was instructed to mark out with a sign those who should be saved from the doomed city of Jerusalem, and then to initiate the city's destruction (Ezek. 9:2–4; 10:2). There is therefore no reason why the vision in Daniel 10 should not be describing the same angelic figure throughout the chapter.

Yet the interpretation that saw the man in the vision as representing God is not entirely wrong. The angelic messengers themselves reflect the image of the glorious God whom they serve, so to look on the angel is tantamount to viewing God himself. This is an important point because (unlike some Hollywood movies) Old Testament visions of God are never produced simply to impress us with special effects. They seek to communicate through the vision some aspect or aspects of God's nature that will be important for the message that will follow. So if we interpret the opening part of the vision as telling us something important about God, we shall not be wrong to do so.

GOD'S HOLINESS AND GLORY

Daniel's vision left him trembling and helpless: "I, Daniel, was the only one who saw the vision; the men with me did not see it, but such terror overwhelmed them that they fled and hid themselves. So I was left alone, gazing at this great vision; I had no strength left, my face turned deathly pale and I was helpless. Then I heard him speaking, and as I listened to him, I fell into a deep sleep, my face to the ground" (Dan. 10:7–9). What did this vision seek to convey about God? Surely the focus is on his holiness and his glory. God's holiness is symbolized in the linen clothing, which was used both for the tabernacle and as priestly attire in the Old Testament (Ex. 36:8; Lev. 16:4). The holiness of God means that God is not like us. He is different, separate from us. The Bible says that he is of purer eyes than to look upon sin (Hab. 1:13). As God himself says: "My thoughts are not your thoughts, neither are your ways my ways.... As the heavens are higher than the earth, so are my ways higher than your ways and my thoughts than your thoughts" (Isa. 55:8–9). In addition to God's holiness, God's glory is equally prominent. This vision shows us a God whose presence, even in mediated form, is overwhelming. The vision pulsates with brightness and reverberates with sound, crushing Daniel to the ground and sending his companions scurrying for cover. The prophet could not stand on his feet before such an awesome vision of God's glory, but must inevitably fall on his face before him.

This is a very different depiction of God from what we see in the culture around us. We live in a culture that is on very friendly terms with their god, a mild-mannered deity who is far too mellow and kindly to send anyone to hell. We have transformed God into a cosmic "Mr. Nice Guy," eager to welcome all comers to his neighborhood. Our culture's god is just like Santa Claus: he may perhaps threaten to put coal in your stocking if you are bad, but we all know that it is merely an empty threat. After all, we know of no one who has ever awakened on Christmas morning to be greeted by the dreaded black stuff! In the final analysis, this god is too soft to judge anyone.

This is not the God whose attributes Daniel sees reflected in his vision, however. He is the God of a glorious holiness that blazes with fire, whose presence is scarcely bearable, even by those who, like Daniel, have devoted their lives to serving him.

GOD'S GLORIOUS HOLINESS AND PERSECUTION

The reality of God's blazingly glorious holiness is an important truth to remember in times of trial and persecution. Satan wants us to think that obedience to God really doesn't matter very much—that it doesn't make much difference whether we follow God or assimilate into the culture around us. Life is so hard; why not just follow the easy path and go with the flow? Why endure persecution for the "Mr. Nice Guy" image of God? It wouldn't even be worth making such a minor sacrifice as giving up your favorite drink for a deity like that!

However, if the God we serve is blazingly and gloriously holy, then obedience to his will is not just a minor matter. He is passionately committed to our holiness and to saving a people for himself, and thus he demands a commensurate commitment on the part of his church. The inheritance that he offers his saints is an eternity experiencing the glory of that holiness. A God like this is worth leaving the comforts of Babylon for, to go and endure the difficulties of rebuilding Jerusalem. A God like this is worth struggling on through the difficult times for. He is worth leaving the security of our own comfortable homes, in order to go and labor for his kingdom in cities and towns and villages around the world, whether or not we see much of a response to our labors. A God like this is even worth giving up our lives for, if that is what it takes. After all, that is precisely what he was willing to do for us, in the person of Jesus, in order to save us from our sins. He left the comfort and ease of heaven and came down into this frustrating and difficult world. He labored on through the good times and the bad times, all the way to death on the cross. Such a God is worthy of great sacrifices.

God's purpose in revealing himself to Daniel in this glorious manner was not to crush him but to encourage him. God wants us to see our own weakness before him so that we will not trust in ourselves but will look to him for our strength. So the awe-inspiring messenger reached out his hand and touched Daniel, speaking encouraging words to him that enabled him to stand, albeit still with trembling: "A hand touched me and set me trembling on my hands and knees. He said, 'Daniel, you who are highly esteemed, consider carefully the words I am about to speak to you, and stand up, for I have now been sent to you.' And when he said this to me, I stood up trembling" (Dan. 10:10–11). The angel encouraged Daniel with the affirmation that he was highly esteemed by God. Furthermore, the angel had been sent to Daniel in response to his prayers, in order to give him insight and understanding. In other words, the vision that follows in chapter 11 will be one that is intended to encourage Daniel in response to his mourning and meditation over the present situation in Jerusalem.

A MESSAGE DELAYED

If this angelic messenger was first sent to minister to Daniel at the point when he began to humble himself and pray, why did he not come until three weeks later? The answer given in the vision is that he was delayed on his journey twenty-one days by the prince of the Persian kingdom:

> Do not be afraid, Daniel. Since the first day that you set your mind to gain understanding and to humble yourself before your God, your words were heard, and I have come in response to them. But the prince of the Persian kingdom resisted me twenty-one days. Then Michael, one of the chief princes, came to help me, because I was detained there with the king of Persia. Now I have come to explain to you what will happen to your people in the future, for the vision concerns a time yet to come. (Dan. 10:12–14)

The "prince of the Persian kingdom" is an angelic figure who is associated with the Persian empire and who resists God's purposes. He is therefore an evil angel, an agent of Satan. Satan's enmity against God's people is sometimes manifested through the rulers and powers of this present age, and the church's present experiences are the earthly working out of a parallel conflict in heaven. The vision explains one reason why there is a delay in the fulfillment of God's promises: the "prince of the Persian kingdom" is a powerful adversary—powerful enough to delay God's own messenger for a period of three weeks. Yet in the end all he could do was to *delay* God's messenger: When the archangel Michael came to help him, the angel who spoke to Daniel was finally able to complete his journey and bring the message of encouragement to Daniel. Ultimately, Satan's most strenuous activity cannot overthrow God's purposes or harm his people.

Daniel's response to the news of this heavenly conflict was to be overtaken again by such an overwhelming sense of weakness that once again he was bowed to the ground. The vision knocked the strength and breath out of him—so much so that he wasn't even able to speak until the angel touched him on the lips:

> While he was saying this to me, I bowed with my face toward the ground and was speechless. Then one who looked like a man touched my lips, and I opened my mouth and began to speak. I said to the one standing before me, "I am overcome with anguish because of the vision, my lord, and I am helpless. How can I, your servant, talk with you, my lord?
>
> My strength is gone and I can hardly breathe." Again the one who looked like a man touched me and gave me strength. "Do not be afraid, O man highly esteemed," he said. "Peace! Be strong now; be strong."
>
> When he spoke to me, I was strengthened and said, "Speak, my lord, since you have given me strength." (Dan. 10:15–19)

The magnitude and power of the spiritual forces ranged against God's people were sobering, and the angel's words opened up a whole new vista on the difficulties facing God's people who were trying to rebuild Jerusalem. They were not simply facing human opposition and enmity, but opposition and enmity on the part of powerful spiritual beings in the heavenly realms. This explains why the progress in rebuilding their city was so slow. Behind the intrigue at the earthly court of the Persian king lay the satanic "prince of the Persian kingdom."

What is more, the spiritual struggle would not soon be over. After communicating with Daniel, the angel would soon return to the fray against the prince of Persia, and after that against the prince of Greece, the next world power to arise:

> So he said, "Do you know why I have come to you? Soon I will return to fight against the prince of Persia, and when I go, the prince of Greece will come; but first I will tell you what is written in the Book of Truth. (No one supports me against them except Michael, your prince. And in the first year of Darius the Mede, I took my stand to support and protect him)." (Dan. 10:20–11:1)

Nor should we suppose that since Persia and Greece are ancient history, these angels are now resting on their laurels. The satanic forces opposed to the church continue to use the powers and institutions of this world in their struggle against God's people. Throughout history, Satan's enmity against the church will be vented time and again. Time and again, however, though the church is bowed to the ground and may feel abandoned and alone, it is not destroyed because God continues to support and sustain it through the strengthening ministry of his own angels. We are not alone in our conflict, and though the promises of God seem slow in being fulfilled, they are nonetheless sure (2 Peter 3:8–10). God's decrees—the edicts that are written in "the Book of Truth" (Dan. 10:21)—are the ultimate determiner of future realities.

We need to see that the root cause of our difficulties is not the husband or wife that is being so unreasonable, or the work situation that seems impossible, or the rebellious child that is making life miserable. The root cause is not even our own bad habits and the sins that frustrate us so greatly. Rather, it is the underlying spiritual battle in which we are engaged against powerful forces in the heavenly realms. As the apostle Paul put it: "Our struggle is not against flesh and blood, but against the rulers, against the authorities, against the powers of this dark world and against the spiritual forces of evil in the heavenly realms" (Eph. 6:12). Does that supernatural struggle sound frightening and intimidating? It is meant to! God wants us to see clearly that life isn't a picnic but a battleground. The devil is a powerful opponent, far too powerful for us to take on in our own strength. We will need patience to endure much while we await the fullness of God's promise. Arrayed on our side, however, is God's strength—the might and the power of the blazingly glorious God, who created heaven and earth out of nothing. His triumph may seem slow in appearing, but it will not be denied.

DISCERNING SATAN'S STRATEGIES

It is important that we have a proper perspective on the devil's power if we are to stand firm against the devil's schemes. The devil seems to have two basic strategies of operation. The first strategy is the "demon behind every bush syndrome," where he tries to persuade people that he is all-powerful and that to resist him is therefore pointless. The apostle Peter describes him as a roaring lion, going about seeking whom he can devour (1 Peter 5:8). Satan pretends to have awesome power and authority. This approach is prominent in developing countries, where the work of sharing the gospel often seems to be a power struggle; it needs to be demonstrated for all to see that God's power is greater than the devil's power. But the devil also uses this strategy effectively on us when he presents a temptation as being irresistible because (as he suggests to us) "You simply can't help yourself. It's the way you were made. It is in your genes or it has become an ingrained habit. What is the point of resisting? You know you are going to lose in the end."

Another aspect of this satanic strategy is the tendency in some parts of the church to blame every negative event on the work of demons. If someone is an alcoholic, it is because he is possessed by a spirit of alcoholism; or if someone is bitter, she is possessed by a spirit of bitterness, which needs to be prayed against and cast out. Even closer to the interests of Daniel 10, difficulties in presenting the gospel in a particular place are attributed to a territorial spirit that is blocking the work there, and the solution is to pray against that particular evil spirit.

While it is undoubtedly true that Satan and his minions are behind much that is evil in our world, and we should certainly pray for God to frustrate their efforts, this approach seems to give Satan altogether too much credit. The angel does not urge Daniel to pray against the prince of Persia. Rather, the proper answer to this strategy is to recognize and celebrate and remind ourselves of God's awesome power, which is being communicated to us. Just as the angel says to Daniel, "Peace! Be strong" (Dan. 10:19), so Paul urges the Ephesians, "Be strong in the Lord and in his mighty power. Put on the full armor of God so that . . . when the day of evil comes, you may be able to stand your ground and after you have done everything, to stand" (Eph. 6:10–13). When evil does its worst, God's strength has been given us so that *we may stand!* No temptation is irresistible, no matter how it may appear to us, because the awesome power of God is at work in us to make us new people. No situation that faces us is impossible, no matter what the satanic opposition, for God will build his church and the gates of hell shall not prevail against it (Matt. 16:18). Satan and his forces are great and dangerous, but they are not all-powerful.

Satan's second strategy, though, is the exact opposite of the first. If in his first strategy Satan hides behind a magnifying glass, in his second strategy he shrinks out of sight altogether. This is probably his dominant strategy in our society. It is all too convenient for him when people don't believe in his existence. He can carry out his work unsuspected and undetected. In this strategy, Satan goes around dressed not as a roaring lion but as an angel of light. He enslaves us not by dominant force but by sweet seduction, in the same way a mouse is allured to the trap by a tasty piece of cheese. So too Satan sets his traps around unseen, attractively baited, and we rush eagerly right into them. How can it be wrong when it feels so right? Snap! The trap closes. When we don't recognize the existence and reality of the devil and his schemes, then we don't see the need to be encumbered with the whole armor of God. He finds us unprepared and easily overcomes us.

The answer to this strategy is to see the reality of what Daniel saw in chapter 10: "Be convinced of the reality of the devil and his very real power. Be aware of the heavenly dimension of the struggle. But remember too that you don't struggle alone." Michael and the other heavenly figure had been engaged in this conflict together on behalf of God's people since the first year of Darius (538 B.C.), the time when the decree to allow the Jews to return to their homeland had been issued and several years before Daniel's prayer. Day by day and year after year, there are powerful heavenly forces engaged on our side of the struggle as well as that of the enemy.

TAKING OUR STAND

So is this simply a heavenly battle in which we are helpless bystanders? It might seem so at first sight. After all, the heavenly contenders are so much more powerful than we are: what part could we possibly play in all of this? The answer, however, lies in Daniel's revolutionary act that triggered the vision in the first place: Daniel prayed. When we pray, we who are merely weak, trembling human beings engage in the cosmic conflict in a way that has vast though often unseen repercussions. That is why, when Paul urged the Ephesians to be properly dressed for spiritual conflict in the whole armor of God, he ended by urging them to pray always with all kinds of prayers and requests (Eph. 6:18). In the face of overwhelming situations, unbearable trials, and frustrating difficulties, what can we do? We can pray.

In contrast to Paul's urging to pray *always* with *all* kinds of prayers and requests, we tend instead to pray *rarely* with *small* kinds of requests. Our prayers are often limited by small imaginations and little faith. We don't pray for big things, because we don't really believe in our heart of hearts that God can or will do them. This is especially true during those difficult and discouraging times when life is hard and spiritual progress seems so slow. We pray for small sinners to become Christians, but not for big sinners. We pray for victory over the small sins in our lives, while we leave those large ingrained sinful habits untouched. We pray for change in our small corner of our state but not in the country at large, or throughout the world. Wake up your vision! This is the great and mighty God whom we serve. He causes kingdoms to rise and kingdoms to fall. He controls the detailed events of world history, as we shall see in Daniel 11. And this God chooses to work in response to the prayers of his people.

The Decisive Victory

Ultimately, though, our victory doesn't rest on our faithfulness to pray, or even on the power of the angels who are fighting for us. Jesus Christ is the one who has himself won the victory for us. He took his stand all alone, wearing God's armor in the decisive battle for our souls. At the cross, Satan did his worst against him and was defeated. Since Jesus won that victory on the cross, no one and nothing can stand against him. Therefore, as Paul tells us in Romans 8, neither life nor death, nor angels, nor principalities and powers, nor anything in all creation can separate us from that victory in Christ. Even now, Jesus is exalted to the right hand of the Father and is no longer engaged in hand-to-hand conflict with the devil. Rather, he is seated, at rest. It is in him that we are "highly esteemed," precious in God's sight, and therefore assured of ultimate victory.

Here is great cause for rejoicing and praise, even during the difficult and frustrating conflicts of life! The decisive battle is already over and God has won the victory. As a result, at the end of our earthly conflict, however fierce that may be, our glorious rest in heaven is firmly assured. The vision of glorious rest that we need to hold before us during those hard times is perfectly captured in the classic hymn:

For all the saints, who from their labors rest,
Who Thee by faith before the world confessed,
Thy Name, O Jesus, be forever blessed. Alleluia, Alleluia!

O may Thy soldiers, faithful, true and bold,
Fight as the saints who nobly fought of old,
And win with them the victor's crown of gold. Alleluia, Alleluia!

From earth's wide bounds, from ocean's farthest coast,
Through gates of pearl streams in the countless host,
And singing to Father, Son and Holy Ghost: Alleluia, Alleluia![3]

Yes, the strife is fierce and the warfare is long. Sometimes it may seem that it will never be over. But lift up your eyes to see the coming dawn!

3. William Walsham How (1864).

Open your ears to hear afresh the distant triumph song. The day is coming when at last the King of glory will come to claim his kingdom. At last, he will lead in the countless host of saints, who have come to receive their glorious inheritance. On that day, may we too be found among those who come in to God's kingdom triumphantly "singing to Father, Son and Holy Ghost: Alleluia, Alleluia!"

14

WARS AND RUMORS OF WARS

Daniel 11:2—12:3

*Now then, I tell you the truth: Three more kings will appear
in Persia, and then a fourth, who will be far richer than all the
others. When he has gained power by his wealth, he will stir up
everyone against the kingdom of Greece. Then a mighty king will
appear, who will rule with great power and do as he pleases. After
he has appeared, his empire will be broken up and parceled out
toward the four winds of heaven. It will not go to his descendants,
nor will it have the power he exercised, because his empire will be
uprooted and given to others.* (Dan. 11:2–4)

hat is history and why do we need it? The dictum of Henry Ford that history is "more or less bunk" is well known. The essence of Ford's disdain was that a preoccupation with history gets in the way of living life here and now. For him, nothing in the past was of any conceivable use in the task of living in the present. He thought that history was simply irrelevant.

Others, however, have argued not only that history is irrelevant but also that it is essentially meaningless. Joseph Heller once vividly described history as "a trash bag of random coincidences torn open in a wind."[1] On this view, "stuff happens" with no particular pattern or significance. Our attempts to discern such meaning are simply a desperate effort to make our own lives meaningful. If that view is correct, then history has no lessons to teach.

I suspect that many people disdain history not so much because they have decided on philosophical grounds that it is irrelevant and meaningless but rather because they have concluded that it is dull and boring. One of the characters in Jane Austen's novel *Northanger Abbey* says it best: "History, real solemn history, I cannot be interested in. . . . I read it a little as a duty; but it tells me nothing that does not either vex or weary me. The quarrels of popes and kings, with wars and pestilences in every page; the men all so good for nothing, and hardly any women at all—it is very tiresome."[2] It has to be admitted at once that studying people and events that took place long ago and far away can very easily be presented in a wearying way. What is more, Daniel 11 seems at first reading to be exactly the kind of dull history that this person has in mind, an account of "the quarrels of [long dead] popes and kings, with wars and pestilences on every page." It presents a dizzying and confusing array of alliances and conflicts, of wars and rumors of wars, the kind that could easily seem to have been simply ripped from "a trash bag of random coincidences." Is there really something that we can learn from this history that will actually be relevant and meaningful to living our lives in the here and now? If so, what on earth is it?

The Context of Daniel 11

The place to start in understanding Daniel 11 is to review its context. As we said in our last study, this chapter is part of a larger single unit that runs from Daniel 10 to 12, a vision given to Daniel in the third year of Cyrus (Dan. 10:1). The third year of Cyrus was a time when the Jews had begun to return from their places of exile to Jerusalem to rebuild the temple and reestablish their life in the Promised Land. However, faced with great opposition from their enemies all around, the rebuilding work had swiftly ground to a halt and people had subsided into a "maintenance" lifestyle,

1. *Good as Gold* (New York: Simon & Schuster, 1979), 74.
2. *Northanger Abbey* (New York: Barnes & Noble Classics, 2005), 102.

focused on bare survival. The glorious optimism present immediately after the people returned to Jerusalem had faded into a general attitude of discouragement and despair.

In response to these difficulties, Daniel set apart three weeks at the beginning of that year to mourn and to fast, devoting himself to prayer. The vision of chapter 11 was a direct response from God to that prayer, so we should expect it to have a message that would speak powerfully to Daniel, and also to other discouraged believers. If your Christian life moves daily from triumph to triumph, as you effortlessly grow in your knowledge of God and your victory over sin, then you can probably skip this chapter. However, if you know what it is to struggle and fail when you attempt to do what God has told you to do, so that you find yourself wondering why you should even bother to try again, then this chapter is designed for you. If you ever wonder where God is in your life, and how to make sense of the gap between his glorious promises of a new and triumphant experience of blessing on the one hand, and the grinding difficulty and discouragement of your daily life on the other, then read on. The Greek historian Thucydides suggested that history is philosophy teaching by examples;[3] so, too, Israel's history provides an example from which we can learn how God works in the world and thus discern how he may be at work in our own little lives.

A PROPHETIC OVERVIEW OF HISTORY

The message Daniel received was a prophetic (and very selective) overview of the flow of history from the time of Daniel in the late sixth century B.C. until the end of the world, the final climactic conflict and victory of God. In its breadth, this history is far from unique. Daniel 8 provided an overview of world history that was similar in its sweeping scope. Yet what is immediately remarkable about Daniel 11 is the depth of detail and specificity with which it covers some of the predicted events. In fact, so accurate are some of these details that many scholars have argued that the chapter must have been written *after* the events that it purports to anticipate. Since even evangelical scholars such as John Goldingay and Ernest Lucas have followed this line of argument, it is necessary to take the time to answer it.

3. Quoted by Dionysius of Halicarnassus, *Ars Rhetorica*, 11.2.

Essentially, the argument runs like this. There are many parallels between Daniel 11 and other "pseudo-prophecies" in other ancient Near Eastern literature, which, according to proponents of this idea, suggests that pseudo-prophecy was a familiar and accepted literary genre whose purpose was not to predict history but interpret it.[4] Moreover, they suggest that elsewhere in the Old Testament prophecy is always directed to the immediate situation of the prophet, not to providing specific and concrete predictions of events in the distant future.[5] These authors accept the possibility that God could reveal in detail future events, but they do not think that he does so in practice; instead, he calls his people to live by faith in the face of a future that is not disclosed.[6]

Answering each of these concerns in turn, it is certainly true that there are parallels in form between Daniel 11 and the ancient Near Eastern pseudo-prophecies. Yet such prophecies almost inevitably relied for their effect on their acceptance as true prophecy, rather than pseudo-prophecy.[7] They do not present themselves simply as an interpretation of past history but as a demonstration of the deity's power to predict, and thus control, history. Interestingly enough, the closest parallels to the Book of Daniel suggest that the author was familiar with ancient and rather obscure second-millennium texts that would likely have been available only in Akkadian and only in Babylon.[8] This exactly fits the kind of literature in which Daniel himself was trained (Dan. 1:4); it is far less likely that an author in the second century B.C., whether in Judea (Goldingay) or Babylon (Lucas), would have had access to it. The Book of Daniel thus has closer connections to the Babylonian world of the sixth century than to anything that came later.

What is more, the Old Testament does not argue that there is always a difference in form between true and false prophecy; rather, pseudo-prophecies often adopted identical forms to true prophecies (see 1 Kings 22:11–12 for one example). So the existence of parallel forms of "proph-

4. John Goldingay, *Daniel*, Word Biblical Commentary (Dallas: Word, 1989), 282; E. C. Lucas, *Daniel*, Apollos Old Testament Commentary (Downers Grove, IL: InterVarsity, 2002), 272.
5. Goldingay, *Daniel*, 321.
6. See John Goldingay, "The Book of Daniel," *Themelios* 2 (1977): 49.
7. Tremper Longman III, *Daniel*, New International Version Application Commentary (Grand Rapids: Zondervan, 1999), 272.
8. As Lucas himself demonstrates (*Daniel*, 272).

ecy" elsewhere in the ancient Near East is not relevant to the question of Daniel's authenticity. In the Bible, the difference between true and false prophecy lies in the content—specifically, the fact that the words of a true prophet come to pass (Deut. 18:22). This test, difficult though it may have been to apply in many circumstances, implies that the work of a true prophet will often be in the form of specific and concrete (i.e., verifiable) predictions of the future. Nor are all of these predictions for the immediate future, either. First Kings 16:34 records that "the word of the Lord he had spoken by Joshua son of Nun" was specifically fulfilled during the reign of King Ahab, in the death of the firstborn and youngest sons of the man who rebuilt Jericho. The fulfillment of this specific word postdated the prophecy by around five hundred years!

Finally, the argument that prophecy is always directed to the immediate, concrete situation of the prophet's audience is not unique to this passage. Goldingay advances exactly the same argument in favor of a late dating of Isaiah 40–55.[9] However, the more frequently this argument is used, the more its initial premise becomes open to question. If in several different books, the prophets *do* appear to address the situations of much later audiences, either they are *all* pseudo-prophecies (but that would now have to be established on some other grounds), or the prophets were called to give genuine prophecies of the future for which we need to find a theological explanation. Such an explanation is not hard to find. In the words of Isaiah 44:6–7: "This is what the LORD says—Israel's King and Redeemer, the LORD Almighty: I am the first and I am the last; apart from me there is no God. Who then is like me? Let him proclaim it. Let him declare and lay out before me what has happened since I established my ancient people, and what is yet to come—yes, let him foretell what will come." The fact that these events lie far in the future does not make them irrelevant to the original audience, any more than the fact that these events are now far in the past makes them irrelevant for us. Whether far in the future or far in the past, they tell us something about God's sovereign control of history that is profoundly relevant for our journey of faith in the present. I therefore take these events to be genuine prophecy from the perspective of the sixth-century author, not pseudo-prophecy from an author writing in the Maccabean period.

9. See John Goldingay, *God's Prophet, God's Servant: A Study in Jeremiah & Isaiah 40–55* (Carlisle, UK: Paternoster, 1984), 11.

Daniel's Vision

Daniel's vision begins as chapter 8 did, with a brief summary of the Persian and Greek empires: "Now then, I tell you the truth: Three more kings will appear in Persia, and then a fourth, who will be far richer than all the others. When he has gained power by his wealth, he will stir up everyone against the kingdom of Greece. Then a mighty king will appear, who will rule with great power and do as he pleases" (Dan. 11:2–3). After Cyrus, the present Persian ruler, three more kings would arise in Persia and then a fourth, who would be richer and more powerful than the others and would enter into conflict with Greece. This fourth king is generally recognized as Xerxes I (486–465 B.C.), the husband of Esther. He was a great and mighty king, under whom Persian power reached its pinnacle, but he is also remembered for invading Greece, only to be defeated at the battle of Salamis.[10] This began the conflict that would ultimately lead to the downfall of the Persian empire. There were several other lesser Persian kings after Xerxes, but they are passed over without mention as the prophecy moves on quickly to the next significant ruler, the warrior king who would rule a vast realm, namely, Alexander the Great. He died in 323 B.C. shortly after establishing an enormous empire encompassing much of the then known world. Alexander's empire was then divided among his four generals, none of whom were related to him, exactly as anticipated in Daniel 11:4–5: "After he has appeared, his empire will be broken up and parceled out toward the four winds of heaven. It will not go to his descendants, nor will it have the power he exercised, because his empire will be uprooted and given to others. The king of the South will become strong, but one of his commanders will become even stronger than he and will rule his own kingdom with great power."

Two of the four kingdoms that emerged out of Alexander's empire were the kingdom of the Ptolemies, based in Egypt, and the kingdom of the Seleucids, based in Syria and Babylonia. From an Israelite perspective, the conflicts of these two dynasties—the kings of the South (the Ptolemies) and the kings of the North (the Seleucids)—were the most significant events in world history during the third and second

10. Goldingay, *Daniel*, 294.

centuries B.C. These events are at the heart of this chapter, for reasons we will explore in a moment.

The precision of the predictions in this chapter is truly astonishing. To take just one example, consider Daniel 11:6–8:

> After some years, they will become allies. The daughter of the king of the South will go to the king of the North to make an alliance, but she will not retain her power, and he and his power will not last. In those days she will be handed over, together with her royal escort and her father and the one who supported her.
>
> One from her family line will arise to take her place. He will attack the forces of the king of the North and enter his fortress; he will fight against them and be victorious. He will also seize their gods, their metal images and their valuable articles of silver and gold and carry them off to Egypt. For some years he will leave the king of the North alone.

These predictions were fulfilled to the letter. Around 250 B.C., Ptolemy II (the king of the South) attempted to make peace with Antiochus II (the king of the North) by sending his daughter Berenice to marry him. The plan was that Antiochus would divorce his first wife, Laodice, and disinherit her sons. Laodice discovered the plot, however, and she had Antiochus and Berenice poisoned, along with their young son. In the same year, Berenice's father died in Egypt. He was succeeded by Berenice's brother, "someone from her own family," who then invaded the Seleucid kingdom and conquered its capital, Antioch, exactly as Daniel 11 had predicted.[11]

This is just one example. If we work our way through the passage, we see the same phenomenon repeated over and over again:

> Then the king of the North will invade the realm of the king of the South but will retreat to his own country. His sons will prepare for war and assemble a great army, which will sweep on like an irresistible flood and carry the battle as far as his fortress.
>
> Then the king of the South will march out in a rage and fight against the king of the North, who will raise a large army, but it will be defeated. When the army is carried off, the king of the South will be filled with pride and will slaughter many thousands, yet he will not remain triumphant. For the king

11. Norman Porteous, *Daniel*, Old Testament Library (Philadelphia: Westminster, 1965), 160.

197

of the North will muster another army, larger than the first; and after several years, he will advance with a huge army fully equipped.

In those times many will rise against the king of the South. The violent men among your own people will rebel in fulfillment of the vision, but without success. Then the king of the North will come and build up siege ramps and will capture a fortified city. The forces of the South will be powerless to resist; even their best troops will not have the strength to stand. The invader will do as he pleases; no one will be able to stand against him. He will establish himself in the Beautiful Land and will have the power to destroy it. He will determine to come with the might of his entire kingdom and will make an alliance with the king of the South. And he will give him a daughter in marriage in order to overthrow the kingdom, but his plans will not succeed or help him. Then he will turn his attention to the coastlands and will take many of them, but a commander will put an end to his insolence and will turn his insolence back upon him. After this, he will turn back toward the fortresses of his own country but will stumble and fall, to be seen no more.

His successor will send out a tax collector to maintain the royal splendor. In a few years, however, he will be destroyed, yet not in anger or in battle.

He will be succeeded by a contemptible person who has not been given the honor of royalty. He will invade the kingdom when its people feel secure, and he will seize it through intrigue. Then an overwhelming army will be swept away before him; both it and a prince of the covenant will be destroyed. After coming to an agreement with him, he will act deceitfully, and with only a few people he will rise to power. When the richest provinces feel secure, he will invade them and will achieve what neither his fathers nor his forefathers did. He will distribute plunder, loot and wealth among his followers. He will plot the overthrow of fortresses—but only for a time.

With a large army he will stir up his strength and courage against the king of the South. The king of the South will wage war with a large and very powerful army, but he will not be able to stand because of the plots devised against him. Those who eat from the king's provisions will try to destroy him; his army will be swept away, and many will fall in battle. The two kings, with their hearts bent on evil, will sit at the same table and lie to each other, but to no avail, because an end will still come at the appointed time. The king of the North will return to his own country with great wealth, but his heart will be set against the holy covenant. He will take action against it and then return to his own country.

At the appointed time he will invade the South again, but this time the outcome will be different from what it was before. Ships of the western coastlands will oppose him, and he will lose heart. Then he will turn back and vent his fury against the holy covenant. He will return and show favor to those who forsake the holy covenant.

His armed forces will rise up to desecrate the temple fortress and will abolish the daily sacrifice. Then they will set up the abomination that causes desolation. With flattery he will corrupt those who have violated the covenant, but the people who know their God will firmly resist him.

Those who are wise will instruct many, though for a time they will fall by the sword or be burned or captured or plundered. When they fall, they will receive a little help, and many who are not sincere will join them. (Dan. 11:9–34)

According to John Goldingay, Daniel 11 refers in a specific, historically identifiable way to thirteen of the sixteen rulers of these two kingdoms between 322 and 163 B.C.[12] A detailed verse-by-verse study of the fulfillment of each prediction would have its merits. It would also run the risk of becoming a tedious and confusing recounting of dates and names and places.[13] Instead, our goal will be to look at the flow of the events that are recorded for us and ask what the significance of this history was for Daniel and what it is for us.

THE FIRST PHASE: WARS AND RUMORS OF WARS

The first phase of the history runs from verse 5 to verse 20, covering the conflict of the kingdoms of the North and the South from their establishment in 322 B.C. down to the assassination of Seleucus IV in 175 B.C. The elements that are highlighted in this part of the history are a seemingly endless sequence of grand conflicts, wars, and politics, which never reach a conclusion. The balance of power ebbs back and forth between the two superpowers, but for all their best efforts and the vast expenditure of lives and wealth, neither one of these superpowers is able to conquer the other. Nor are they able to live in peace with one another: their best efforts to forge a unity through politically motivated marriage unions and other strategies are equally unsuccessful.

12. Goldingay, *Daniel*, 295–96.
13. Calvin devotes some forty pages to a full analysis, which would stretch a sermon well beyond the limits of most people's patience!

199

This summary gives us a profound perspective on history. On one level, it is the continual story of wars and rumors of wars, as one human ruler and empire after another seeks to gain power by cunning or force. Yet though the tide in the affairs of men comes in and goes out, in the end it accomplishes precisely nothing. The balance of power in earthly politics may shift but it never comes to a permanent rest. On the one hand, therefore, Daniel 11 shows us the fallen world pursuing the wind and finding it elusive. What do power and politics gain for all their toil? All this, as the writer of Ecclesiastes noted, is vanity.

Nor is this a history that God's people could watch from the safety of the sidelines. Some of the Jews were caught up in the conflict directly, seeking to take one side or another, but without success (Dan. 11:14). Others were indirectly affected as the forces of one side or the other swept through Judah ("the Beautiful Land," 11:16), leaving a trail of destruction in their wake.

Trials and Endurance

Why did Daniel need to hear about this history in his situation? The goal was to put the difficulties that the Jews were facing in 536 B.C. in perspective. There was nothing unique about the trials and tribulations that faced them. The court intrigues that delayed the building work on the temple in Jerusalem and the opposition from powerful enemies that they encountered were not merely a temporary hiccup but would be an ongoing feature of life in this world. Their experience should therefore not surprise them, as if something unexpected and out of control were happening to them. God was in control of these machinations as well. Nor should they seek to take matters into their own hands, as if by rising up against the authorities they could bring about the establishment of God's kingdom more swiftly. Patient endurance would continue to be the order of the day until God intervened to set up his kingdom.

This is an important lesson for us also to learn from this history. The kingdoms of this world often seem overwhelming in their power to accomplish great things, a power that can easily either cow Christians into a state of depressed submission or, alternatively, seduce them into trying to use the world's power to do God's work. Some Christians seem to believe that they can hasten the coming of God's kingdom by achieving certain political goals. Yet at the end of the story, and for all their vaunted power, the kingdoms of this world can neither destroy God's work nor establish it. They are merely tools in the hand of a sovereign God who is able to declare the end from the beginning because he alone ultimately controls the affairs of men and nations.

This truth is of great practical value in each of our lives. We all experience times when our existence seems caught up in a larger conflict that is completely out of our control. Perhaps our job is threatened when a manufacturing plant is closed by corporate authorities located thousands of miles away. Perhaps political decisions or terrorist acts that are beyond our power to influence threaten our freedoms and lifestyle. Our health, or the health of someone we love, may be threatened by a disease against which we have no ability to guard. We live in a great big world and we are ever so small.

In such times of personal uncertainty, we need to cling firmly onto the knowledge that all of world events, from the greatest to the least, are not only known ahead of time to God but are under his sovereign power to control. Even those actions that are initiated by godless men and women in pursuit of their own wicked purposes will ultimately achieve the Lord's holy purposes (see Acts 4:27–28). He is the first and the last; apart from him there is no God. He alone can foretell what the future holds because he holds it in his sovereign hand (see Isa. 44:6–7).

THE SECOND PHASE: ANTIOCHUS IV

After fifteen verses that cover the reigns of seven Seleucid kings over a period of around 150 years, the next fifteen verses focus our attention on the reign of a single Seleucid king, Antiochus IV. Although he was not next in line for the throne after the death of his brother Seleucus IV, Antiochus gained it through intrigue:

> He will be succeeded by a contemptible person who has not been given the honor of royalty. He will invade the kingdom when its people feel secure, and he will seize it through intrigue. Then an overwhelming army will be swept

away before him; both it and a prince of the covenant will be destroyed. After coming to an agreement with him, he will act deceitfully, and with only a few people he will rise to power. (Dan. 11:21–23)

Antiochus started with limited support but gradually grew in power, making strategic alliances but keeping them only as long as suited him (11:23). Those who tried to resist him were swept away including the then Jewish high priest Onias III, who may be the "covenant prince" mentioned in verse 22.[14] Onias vainly attempted to resist the growing pressure from the Seleucid authorities towards the hellenization of their empire, which involved the adoption of Greek customs and practices that were antithetical to God's laws. He was removed from office and replaced by a more compliant high priest.

During this time there was also a fresh outbreak of the old hostilities between the Seleucids and the Ptolemies, the kings of the North and the South: ("With a large army he will stir up his strength and courage against the king of the South. The king of the South will wage war with a large and very powerful army, but he will not be able to stand because of the plots devised against him," Dan. 11:25). Ptolemy VI, the king of the South, initiated the hostilities but he was defeated by Antiochus and captured. A few years later, though (in 168 B.C.), Antiochus invaded Egypt again, this time with disastrous results. The rising Mediterranean power of the day, the Romans ("the ships of the western coastlands," 11:30) became involved in the dispute. Their delegate, Gaius Popillius Laenas, faced down Antiochus as he approached Alexandria. He drew a circle in the sand around Antiochus, insisting that he had to agree to withdraw from Egypt before he left the circle.[15] Antiochus was no stranger to the power of Rome, having spent his childhood in Rome as a political hostage. Humiliated, he was forced to withdraw.

Meanwhile, during Antiochus's campaign in Egypt, rumors had circulated in Judah of his assassination, which led to an attempted uprising by the Jews. On his return, Antiochus stormed Jerusalem and slaughtered many, erecting a fortress for his troops there. He banned Jewish practices such as circumcision and eliminated the regular daily offerings at the temple, offering pig's flesh on the altar instead. He desecrated the Holy of Holies and dedicated the temple to the worship of Zeus (Dan. 11:31). Some of the Jew-

---

14. André Lacocque, *The Book of Daniel*, trans. D. Pellauer (Atlanta: John Knox, 1979), 226.
15. Lucas, *Daniel*, 286.

ish people caved under the pressure and collaborated with his forces, while others faithfully resisted him at great personal cost, falling by the sword or being burned (11:33).

THE THIRD PHASE: ONE GREATER THAN ANTIOCHUS

Bad though things have become by this point, there is worse yet to come:

> The king will do as he pleases. He will exalt and magnify himself above every god and will say unheard-of things against the God of gods. He will be successful until the time of wrath is completed, for what has been determined must take place. He will show no regard for the gods of his fathers or for the one desired by women, nor will he regard any god, but will exalt himself above them all. Instead of them, he will honor a god of fortresses; a god unknown to his fathers he will honor with gold and silver, with precious stones and costly gifts. He will attack the mightiest fortresses with the help of a foreign god and will greatly honor those who acknowledge him. He will make them rulers over many people and will distribute the land at a price.
>
> At the time of the end the king of the South will engage him in battle, and the king of the North will storm out against him with chariots and cavalry and a great fleet of ships. He will invade many countries and sweep through them like a flood. He will also invade the Beautiful Land. Many countries will fall, but Edom, Moab and the leaders of Ammon will be delivered from his hand. He will extend his power over many countries; Egypt will not escape. He will gain control of the treasures of gold and silver and all the riches of Egypt, with the Libyans and Nubians in submission. But reports from the east and the north will alarm him, and he will set out in a great rage to destroy and annihilate many. He will pitch his royal tents between the seas at the beautiful holy mountain. Yet he will come to his end, and no one will help him. (Dan. 11:36–45)

As we progress through this vision towards the conclusion of the prophecy, there is the growing sense on the part of many interpreters that even while the vision addresses the situation under Antiochus, it is not simply about him.[16] Antiochus was powerful, able to "do as he pleased" (Dan. 11:36)

16. Longman, *Daniel*, 282.

up to a point, but throughout his reign the power of the Romans was far greater than his, as his retreat from Egypt made clear. Antiochus certainly viewed himself as a god—his nickname "Epiphanes" means "[god] made manifest"—but so too did many ancient rulers. Antiochus abandoned the god that his fathers worshiped, Apollo, and showed no regard for the "one desired by women," which is probably a reference to the worship of the god Adonis or Dionysius, which was common in Egypt.[17] He thus could be said to have turned his back on the traditional deities of the kings of the North and the kings of the South, in favor of the worship of Zeus, a god who embodied military strength. Yet at the same time, even while aspects of the language of Daniel 11:36–39 seem to fit Antiochus, the passage as a whole seems to be speaking of a king who will be a larger and more ultimate version of Antiochus. This coming ruler will truly "do as he pleases," "attack the mightiest fortresses," and make his followers "rulers over many."

There is no clear shift in the language of Daniel 11 that marks the transition from Antiochus to the final king, perhaps because Antiochus forms a model with which to compare the ultimate ruler. One striking difference between them, though, lies in the events surrounding the king's death in verses 40 to 45, which do not fit what we know of the death of Antiochus. He met his end during a relatively minor campaign against Persia in 164 B.C., not between the sea and Jerusalem after a grand and successful assault on Egypt. Particularly when compared to the precision of fulfillment of the previous verses of Daniel 11, therefore, these verses seem still to be looking for a greater fulfillment that is yet to come. Matthew 24 similarly anticipates a dual fulfillment, referring both to the events of the fall of Jerusalem in A.D. 70 and also to events that will mark the end of all things. History will not come to a conclusion, it appears, until the coming of another Antiochus-like king.[18]

Believe, Resist, Teach, and Pray

What does this prophecy of the coming of the dark days of Antiochus IV and of another greater Antiochus yet to come have to say to Daniel and to us? The goal of this history is to put our lives into perspective. Is

---

17. Goldingay, *Daniel*, 304.

18. E. J. Young, *The Prophecy of Daniel: An Introduction and Commentary* (Grand Rapids: Eerdmans, 1949), 251–53.

Daniel troubled by the real difficulties of his own day? The Lord responds by announcing that there are even more trying times yet to come. Are we troubled by the problems that we face? Cheer up, they could easily be worse. In fact, we don't even have to wait for the coming of the final antichrist to find greater distress than ours: there are believers in many parts of the world today whose possessions are being plundered and family members kidnapped and enslaved. Even today there are believers who are faithfully laying down their lives by the sword or by fire. If that is true, then what do we really have to complain about?

Yet Daniel 11 doesn't simply want to make us ashamed of our grumbling because other believers are faithfully enduring far worse trials than the ones we are so bitter about. It also wants to teach us how to live faithfully in the midst of the worst trials, lessons that will be equally valid in the midst of our far lesser tribulations. The lessons of Daniel 11 can be summed up in the form of four imperatives that, though not explicit in the text, summarize its message: believe, resist, teach, and pray.

First, we are called to believe. In Daniel 11, it is those who know their God who will be strong and take action: " . . . the people who know their God will firmly resist" (Dan. 11:32). Faith in God's sovereign power, as it is clearly displayed in Daniel 11, is the foundation and basis for all of our hope and all of our activity for God. History is not simply a wind-blown medley of random coincidences. Nor is it merely the account of the struggles of long dead popes and kings, involving good-for-nothing men and hardly any women. Rather, it is the account of the working of God's hand accomplishing his sovereign purposes in the lives of men and women in every era. Do you believe this? It is the foundation for everything else.

Second, we are called to resist faithfully, even unto death. In the days of Antiochus, some would be seduced or pressured into abandoning the covenant and going over to the dark side: "His armed forces will rise up to desecrate the temple fortress and will abolish the daily sacrifice. Then they will set up the abomination that causes desolation" (Dan. 11:31). Power can be very attractive, yet those who know God resist its seductions, even if it means death: "With flattery he will corrupt those who have violated the covenant, but the people who know their God will firmly resist him. Those who are wise will instruct many, though for a time they will fall by the sword or be burned or captured or plundered" (11:32–33). Sometimes

205

obedience to God will mean a lifetime of faithfulness in a hostile environment, as it did for Daniel himself. Sometimes it will mean literal martyrdom for the faith, by the sword or the flame, with no dramatic rescue at the last minute, as there was for Daniel and his three friends. Such an act of laying down your life for what you believe looks like the ultimate foolishness to the world. The Lord, however, calls it wisdom. How can such a horrific death be wise? It is wise because the persecutor's fire has no power to inflict real hurt on the believer: the fire of persecution is the means by which God's people are refined, purified, and made spotless for the time of the end: "Some of the wise will stumble, so that they may be refined, purified and made spotless until the time of the end, for it will still come at the appointed time" (11:35). As Jesus said in Matthew 10:28: "Do not be afraid of those who kill the body but cannot kill the soul. Rather, be afraid of the One who can destroy both soul and body in hell."

Our view of history is foundational to the way we live. If history is an assortment of random circumstances, coming from nowhere and going nowhere, then faithful suffering has no possible meaning. It is a wasted life that could have been better spent on pursuing pleasure instead. But if history is actually following God's predetermined course to a final end, then our actions are filled with meaning. Any sacrifices that are demanded of us will be made more than worthwhile by our hope of glory on the last day, when the dead shall rise: "Multitudes who sleep in the dust of the earth will awake: some to everlasting life, others to shame and everlasting contempt. Those who are wise will shine like the brightness of the heavens, and those who lead many to righteousness, like the stars for ever and ever" (Dan. 12:2–3).

As Paul says in 1 Corinthians, if it is only for this life that we have hope, then we are of all men most to be pitied (1 Cor. 15:19). If all of God's plans are being worked out within the scope of time and space, then persecuted believers are being short-changed and missing out on much that life has to offer. But if there is a heaven to come, in which earthly deeds will be judged and faithfulness to God will be rewarded, then those who are faithful to God, even unto death, have made the best choice of all. As Jim Elliot once said, not long before he was martyred by the Auca Indians of South America, "He is no fool who gives up what he cannot keep to gain what he cannot lose."[19] The hope of glory, rooted in God's sovereign control of history, makes any sacrifice worthwhile for the sake of faithfulness to God.

Third, we are called to teach those around us. Others need to know that history has a goal and purpose that has been set by God, and we are called to instruct them: "Those who are wise will instruct many . . ." (Dan. 11:33). This has implications for our witness locally. We are constantly surrounded by people whose thoughts are shaped entirely by present realities rather than ultimate realities. Many of our friends and neighbors go through life with no thought for the final resurrection and the day when they will stand before God to give an account for their lives. Who else is going to share that news with them? Who is in a better position to speak to them of the power and sovereignty of a holy God, the seriousness of the last judgment, and their need to live their lives in the light of eternity? How much of our conversation is "wise," when measured in those terms, and how much of it is prattling foolishness, taken up with mere trivialities?

Fourth, we are to pray. The victory in this conflict is not won by the wise among God's people overcoming the evil one through their own strength. Rather, victory comes when the heavenly hosts, led by the archangel Michael, rise up to deliver the saints (Dan. 12:1). In fact, Daniel 11 is bracketed by mention of Michael and the heavenly conflict in which he is engaged. As we saw in our last study, our part in that conflict is to pray, just as Daniel had been doing. Prayer is the revolutionary activity by which weak, mortal creatures take our stand in the great cosmic battle and do our part to move heaven and earth towards God's final victory. In the light of the ultimate victory of God and the resurrection of the saints, the wise will commit themselves to pray for that final victory to come soon.

There's an old saying, "All good things must come to an end." Fortunately, the same is true for all bad things as well. Antiochus Epiphanes was a powerful foe for God's people in his own day, but his reign eventually came to an end. Tyrants rise and fall, empires come and go, but the Lord's kingdom endures forever, and with it, those whom God has redeemed by his grace. Our present circumstances will pass away, whether they are good or bad. Our life will come to an end, perhaps sooner, perhaps later. But those who have placed their trust in the Lord and have been redeemed by his

19. *The Journals of Jim Elliot* (Old Tappan, NJ: Fleming H. Revell, 1978), 174.

mercy will endure forever. Those who have washed their robes and made them clean in the blood of the Lamb will shine for all eternity, endued with the glory of God.

The saints will not endure forever because of their own faithfulness and suffering, however. There is no redeeming power intrinsic to the blood of the martyrs. Those who enter heaven, whether as martyrs or as regular believers, do so through the power of the blood of the Lamb (Rev. 7:14; 12:11). It is because Christ has suffered and died and has risen again that history has meaning and purpose. It is because Christ has shed his blood for me that I can look forward to spending eternity in his light. Our heavenly inheritance is all of grace, and that glorious prospect will make any sacrifice God calls us to make in this life more than worthwhile.

The prospect of heaven is the answer to Satan's temptations to compromise and submit to his ways. The anticipation of seeing God's face shining on us with the same warmth and love that he has for his own Son is the answer to our present discouragement, difficulty, and despair. Lift up your eyes from the trials and difficulties of the present and behold the glorious inheritance God has prepared for you. Gaze intently upon that glorious sight and let it strengthen your weak knees and encourage your failing arms for the battle that is still set before you.

15

HOW LONG WILL I BE BROKEN?

Daniel 12:4–13

At that time Michael, the great prince who protects your people,
will arise. There will be a time of distress such as has not
happened from the beginning of nations until then. But at that
time your people—everyone whose name is found written in
the book—will be delivered. Multitudes who sleep in the dust of
the earth will awake: some to everlasting life, others to shame
and everlasting contempt. Those who are wise will shine like the
brightness of the heavens, and those who lead many to righteous-
ness, like the stars for ever and ever. (Dan. 12:1–3)

e live in an age in which we expect everything to be fixable. There is a pervasive air of pragmatic optimism in our society, born out of a generation steeped in the notion that if every morning you just repeat the saying "In every way and every day I am getting better and better," you surely will. If your teeth aren't straight, orthodontics will set them right. If you don't like your body shape, try cosmetic surgery. If your job frustrates you, search the classified advertisements for new opportunities that will fulfill your potential. If you can't get along with your wife, get a different one. Whatever our problem is, we have been trained to believe that someone out there has the answer that will fix it.

This is true on a national and global scale as well as a personal scale. Whether the problem is global warming, or world poverty, or dictatorial and oppressive governments, we think we can fix it. Perhaps we don't have the solutions to all of the world's problems worked out yet, but just give us a few more years and we will surely figure it out. This attitude is equally prevalent on both ends of the political spectrum: political liberals generally think that a little more government money and intervention will solve the world's problems, while political conservatives think that a little more capitalism and personal freedom will do the trick. The idea that evil is intractable and powerful, with deep roots and sharp claws, and that no amount of education, activism, or democratic reform will ever eliminate it, is distinctly countercultural.

The same attitude of pragmatic optimism has affected evangelical churches as well. Encouraged by well-meaning Christian counselors and Christian political action committees, we too have come to believe that whatever is broken, we can fix. Just buy this book, vote for these politicians, come to these meetings, or pray this prayer, and everything will turn out well. You too can be slim, healthy, and sin-free in six weeks by following these simple steps. We have reduced sanctification and spiritual victory to a technique to be learned and mastered, almost like a golf swing.[1] Therefore, if you haven't yet attained perfection, there is evidently something wrong with you! It is clearly your fault for failing to take advantage of all of the resources available to you at your local Christian bookstore. You need to get with the program!

"IT CAN'T BE FIXED"

Real life, however, doesn't always match our theories. When my son Jamie was about eighteen months old, he went out for a walk with his mother. As they walked along, they came across a dead bird lying beside

---

1. Lynn Garrett of *Publishers Weekly* said about the runaway bestseller *The Prayer of Jabez*: "It's very evangelical and very American, this whole notion that if you know the right technique, the right form, that prayer will be efficient and effective. Kind of like golf." See David Van Biema, "A Prayer with Wings: How Did an Ancient Entreaty Become a Best Seller?" *Time*, May 14, 2001. <http://www.time.com/time/pacific/magazine/20010514/wings.html>, accessed February 7, 2006.

the road. After bending over it and examining it closely with all of the seriousness of a toddler encountering something that he had never experienced before, Jamie looked up at my wife and said, "It can't be fixed, Mommy, can it?" To which she could only respond, "No, Jamie. It can't be fixed."

The apocalyptic parts of the Bible, like the Book of Daniel, remind us that we live in a world that cannot simply be fixed. It needs to be recreated. To be sure, God will eliminate all evil in the end, but sin and sickness will be defeated according to his timetable, not ours. In the end, the broken shall be made whole and all tears will be wiped away. But until the coming of God's kingdom, brokenness and suffering, pain and persecution will continue to be the normal state for believers. We live in a world that is profoundly broken.

This has been the message of the Book of Daniel from the beginning, and it is still its focus as the book draws to a close. Remember, this closing chapter is part of God's answer to Daniel's concerns in the third year of Cyrus. At this time, God's people had returned to Jerusalem, yet had found progress frustratingly slow and difficult in the face of powerful and entrenched opposition. As a result, the people had started to despair. The prophet Isaiah had foretold a glorious future in which there would be a new heavens and a new earth:

> Behold, I will create new heavens and a new earth. The former things will not be remembered, nor will they come to mind. But be glad and rejoice forever in what I will create, for I will create Jerusalem to be a delight and its people a joy. I will rejoice over Jerusalem and take delight in my people; the sound of weeping and of crying will be heard in it no more. (Isa. 65:17–19)

Similarly, Jeremiah anticipated a new covenant in which God's law would be written on the people's hearts: "This is the covenant I will make with the house of Israel after that time," declares the LORD. "I will put my law in their minds and write it on their hearts. I will be their God, and they will be my people" (Jer. 31:33). Ezekiel also foretold a new heart and new spirit for the people that would be accomplished through the cleansing work of the Holy Spirit: "I will give you a new heart and put a new spirit in you; I will remove from you your heart of stone and give you a heart of flesh. And I will put my Spirit in you and move you to follow my decrees and be careful to keep my laws" (Ezek. 36:26–27).

When were these glorious prophecies going to find their fulfillment? The people had returned to their land but it seemed that nothing had really changed. Internally, they wrestled with the same sins as before, and externally they were faced with the same trials and problems. How long before their expectations of real change and healing were realized? How long would they be broken?

This is a message that we need to hear as well, especially when our own progress in sanctification is slow and difficult, or when we face powerful opposition and persecution for the sake of the gospel. We inhabit a world where church services may be interrupted by crazed gunmen, who shoot to kill. Innocent children can be abducted from their beds and murdered. Cancer ravages the body of believers as well as unbelievers, leaving them in excruciating pain for which they have no answers and no reasons. The effects of dysfunctional childhoods and longstanding sinful patterns of behavior continue to bear their bitter fruit in ourselves and in our marriages and families, even after we have followed Christ for many years. We find obedience to God's law hard, while sin is constantly attractive, and we cry out for a cure. We rightly agonize over these signs of the powerful work of the beast in our world, seeking to wreck and destroy everything that is good, and noble, and pure.

The Book of Daniel never assumes that we would find living in a world like this easy. On the contrary, it anticipates the fact that we will frequently find ourselves crying out, "How long, O Lord? Where are you? What are you doing? Why are your people dying and despairing? Why are they not prospering and victorious? How long do you think that we can hold on?" These are the questions that Daniel 12 is designed to address.

How do we live as broken people in a broken world? Should we give in to despair and assume that this is the way things will always be? Should we simply seek to anesthetize our pain through whatever pleasures and comforts we can find in this world, looking to make the best of a bad job? By no means. The Book of Daniel is very far from being a sedative given to the suffering in order to dull their pain. On the contrary, it is a wake-up call to all of us to live with wisdom in this broken world. By all means, we should pursue obedience to God with heartfelt passion using whatever resources are available to us. Yet at the same time, we should recognize that even as we grow in grace, we will continue to be profoundly broken.

THE WISE AND THE WICKED

The foundational obligation upon us to live as God's people in this broken world is to be wise. According to Daniel 12, there are only two kinds of people in this world, the wise and the wicked (see 12:10). This is not the pairing that we would normally put together. We tend to think that the opposite of "wicked" is "righteous," but here it is wisdom and understanding that distinguishes God's people from the wicked.

Nor is it simply the pursuit of wisdom and understanding that marks out God's people: in contrast to the wicked, God's people actually achieve wisdom. So in verse 4 we read that "Many will go here and there to increase knowledge." This is an allusion to Amos 8:11–12: "The days are coming," declares the Sovereign LORD, "when I will send a famine through the land—not a famine of food or a thirst for water, but a famine of hearing the words of the LORD. Men will stagger from sea to sea and wander from north to east, searching for the word of the LORD, but they will not find it." Similarly, the Lord was telling Daniel that people will seek for wisdom in all kinds of places but will not find it. They will go "here and there" looking for knowledge, when all the while it was right in front of their noses. God's people know where to find true wisdom, while the wicked search for it in vain, for "The fear of the LORD is the beginning of knowledge" (Prov. 1:7).

It is not because God's Word is hidden away that men cannot find it, either. Daniel was instructed, "But you, Daniel, close up and seal the words of the scroll until the time of the end. Many will go here and there to increase knowledge" (Dan. 12:4). It was not merely a matter of keeping these words secret, but rather of storing them safely for future generations of God's people to read.[2] God's truth is often hidden in plain sight. The Bible displays its riches so clearly that the simplest believer can grasp its essential message, while the most brilliant unbelieving intellect reads the same words but fails to discern their truth. As a result, men and women

---

2. Tremper Longman III, *Daniel*, New International Version Application Commentary (Grand Rapids: Zondervan, 1999), 285.

go searching for spiritual insight in all manner of religious experiences and teachings, but fail to find it. God's Word is the only source of true spiritual insight: the wise read it and understand who God is and what he is doing in this world.

This stress on the wisdom, understanding, and knowledge of God's people is an important point for us to grasp because we live in an age that despises doctrine and plays down knowledge in favor of the claims of experience. Our postmodern era is profoundly a time when people are going here and there seeking knowledge. Our age affirms the validity of every possible form of spirituality because it views all truth as relative and our experience as normative. Truth becomes whatever philosophy gives me the experiences that I desire. In our age, the idea of unique, authoritative Truth revealed once and for all in God's inspired Word, the Bible, is therefore highly countercultural. Yet Daniel is repeatedly told to be wise and to understand the things revealed to him by God, and to teach these things to others (Dan. 11:33), for such understanding will help both him and his hearers to stand firm in the midst of the challenges and messiness of living in a broken world. The wise know where to find true wisdom: in the objective standard of the revealed Word of God.

How Long?

Daniel's final vision took place beside the banks of a river:

Then I, Daniel, looked, and there before me stood two others, one on this bank of the river and one on the opposite bank. One of them said to the man clothed in linen, who was above the waters of the river, "How long will it be before these astonishing things are fulfilled?"

The man clothed in linen, who was above the waters of the river, lifted his right hand and his left hand toward heaven, and I heard him swear by him who lives forever, saying, "It will be for a time, times and half a time. When the power of the holy people has been finally broken, all these things will be completed."

I heard, but I did not understand. So I asked, "My lord, what will the outcome of all this be?"

He replied, "Go your way, Daniel, because the words are closed up and sealed until the time of the end. Many will be purified, made spotless and refined, but the wicked will continue to be wicked. None of the wicked will understand, but those who are wise will understand.

"From the time that the daily sacrifice is abolished and the abomination that causes desolation is set up, there will be 1,290 days. Blessed is the one who waits for and reaches the end of the 1,335 days." (Dan. 12:5–12)

True wisdom for living in a broken world is central to the two questions that are asked of God in this passage—one by the angel and one by Daniel himself. The two questions are essentially parallel, as can be seen from the fact that Daniel asked his question because he didn't understand the answer given to the angel. The angel asked: "How long will it be before these astonishing things are fulfilled?" while Daniel inquired: "My lord, what will the outcome of all this be?" (12:6, 8). Taken together, the answers to these two questions unfold two aspects of living wisely in a broken world, the issues of "How long?" and "How?" These are the two things that Daniel needed to understand, and that we too need to understand if we are to live with wisdom in a broken world.

The answer to the question "How long?" has two parts: it will be "for a time, times and half a time" (Dan. 12:7), and it will be for 1,290 days (12:11). Broadly speaking, both of these terms can be used to describe periods that are around three and a half years.[3] What is more significant here, however, is the different terms that are used to describe the same time span. Three and a half times focuses on this period as half of seven times, which would be a complete period of judgment (see Dan. 4:25). In contrast to such a complete period of judgment, this period of trials is limited, cut short in its length. Meanwhile, 1,290 days focuses on the precision with which the period is measured. It is not just a vague period of judgment but one that is predetermined by God down to the very day when it will end. A third note is sounded by the inclusion of the additional figure of 1,335 days in Daniel 12:12, which adds 45 days to the 1,290-day period and tells us that the saints will need to persevere all the way to the end of this longer period. The inclusion of this number seems designed to heighten the sense of mystery that surrounds the Lord's timing and the

3. A variety of calendars were in use during this period of history. If a luni-solar calendar of 360 days was intended, with an intercalary month to adjust for differences between this figure and the true period of the earth's orbit around the sun, then three and a half years (with one month intercalated) is exactly 1,290 days. See Goldingay, *Daniel*, Word Biblical Commentary (Dallas: Word, 1989), 310.

need for faithful perseverance on the part of the saints, even when according to human wisdom God's arrival seems to be overdue. Though the time for God to complete his work may seem to have come, his people will still have to wait patiently for the end.

Taken together, then, these numbers characterize history as a whole as a time of judgment and trial. At the same time, they remind us that this time of trial is limited by the Lord's mercy, that its precise end is known to the Lord though utterly impenetrable by human logic, and that we need to persevere in faith until the very end. What significance does each of these points have for our struggle with brokenness?

Limited by the Lord's Mercy

In the first place, it is imperative to remember that our struggle with brokenness is limited by the Lord's mercy. When I was a pastor in California, a member of my congregation would habitually respond to the question "How are you doing?" with the answer "Better than I deserve." This could be said glibly, yet on a profound level this is true for all of us, whatever our circumstances: they are better than we deserve. Are we experiencing physical pain and suffering? It is far less than the physical pain and suffering we deserve in hell, so that is better than we deserve. Is our progress in sanctification slow and frustrating? Whatever progress we do see is a work of God's Spirit in our hearts for which we should give thanks, even if it is only the ability to see our sin and mourn for it. We have the promise that ultimately his sanctifying work in us will be complete, and we will be purified forever. That too is better than we deserve. Are our earthly relationships damaged and broken? Nevertheless, through Jesus we have peace with God, our Father in heaven, which is better than we deserve. No matter how challenging our lives may be, our trials are limited by the Lord's mercy.

Precisely Known by the Lord

Second, the timing of the exact end of our trials is known precisely to the Lord, though it is impenetrable to human logic. If that is true, then I should trust that my Father will not put me through any unnecessary trials, nor will he keep me in them any longer than is necessary for my good, even when I cannot see that good myself. We understand this instinctively on the human level. As parents, we know that there are times when we deliberately cause pain to our children in a variety of ways they cannot understand, for their own good. For example, we take babies to the doctor for inoculations, even though we know they will cry when the needle goes in. We take our children to the dentist, even though we know that drilling out a cavity in a diseased tooth is painful and unpleasant. Our children often don't understand these things, but we do them nonetheless, because it is our responsibility as parents who love our children very much.

In the same way, our heavenly Father brings trials into our lives and exposes our brokenness in a variety of ways for exactly the right period of time. He knows what challenges are necessary to move his work forward in our hearts, and for how long they need to be applied. What is more, the right period of time for our trials to continue is the one that makes sense to him, not to us—just as the right period of time for the dentist to drill is determined by him and not by the patient. The end will come when God is done with the process, not when we think he should be done. Yet at the same time, when it finally does arrive, the time of the end will be perfect for us, even though we cannot see how it should be so.

PERSEVERING IN FAITH AND TRUST

Third, our part in the face of this is to persevere in faith and trust. What does a parent expect of young children when they go to the dentist? Children don't have to like the experience, but they do have to persevere with it. They are certainly allowed to feel the pain and to cry out to their father for reassurance; to let them do anything less would be inhuman. Yet at the same time, they also need to keep on sitting in the dentist's chair because that is where their father has placed them. They must trust their father's wisdom, even when they cannot possibly understand what is going on.

So too in the face of the incomprehensible experiences that come to us as broken people living in a broken world, we don't have to like them but we do have to persevere. We can certainly cry out to our heavenly Father, "How long, O Lord?" We can seek reassurance from him, pleading with him to show his presence with us in our pain and suffering. Yet at the same time, we also need to persevere in obedient trust, seeking to obey him in the midst of our pain, trusting that his wisdom is greater than ours. We need to remind ourselves daily that the trials we face in our lives do not come to us from random chance and circumstances, but from our heavenly Father, who has fitted these trials to our needs, to shape us into the people he wants us to be.

How Will the End Come?

In addition to the question "How long?" there is also the question "How?" The response that the angel received is "when the power of the holy people has been finally broken" (Dan. 12:7). Does this response surprise you? It is certainly counterintuitive: we expect the end to come when the power of the wicked people has been finally broken, not the power of the holy people. Yet this statement is further elaborated in the answer given to Daniel. The angel told him that there will be continuing persecution to purify and refine the wise (12:10; cf. 11:33–35) and continuing wickedness on the part of the wicked. Even after the time when the temple sacrifices would come to an end and the abominating desolation would be established,[4] there would continue to be trials. Certainly there is no expectation here of a gradual Christianization of the world. The prerequisite for the end is not the final fixing of our world's brokenness; rather, it is the final breaking of the holy people's strength.

Such a statement may sound paradoxical, but it is God's consistent pattern of working in this world, moving through suffering to glory. The world's wisdom is constantly focused on strength and glory in the present. It tells me to have my best life right now. Yet if there is anything at all to be learned from the vision that Daniel has just seen in chapter 11, it is that the lives of God's people in this world will frequently be anything but "the best." There are wars and rumors of wars, persecutions and trials, the temple in Jerusalem being desecrated all over again and the faithful facing martyrdom by the sword and at the stake (see Matt. 24). God's wisdom is not the wisdom of the world, and in God's wisdom the way in which we are cured of our brokenness is precisely through fiery trials.

We need to be careful at this point, however. There is nothing intrinsically purifying about fiery trials in themselves, and we should not seek them for

4. On these events, see the discussion of Dan. 9:20–27.

their own sake. The refiner's fire does not create the pure metal, it simply reveals it. If you put metallic ore into the crucible, the pure metal will sink to the bottom and you can remove the slag from the top. However, if what you put into the crucible is dross to begin with, you will get out nothing but dross. The fire simply reveals the true nature of the material being refined. So too in Daniel 12:10, when those who are wise go through trials, they are "purified, made spotless and refined" by them; yet in the same circumstances, the wicked continue to be wicked. Trials thus serve to reveal the difference between the wise and the wicked. As the apostle Peter reminds us, this is a key purpose of our trials: so that "your faith—of greater worth than gold, which perishes even though refined by fire—may be proved genuine and may result in praise, glory and honor when Jesus Christ is revealed" (1 Peter 1:7). In a mysterious way, the trials that we face—trials that come from the fallenness and brokenness of this world—refine our faith and demonstrate its genuineness, making us more fit for the presence of God.

THE HEAVENLY WITNESSES

What is more, we humans are not the only witnesses to these events. It is the angel who asks, "How long will it be before these astonishing things are fulfilled?" (Dan. 12:6). In other words, there is not only a heavenly conflict going on that parallels our earthly struggles, as we saw in Daniel 10, but there is also a heavenly audience that is watching earthly events play themselves out, waiting to see what happens next. We are actors on a cosmic stage, under the constant gaze of the heavenly beings.

What can angels learn from beholding the likes of us? Surely they can learn the power of God's grace that takes flawed and broken people and sustains them through the overwhelming trials of life until we arrive safely at our heavenly home. If God were to heal our brokenness this side of heaven, there would be no wondering in heaven over his long-suffering with us, no awe at his patience and mercy shown towards us. Who needs patience and long-suffering to persist with perfect creatures? Yet if God in his mercy can take unmitigated dross like us and transform us into gold, will not the heavens themselves shout aloud to his praise? If God can take weak, compromised human beings and bind them together into a people who will ultimately be spotlessly holy, will not all creation magnify his name?

This age, then, is revealed as a constant period of refining and testing, a time of ongoing and great tribulation in which only God's grace sustains us to the end. But it will be followed by another age, an age of glory and rest for those who have been found faithful. In the age to come, the wise will shine like the brightness of the heavens, and those who lead many to righteousness, like the stars for ever and ever:

> At that time Michael, the great prince who protects your people, will arise. There will be a time of distress such as has not happened from the beginning of nations until then. But at that time your people—everyone whose name is found written in the book—will be delivered. Multitudes who sleep in the dust of the earth will awake: some to everlasting life, others to shame and everlasting contempt. Those who are wise will shine like the brightness of the heavens, and those who lead many to righteousness, like the stars for ever and ever. (Dan. 12:1–3)

There is a rest that awaits Daniel after his earthly work is done, and it awaits us as well. If we persevere by faith, through God's grace, in doing the tasks he has set before us to do in this broken world, then there is a glorious eternal rest prepared for us, when our sin will be done away with and our guilt will be cleansed forever. In that age, all of our brokenness will finally be fixed, along with the brokenness of the present created order. If, however, we are faithless and abandon the truth, we shall rise to judgment that will end in our shame and everlasting destruction. There is no middle ground: our ultimate destiny is bright glory or utter darkness, depending on whether our names are found written in the book of life, the Lamb's record of those who by faith belong to him (see Rev. 21:27).

The doctrine of the personal resurrection of the saints, which perhaps finds its clearest Old Testament expression here in Daniel 12:1–3, is thus not merely a philosophical construct but is the profound answer to our continuing brokenness and the basis for our perseverance. If there is no resurrection from the dead, we are of all people most to be pitied (1 Cor. 15:19), and that sad truth is all the more evident to those who know their own brokenness. People whose lives are working out well may not spend much time thinking about eternal things, but we who know and experience our own brokenness and the brokenness of the cosmos in which we live will delight to do so. We will have hearts that are constantly reaching out for the glorious inheritance that is ours in Jesus Christ. As our physical bodies age and break down, our hearts long all the more intensely for the wholeness of heaven. When we see most clearly that this broken world is not enough, then our eyes turn more eagerly to what God has promised us in the age to come. God has sworn it to us on oath (Dan. 12:7): the one who lives forever cannot lie.

HOW WILL WE BE CURED?

So how will we finally be cured of our brokenness? How will the broken world in which we live be restored to wholeness? Ultimately, it is accomplished through God himself taking flesh in Jesus Christ and being broken for us.

In the time of Antiochus IV, almost four hundred years after Daniel's vision, evil men abolished the sacrifices of the Jerusalem temple and defiled it. They burned pig's flesh on the sacred altar and dedicated the Holy of Holies to Zeus. It was certainly a desolating abomination, probably the greatest abomination up until that point in history. Yet surely the greatest abomination of all time was when wicked men laid hands on Jesus Christ, whose body was God's new temple on earth (John 2:19–21). They desecrated that body, the flesh in which God's own glory had come to dwell among us (John 1:14). They spat upon his face and they scourged his back until his flesh was broken and torn. They hung his body on a tree, the sign of a man who was exposed to the curse of God (Deut. 21:23). While he hung there, they mocked him, saying "Come down from the cross, if you are the Son of God" (Matt. 27:40).

Was there ever a greater display of brokenness than we see at the cross? At the cross we see the brokenness of this fallen world that would take its own Creator and crucify him. On the cross we see the brokenness of God's true Israel: there Jesus Christ personified the holy people of God, and there his power was thoroughly broken. In fact, he was so broken that he needed a stranger to carry his cross up to Golgotha, and then someone else to carry his lifeless corpse down again. Was there ever a greater display of weakness and brokenness than the cross?

Yet the foolishness of God is wiser than the wisdom of men. His broken-ness is stronger than man's strength. For the brokenness of God in our place is the means by which we, his broken people, are healed and restored. It is through the brokenness of God that this fallen and ruined world will be set back to its former glory. On the cross Christ took our sin and broken-ness on himself: he was wounded for our transgressions and beaten for our iniquities. He took into himself the suffering and curse that we deserved for our unrighteousness, and the result of his death is our life. Through his sojourn in darkness, we receive a glory that will enable us to shine forever. By his stripes, we are healed. Through his brokenness, all of our brokenness will be fixed. So whatever your brokenness—whatever form your sins and transgressions have taken and still take—Jesus Christ's death on the cross is more than sufficient to heal them all.

How Then Shall We Live?

How then should we live? As broken people in a broken world, we need to recognize that we live in the time between the times. Like Daniel, we are called to go on our way and be faithful in the present in the tasks to which God has called us. Our brokenness is never to be used as an excuse for giv-ing up in the ongoing battle against sin. We are to pray and to persevere in good works, not growing weary in doing what is right (2 Thess. 3:13). We are to be comforted by God's sovereign power over history, which guaran-tees that our present sufferings will not be in vain (1 Cor. 15:58). We should glory in the physical resurrection of Christ, the first fruits of the saints who will shine forever, and whose glorified body is the pattern after which our own resurrection bodies will be modeled. We are to be exhilarated by the joyful inheritance that has been set before us. If Christ could endure the agonies of the cross for the sake of joy that was set before him (Heb. 12:2), so also we should endure the far lesser agonies that we face with our eyes firmly fixed on heaven's great joys. When we reach heaven's distant shore, it will all have been worth it.

Finally, we must remember that the primary biblical image for the saints is not that of crusaders but martyrs. It is not our task to come along on a white horse and save the world. That job belongs to someone else. The apostle John tells us:

I saw heaven standing open and there before me was a white horse, whose rider is called Faithful and True. With justice he judges and makes war. His eyes are like blazing fire, and on his head are many crowns. He has a name written on him that no one knows but he himself. He is dressed in a robe dipped in blood, and his name is the Word of God. The armies of heaven were following him, riding on white horses and dressed in fine linen, white and clean. Out of his mouth comes a sharp sword with which to strike down the nations. "He will rule them with an iron scepter." He treads the winepress of the fury of the wrath of God Almighty. On his robe and on his thigh he has this name written: KING OF KINGS AND LORD OF LORDS (Rev. 19:11–16).

The day is coming when Jesus Christ will ride out to conquer and to re-create, a day when the kingdom of this world will become the kingdom of our God and of his Christ (Rev. 11:15). In the meantime, our task as martyrs is simply to testify to the Lord's greatness and grace by our words and by our sufferings. As we cling to God in the midst of trials that we do not understand, we testify of God's grace to a watching world and to the heavenly beings. Like Jacob, who wrestled on with God at the fords of the Jabbok even after he had been crippled by the encounter (Gen. 32:24–31), we testify not by our strength and might but simply by our persistence in clinging on to God in the midst of our brokenness.

And when the final trumpet sounds for us, bringing to an end our earthly conflict, then at last we too will hear our Redeemer say to us: "As for you, go your way till the end. You will rest, and then at the end of the days you will rise to receive your allotted inheritance" (Dan. 12:13). We will rise with Daniel—the same Daniel who endured the trials of the lions' den and the challenges of living in an alien land, who prayed daily for the consummation of God's kingdom and who prospered throughout the exile—and with all of the saints, to receive our final reward in Christ.

INDEX OF SCRIPTURE

226

Index of Subjects and Names